CALVIN HARRIS

THE $100 MILLION DJ
THE UNAUTHORISED BIOGRAPHY

Douglas Wight

BLACK & WHITE PUBLISHING

For L, C, G + M

First published 2015
by Black & White Publishing Ltd
29 Ocean Drive, Edinburgh EH6 6JL

1 3 5 7 9 10 8 6 4 2   15 16 17 18

ISBN: 978 1 84502 967 8

Typeset by RefineCatch Ltd, Bungay, Suffolk
Printed and bound by Gutenberg Press, Malta

Contents

Author's Note

CALVIN Harris first came to my attention when in 2007 posters started spreading around London heralding a precocious new talent who had created disco. Those 'fly eye' shades were everywhere. It was refreshingly ballsy and somewhat surprising for a previously little-known Scot.

When a good mate then raved how Calvin had rocked an event in Skye, it struck me that there might be more to this artist than quirky hits like 'Acceptable in the 80s' and 'The Girls' suggested. So when the records started tumbling, I was intrigued to find out what made Calvin Harris tick.

Although Calvin – or Adam Wiles, his real name – was not involved in the writing of this book, he has been so prolific in interviews and on social media that there was no shortage of opinion from him. Sources for the majority of his comments are listed at the back of this book.

Tweets quoted in the book retain their original spelling and punctuation, and expletives have been asterisked as they were in the source material.

Prologue

THE lights dim momentarily but the first chiming beats of 'We Found Love' ignite a flash of colour, sparking frenzied cheers from a grateful crowd.

High up on his huge riser Calvin Harris extends an arm into the air, his other hand clutching headphones to his ear. It is the Coachella Valley Music and Arts Festival in California. It is April 2012 and he has his audience where he wants it, judging the pitch of the room and controlling emotions like a conductor with an orchestra.

The arrival of Rihanna, whose vocals turned Harris's near-perfect fusion of house and pop into a worldwide chart smash, sends the crowd into an even greater frenzy. Now all Harris can see are hands extended into the air and the lights of camera phones, everyone desperate to capture this surprise moment lest their own memories fail them.

As Harris expertly builds the tempo, lifting the audience as one to a higher plain of ecstasy, something catches his eye. It's not Rihanna bouncing maniacally along the stage below him. Another figure is emerging from the crowd, and only as it is carried along on a sea of hands does Calvin see that it is Katy Perry – another pop superstar who would move mountains to work with him.

Harris pauses. As all hell is breaking loose around him he takes a moment to drink in this scene. 'This will never happen again,' he tells himself, 'so remember it for all time.'

Even in the crazy life of Calvin Harris – one that has presented a host of Kodak moments like this – he knows the importance of taking the time to appreciate every last second.

This night, at Coachella, he is a DJ – a superstar one at that – having ditched his band for an altogether more dynamic live performance. But to label him only as such – or brand him a 'knob twiddler', as some unkind journalists do – is to misunderstand completely his contribution to modern music.

Producer, musician, songwriter, singer, performer. He is all of these things, ruthlessly exploiting innovations in sound and technology to bend an at times archaic industry to his will.

It's no surprise that he is now one of the wealthiest musicians on the planet and easily the highest-placed DJ. With a residency at Las Vegas megaclub Hakkasan and some of the biggest hits of 2014 with 'Summer', 'Blame' featuring John Newman, and 'Outside' with Ellie Goulding, he has earned $66 million (£42 million) in the last year, according to American business magazine *Forbes*. To put that into perspective, he has earned more than Taylor Swift ($64 million), Jay-Z ($60 million), Justin Timberlake ($57 million), his collaborator Rihanna ($48 million) and his Coachella crowd-surfer Katy Perry, who raked in $40 million. He's also ahead of Jennifer Lopez ($37 million), Miley Cyrus ($36 million) and Lady Gaga ($33 million), and only just behind Sir Paul McCartney.

How has he done it?

By his own admission, for a man who has stated provocatively 'I Created Disco', the 6 ft 5¾ in. artist is 'not good at interviews', 'not good at dancing' and 'not good at looking like I'm having fun'.

'Luck,' he would say. Being in the right place at the right time.

But it takes more than luck to smash Michael Jackson's twenty-seven-year record for the number of top ten singles from one album. The nine gleaned from Harris's 2012 album *18 Months* beat the seven Jackson scored from 1987's *Bad* and from *Dangerous*, released in 1991.

After that success he announced that having spent the previous two years 'intensely fucking working to try and make singles and hit records' he was planning a change of direction and was working on 'dance music that probably won't get into the charts'.

What happened next? His 2014 album *Motion* spawned six hits, three of them number ones.

Not bad for someone whose intention was never to be behind a microphone or front and centre onstage, or even to be a DJ. The young Calvin Harris harboured dreams instead of becoming a policeman, out of a desire to preserve law and order, or a professional footballer.

How things changed for the unassuming Scot, who was once so shy performing that he hid out of view. Playing live now, he strikes a familiar pose: one hand casually hovering at waist height, attending to the controls on his decks, while the other punches the air in time with the beat. If you ignore the ubiquitous set of headphones, the image isn't a far cry from that of the one he might have pictured in his dreams as a young boy – arm raised aloft, taking the applause from an appreciative crowd. The only difference is that the acclaim is for making music rather than for scoring a match-winning goal. And it's worth noting that such is his success that his earnings have also taken him past those of the world's finest footballer, Lionel Messi.

Harris's is a remarkable rise to fame – a biochemist's son who launched his music career simply by asking people to follow him on the now outdated social networking site Myspace. He only posted his music there because 'everyone else was doing it'.

He entered Myspace as humble Adam Wiles, then only eighteen but already weary of and jaded about the music industry after a succession of rejections, but emerged as Calvin Harris, a cocksure performer ready to take on the world.

Since then he's enjoyed unrivalled success, with a list of collaborators and beneficiaries that reads like a *Who's Who* of pop, from Kelis, Rihanna, Tinie Tempah, Florence Welch, Dizzee Rascal and Example to Kylie Minogue and Cheryl Cole.

At some point a strange metamorphosis took place, after which Harris's life has seemed to exist online, as he expertly uses burgeoning video sites, blogs and social media to further his cause. Yet for a persona that was born in a digital age this is hardly surprising.

What is surprising is that many people still don't know what he actually does.

Calvin has said, 'The large majority of people don't really know what I am or what I do or why my name is, like, first on the record when I'm not singing.'

His own family might not even appreciate exactly the influence he carries in the pop world. In his native Dumfries, a historic and bustling town in south-west Scotland, there's a lovely story of how his father, David Wiles, upon hearing a proud mother tell of what an accomplished musician her son had become, offered a nugget of insight into his own son's achievements.

'My son is also a musician,' he is said to have replied. 'But I don't think you will have heard of him.'

'Mr Wiles,' the woman apparently responded, 'the whole world has heard of your son.'

Calvin himself sometimes even seems unsure of his place. After accepting the Ivor Novello Award for 'Songwriter of the Year' in 2013 and announcing it as 'easily the greatest achievement of my entire life', he went on to say, 'I can't believe I was even let in the door of this whole ceremony. It feels like I shouldn't be here.'

That he is here is something for which we should be grateful. Not only does he come up with banging good tunes and throw one hell of a party but we should also applaud him for the insight he gives us into the music industry. Calvin might fiercely guard his privacy when it comes to relationships and personal matters, but when it comes to the business in which he operates anything is fair game.

In this carefully polished world that trades on image and perfection, here is a guy who isn't afraid to show his workings. From the stars who have turned down his music to the backroom deals, and from trade-offs between talent to spats on Twitter, celebrities snubbing him or what he spends his money on, he's like our insider, revealing the tricks of the trade and what really goes on behind that green curtain in the magical world of Oz.

On Calvin Harris's right arm are tattooed the words 'Enter with Boldness', taken from Law 28 of *The 48 Laws of Power*, a book by American writer Robert Greene and a cult classic that since its publication in 1998 has crossed over into the mainstream, selling over 1.2 million copies in the United States. Greene's early research was inspired by Julius Caesar and his decision to cross the Rubicon River to shape his destiny and that of Rome, and the book examines the traits shared by many of today's power elite and influential figures throughout history. Curiously, it is popular with celebrities and the prison population alike (it is one of the most requested titles in penitentiary libraries in the US). This book could be a metaphor for Calvin Harris in that it too found a niche market but later broke through into the nation's consciousness.

What is most telling, however, is the rule Harris chose with which to mark his skin. Law 28 states: 'If you are unsure of a course of action, do not attempt it. Your doubts and hesitations will infect your execution. Timidity is dangerous: Better to enter with boldness. Any mistakes you commit through audacity are easily corrected with more audacity. Everyone admires the bold; no one honors the timid.'

For Adam Wiles to succeed he had to cross his own Rubicon and become Calvin Harris.

Met with rejection at every turn, he had a decision to make. Hide in the shadows or step forth to claim what was his.

'It was never my plan to even be onstage,' he said. 'I was meant to be a producer.'

To those who have witnessed him onstage, holding an audience in the palm of his hand, which would argue that he was not born to be there?

His is a remarkable story of how to succeed in the modern age. It is now our turn to enter with boldness.

1

Tall Oaks from Little Acorns Grow

Wee, sleekit, cow'rin, tim'rous beastie,
O' what a panic's in thy breastie!

NO sooner had the opening lines of Robert Burns' famous poem left the nervous boy's lips than the sniggering began.

Young children rarely need an excuse to poke fun and Adam Wiles' soft English accent gave some of his classmates all the ammunition they needed.

That those lines, which Burns penned in honour of a small mammal nearly turned over by the tenant farmer's plough, might just have well applied to the young Adam was presumably lost on the class of Calside Primary School in Dumfries. What would also have been lost on them was how significant a moment this was in the lad's development. It was his first public performance – and he required nerves of steel to get through it.

Like the rest of the children, Adam had been required to commit a Burns poem to memory and recite it in front of the whole class. Dumfries is particularly proud of its connection to Scotland's national bard. Although born in Alloway, Ayrshire, the poet made Dumfries his home in 1791 after giving up his lease at Ellisland farm six miles away.

Adam Wiles had a bigger claim than Burns to being a local lad. However, despite being born and raised in Dumfries, Adam's accent – a soft, lilting mix of Scottish and English – betrayed his family's roots south of the border.

Years later, speaking as his new alter ego Calvin Harris, as he

1

prepared his first assault on the charts, he said, 'When I was grow-ing up, because I had English parents with a slight English accent, I would get lots of stick for being the English guy in Scotland.'

Of his recital in particular, he said, 'I'm only one-eighth Scottish, so there I was standing at the front of the class reciting "To a Mouse" in the unmistakable twang of the Auld Enemy. My Scottish class-mates would tease me mercilessly and do ridiculously over-the-top impressions of my accent.

'I'm afraid I can't recite it off by heart any more, but I do remem-ber the first line about a "wee, sleekit, cow'rin, tim'rous beastie" and I'd have to admit it has a certain charm.'

Thanks to that bruising experience, it took Adam Wiles years to appreciate the merits of Burns. As a young boy he was probably more concerned with keeping his head down and not giving the more critical of his classmates any further cause to tease him.

He finds it hard to look back on that period and admits, 'It's weird, though, as I don't have many memories from before I was nine. Something terrible must have happened before that and I've blocked it out.'

It is difficult to imagine what might have caused a young boy to be unhappy. On the surface he seemed to have everything a small child could wish for – a stable, happy home and a loving family.

His dad, David Wiles, a biochemist, and his housewife mum Pamela married in Oxford, and after the birth of two children, Sophie and Edward, moved north and settled in Dumfries. It is not hard to see what would have attracted them to the picturesque town. Historically significant and assured in its own identity, Dumfries is a thriving community with a strong rural influence, while at the same time offering quick access to motorway links north and south of the border.

Rather romantically nicknamed the 'Queen of the South' and strategically situated near the mouth of the River Nith, the town seems almost like a historical touchstone, with many of the country's significant figures and events having some connection, however fleeting, to Dumfries. Aside from the Burns links, it was from here that future king of Scotland Robert the Bruce, who later triumphed at Bannockburn, launched his revolution for Scottish independence in 1306. Bonnie Prince Charlie, whose bid for the Scottish crown in 1745 was somewhat less successful, based his army there. J. M. Barrie, the creator of Peter Pan, was educated there, as was William Charles Wells, who theorised on natural selection before Charles Darwin made it popular. The family of the surgeon who inspired Arthur Conan Doyle to write Sherlock Holmes came from the town, as did John Law Hume, one of the violinists who went down with the RMS *Titanic* in 1912, famously continuing playing as passengers evacuated the sinking liner.

Although the young Adam Wiles might have been teased for his accent, the idea that Doomhamers, as local residents are known, harbour a strong anti-English sentiment seems unfounded. The town is situated seventy-six miles from Glasgow, yet only thirty-three miles from Carlisle, and many people, while proudly Scottish, feel an affinity with their neighbours across the border. A majority of voters regularly favour unionist candidates, and in the 2014 referendum on Scottish independence Dumfries and Galloway returned one of the strongest results to stay part of the United Kingdom, with over 65 per cent voting 'No'.

David and Pamela chose the family-orientated suburb of Georgetown in which to settle and had been married for twelve years when on 17 January 1984 they added to their brood with the birth of their second son, Adam Richard. After living for a short time in Maryfield, they moved to a large detached home up the hill from Calside Primary, the school that Adam would attend.

Those difficult early problems at school aside, Adam enjoyed his childhood.

'It was good when I was a young child. My first home was a nice house in a place called Georgetown,' he said. 'My mum and dad, brother and sister all lived there and it was a happy environment.'

Music seemed to play a big part in creating that atmosphere. Being the youngest of three siblings, Adam was often subjected to the tastes of his older brother and sister. In the late 1980s that pretty much guaranteed a mixed bag of music styles.

At that time popular music was suffering from something of an identity crisis. Traditional pop bands and rock groups had been usurped to a degree by 'manufactured' acts benefitting from the assembly line of hits from producers Stock, Aitken and Waterman (SAW), who enjoyed astonishing success from the decade's end through to 1993. Of those acts, the one that benefitted the most from SAW's Midas touch was Kylie Minogue. The Australian actress was already a household name in Britain, thanks to her role as tomboy Charlene in the television soap opera *Neighbours*.

As Adam was toddling around as a three-year-old, Kylie, then nineteen, was signing to PWL, Pete Waterman's record label. Her first single, 'I Should Be So Lucky', became the biggest-selling of the year.

Her particular brand of pop didn't seem to make an impact in the Wiles household. Little was the young Adam to know that one day he would work closely with the pop princess. And given that Adam did not fully appreciate dance music until his teens it seems unlikely he was aware of another music scene that was just gaining a foothold in the mainstream.

House music was born in Chicago in the early eighties but by 1984 had branched out to other cities in North America and was starting to make an impact in Europe. Characterised by minimalistic electronic beats, synthesised basslines and drum machines, it made its first real crossover in 1987. As Kylie was putting pen to paper on her PWL contract, MARRS were set to unleash 'Pump Up the Volume' on an unsuspecting British public.

Spotting the competition early, SAW attempted to block its release, claiming a sample from their hit single 'Roadblock' amounted to 'wholesale theft'. The legal dispute only served to delay the inevitable and 'Pump Up the Volume' soared to number one, fittingly knocking the SAW act Rick Astley off the top spot.

Although MARRS were never heard of again following their one-hit wonder and SAW's Kylie Minogue ended the year triumphantly, the seeds had been planted for a dance revolution in British pop music – one of which Adam Wiles would be at the forefront.

For the young boy, however, plans of world domination would have to wait. He had other competing interests. 'I was always really into music and sport,' he said. 'I loved playing football.'

Adam's local team was Queen of the South, the local team of Dumfries who play at Palmerston Park and who at the time were in the Scottish Second Division. They weren't having the best of luck then and at one stage, in April 1992, were so short of players for a reserve game that manager Ally MacLeod – aged sixty-two – named himself on the team sheet. MacLeod is best remembered as the Scotland manager who predicted they could win a medal at the 1978 World Cup in Argentina, but on this occasion he played the whole ninety minutes, scoring a penalty in a 7–1 defeat. Slight setbacks aside, however, 'Queens' is a well-run and family-friendly club whose fans steer clear of the senseless bigotry and rivalries that beset other teams, making it the ideal place to go for young kids.

Although Adam had a soft spot for his local team, he also liked Liverpool, who in the late eighties were still dominating English football, winning the last of their eighteen league titles in 1990. 'I was big into football before I got into music and collected Liverpool shirts,' he has since revealed. 'I even had the ecru one, which was a controversial magnolia.'

His favourite player was Steve McManaman, the Liverpool winger who moved to Real Madrid and scored in a Champions League final, and he wished he had the wide man's flowing locks: 'I wanted to be like Steve McManaman, on the left wing, with curly hair. But I never had curly hair, so I got into music. If I'd had curly hair, things would've been different.'

Being tall, one might have expected Adam to make a good target man, but he said, 'Everyone expected me to be brilliant at headers, but they always hurt me.'

Football wasn't the only sport in which Adam was showing prowess. 'I was good at sprints, three-legged races and the egg-and-spoon races at sports day,' he said.

And though he applied himself at school, he suffered from the lack of concentration that can afflict many small boys. 'I could read and write to a reasonable level,' he explained, 'but I've never had a long attention span. I want things to be interesting all the time.'

His short attention span might explain his choice of TV programmes back then. His favourite was *Top Banana*, a Saturday morning kids show broadcast as part of *TV-am*. It was a game show set in a jungle in which children competed against each other to reach the top of the mountain, where the prize was a golden banana. A madcap character called Captain Keyboard provided musical accompaniment. The show only ran for twenty-six weeks in 1990, but the six-year-old Adam was so taken with the zany humour – and the inflatable bananas that littered the studio floor – that he was moved to get in touch.

'I used to get up to watch it before school,' he said. 'It had talking bananas and these big inflatable bananas that they hit each other with. I once wrote to them and asked them to send me one of those inflatable bananas. I never expected to receive one but I did. They included a letter saying that they didn't normally give them out but because it seemed like I was so sure I wasn't going to get one they decided they would surprise me. I was so happy.'

Adam was not a particularly big infant – 'baby-sized' is how he humorously describes his birth weight – but during primary school he started to notice he was shooting up at a faster rate than his peers. 'I wasn't overly tall. But, in primary school, from the photos I can see I was always at the back with the tall people,' he said.

It took him years to feel comfortable in his own skin and as a young kid found everyday activities like skating take on a whole new perspective. 'I once wore [skates] when I was eight and I was frightened as I've got a high centre of gravity – I'm like a giraffe,' he said.

The only advantage he could see at the time was that when he left school he might be able to pursue a career for which being a certain height was a necessity. If Adam wasn't going to make it as a footballer for Queen of the South, there might be another career for him – as a copper. 'I think I would also have made a good police-man,' he said. 'When I was eight, I wanted to be one so I could tell people off.'

Following the turn of the decade, although dance music's influence on the charts was beginning to grow and small independent label 'indie' music was gaining prominence, it was another American import that caught Adam's attention.

Big brother Ed – who is seven years older than Adam – was probably, like many teenagers in Britain in 1991, crying out for some new sound. That all changed with the release of Nirvana's 'Smells Like Teen Spirit'. The brooding verse/crashing riff combination of the Washington band's first single from second album *Nevermind* heralded the arrival in the UK of the Seattle grunge scene. The single became a worldwide anthem for doomed youth, turning Nirvana into one of the biggest bands on the planet and lead singer Kurt Cobain a media-appointed spokesman for a generation. *Nevermind* spawned three more hit singles and sparked interest in their raw debut album *Bleach*. Adam said, 'My big brother Ed was a huge fan. I became pretty much obsessed with Nirvana at a very young age . . . well, along with the rest of my generation, I suppose. I'm a fan still and love *Nevermind* but I couldn't get into *Bleach*. I couldn't handle their harder stuff.'

Adam's favourite song was 'Lithium' and he was desperate to grow his fringe out, à la Kurt Cobain: 'This song had to be my favourite purely on the grounds of the bassline, which I used to play on my wee acoustic guitar. Also, I really wanted Kurt Cobain's hair but my mum always used to pin me down and cut my fringe before it got too long. Gutted.'

Ed was already showing prowess at the piano and, being technically gifted, was looking at ways of producing his own music – as well as appreciating a host of different styles. Adam has always been quick to credit his brother's influence. 'It was Ed who introduced me to music in the first place,' he said. 'He turned me on to Nirvana and a whole lot of other brilliant stuff. But he was actually the musical one. He was a child prodigy on the piano. I just followed on.'

Fame never sat comfortably with Nirvana star Cobain, who was battling heroin addiction. Although the band only produced one other studio album, *In Utero*, and the acclaimed *Unplugged* collection, its place in rock folklore was assured when Cobain shot himself at home on 8 April 1994.

By then, however, Adam preferred a softer sound, and while he appreciated his brother's taste in music, he showed an early leaning to a more traditional funky sound with his first 'official' music purchase – 'Too Young to Die' by Jamiroquai. It wasn't technically the first record he acquired – that seems to have been 'Young at Heart' by the Bluebells, most likely when it was rereleased in April 1993, a month before 'Too Young to Die'. However, Jamiroquai's second single from debut album *Emergency on Planet Earth* must have had more of a lasting impression, and while critics likened it to early Stevie Wonder, nine-year-old Adam must just have liked its soft acid groove. 'The first record I bought,' he said of the single. 'I have memories of crouching down at my mum's tape player to listen to it.'

That purchase was to ignite something inside Adam that would shape his future development – that, and an intrigue in what his brother was moving on to musically.

Ed had acquired a bargain-basement Commodore Amiga computer and, inspired by the thumping big beats of dance pioneers the Prodigy, set about trying to create electronic sounds of his own. As Adam listened to the 'hilarious, bangin', Prodigy-esque rave tracks' pounding from his brother's bedroom, his first reaction was amusement. But his interest in music was starting to take hold and as a consequence other passions fell by the wayside. 'Music took over,' he said, 'and I became rubbish at all sports.' He started learning bass guitar as he grew older.

The transition from child to teenager is awkward for everyone and for Adam it presented its own challenges – not least because by thirteen he was beginning to tower over his other classmates.

'It was hard being the tallest person in class,' he said. 'Especially when you are a teenager. You want to keep your head down. I did, anyway. When you are a spotty, awkward teenager, you don't want people to look at you. It's a self-conscious thing. Everyone looks at you because you are extra gangly. I didn't get picked on less because I was tall. If anything, I would get picked on more. People would call me a "big lanky ****" and all that kind of stuff.'

Despite his size he shied away from confrontation, but when he made the step up to secondary education at Dumfries High School he found there were some boys who were desperate to see how tough the tall kid was. Although he tried to run away from any signs of trouble there was one time when scarpering wasn't an option, so he had to take evasive action.

8

'I couldn't fight,' he said. 'The only fight I was in, I fell down before he hit me. The only thing I was good at was running away because I had long legs.'

Between the ages of fifteen and sixteen Adam shot up even higher, effectively reaching the height he is now, 6 ft 5¾ in. One might think, being that tall, the extra ¾ inch would not be important, but for Adam it was very significant. 'It's a touchy subject,' he said, 'because if I had that other quarter I would be a certified giant and I would get a certificate and documentation that I could show airport officials.'

These days Adam does not have to worry about convincing check-in desks about his need for extra legroom. He flies mostly by private jet. Yet there was a time when being that tall was awkward.

'For a while I was walking down like Lurch,' he recalled. 'It wasn't until I was sixteen or seventeen that I became too tall compared to everyone else. But I have never been a fighter and never will be. I was the softest person in school and I'm still rubbish at fighting.'

The school holidays brought some respite, and every summer the family would make the long journey down the M6 to visit his grandmother in Devon. Adam loved the change of scene, but by the time he reached his teens he was itching to experience something new. 'It was good when I was a young child,' he said of his annual trips south, 'but by the time I was thirteen I was ready for a change.'

Adam might have preferred to stay at home – after all, his siblings were preparing to leave the nest and go off to university – but his parents had other ideas. Perhaps as a compromise, David and Pamela took Adam to London for a day trip. On their whistlestop visit there was only time to see the main tourist attraction, but as Adam stood outside Buckingham Palace in his Liverpool shirt and looked around at the splendour of Westminster, could he have imagined that in just five years' time he would be back there, trying to make a name for himself?

London would have to wait for now. The main family holiday remained the customary trip to Devon. Little did he know it, but something was to happen on that trip that would set his life on a course he is following to this day.

2

Music Sounds Better With Me

THE car park of a zoo does not at first seem like the ideal location for a musical awakening, but it was there that Calvin Harris was born.

Sitting in his parents' car after a day watching the animals at the park near Torquay, in Devon, during their annual summer holiday, Adam was listening to the radio when some bouncy, funky chords started chiming from the speakers. The song was 'Music Sounds Better with You' by Stardust, and Adam was smitten.

'It's full of soulful, happy chords, and it was one of the first housey dance tunes I really liked,' Calvin later recalled. 'I first heard it on Radio 1, sitting in my mum and dad's car in the car park of Torquay zoo when we were on holiday. I was fourteen and not actually into music back then, but when I heard that, I thought it was amazing and bought it as soon as I got home. It was a gateway into the world of dance music.'

The tune could not have been more relevant. Stardust, like MARRS years earlier, was a one-off venture uniting French electropop wizards Thomas Bangalter and Alan Braxe and vocalist Benjamin Diamond. Bangalter was one half of curious dance duo Daft Punk, whose infuriatingly catchy 'Around the World' had been a hit the year before. They had styled themselves as a sort of computerised Chic ('Around the World' borrows the bassline from the New York funk maestros' disco classic 'Good Times'). And it was to the past Bangalter looked again for inspiration for 'Music Sounds Better with You'. The catchy hook is based on a two-second sample of 'Queen of Funk' Chaka Khan's 1981 hit 'Fate' looped over and over.

Adam was not alone in appreciating its greatness. It has gone on to become one of the biggest-selling house tracks of all time. Although the collaborators were reportedly offered millions of pounds to produce an album together, they declined. But the die was cast – the song's place in music history was assured.

Back home in Dumfries, Adam had the inspiration to start making his own music. He knew the sounds he wanted to produce – he just needed the equipment. Ed had left home to study at university and had left his Commodore Amiga for his little brother to tinker with. It was all the invitation Adam needed.

When it was launched in 1985, few people could appreciate the capabilities of the Amiga – not least Commodore themselves. These days, thanks to the rise of Apple, we are used to slick device launches with manufacturers selling consumers technological advances they never thought they needed, let alone desired. Back in the 1980s computer technology was a lot simpler, but the know-how was there for people who dared to dream.

By the early nineties, the Amiga – named after the Spanish for (female) friend – was the bestselling home computer in Europe. However, in just a few years Commodore had surrendered its place in the market in the face of stiff competition from Apple, IBM and the development of games consoles. In 1994 the last Amigas were produced and Commodore went bust. The Amiga might have fallen out of fashion, but in some regards it broke the mould.

Writing in *Byte* magazine in 1994 on the demise of Commdore, Tom R. Halfhill said, 'The Amiga was so far ahead of its time that almost nobody – including Commodore's marketing department – could fully articulate what it was all about. Today, it's obvious the Amiga was the first multimedia computer, but in those days it was derided as a game machine because few people grasped the importance of advanced graphics, sound, and video.'

Luckily for Adam, Ed knew the potential of the little PC. Incredibly, the software he used then for his Prodigy-inspired banging dance tunes came free with a magazine. 'Ed had the Amiga for years before I got it,' Adam said. 'He's a proper computer boffin so he was always writing programs for it. He got the music-sequencing software off a magazine and let me use it. It was a bit quirky and took four times as long as the more modern equivalent, but it did the job.'

Left to his own devices, Adam set about trying to construct tracks of his own. 'It was one of the things I dreamt about as a boy,' he said. Adam started to spend hours locked in his bedroom working on music.

'Right at the start, when I was about thirteen or fourteen, I only had an Amiga 500 Plus running a bit of tracker software called OctaMED. My brother was big into his computers, and when he moved up to a proper PC, I took charge of the Amiga. With the right interface, you could sample things off CD, so I used to nick loads of loops from Fatboy Slim albums and make my own tunes.

'In a sense, I suppose you could say that I immediately went on board. I was working inside the computer. That computer just happened to be an 8-bit Amiga! I know we get all nostalgic about 8-bit samples, but, rest assured, the Amiga didn't sound lo-fi and gritty. It just sounded . . . a bit rubbish. It probably didn't help that the only monitors were the TV speakers from the second-hand TV in my bedroom.'

Adam started to use Christmas and birthdays as a way of acquiring new kit. 'I moved up to an Amiga 1200 and, at Christmas, persuaded my parents to get me my first keyboard . . . a Korg M5. That was the great thing about being a kid. You could ask for bits of kit for Christmas and birthdays. I also managed to get a Zoom 1201 – an amazing little effects box – for ninety-nine quid and an Electrix Filter Queen.

'Without a doubt, that was the best present anyone has ever bought me! Sadly, it broke after about two weeks, but they were the greatest two weeks of my life. A real filter! A filter! I stuck everything through it. Twiddling and tweaking. To my young ears, it made everything sound fucking brilliant! I have to mention the M5, too. I've still got it and I still consider it one of the best all-round keyboards you can get. I sometimes dig it out, just for old times' sake. The piano sounds on it are amazing. Bizarrely, my early studio set-up also included a lot of stuff from school. I had a very understanding music teacher who let me take home things like mics, mic stands, a mixer and an eight-track MiniDisc recorder.

That eight-track was a revelation. That's how I learned to mix,' he said.

Lee McQueen, who was in many of Adam's classes throughout secondary school and sat next to him in many lessons, bonded with him over music. And he was immediately impressed by what he saw: 'During music class you move around instruments and try different ones, and although Adam played bass he seemed to do well with all the instruments – guitar and keyboards. It didn't matter what the instrument, he seemed to be able to play them all to quite a high standard. He had an interest in music but he was interested in all areas.'

Lee, who was following a more traditional route, learning the accordion at the time, remembers Adam as a quiet lad who, despite his stature, was keen to sit in the background. His memories are startlingly at odds with the self-assured pop star we see today.

Lee recalled, 'He was quite shy, especially around people he didn't know. Once you knew him he was quite funny, but he was certainly in the background, not at the forefront of things. He just got on with it. He was quite clever and he was one of those people you don't notice how he's getting on, he just quietly did his stuff.'

Coming from different primary schools, it might have taken Lee and Adam a while to warm to each other, but a shared sense of humour, as well as musical taste, sped up the process.

'We hit it off quite quickly,' Lee said. 'When you sit together you get to know someone quite well. We got to know each other better through music. He played the bass guitar and I played the accordion, but he was interested in all kinds of music. I remember there was an advert on TV that used Nat King Cole's "L-O-V-E" and I remember we had a go at singing that and sang the opposite words, or mucking about with it in first year. He was aware of who Nat King Cole was and knew the song. I listened to anything and it was good to meet someone who was also into jazz and other types of music.

'We also connected over our shared sense of humour. He could really be quite funny. His sense of humour was such that not everyone would get it, but to me it seemed to make sense. Not only did he have an eclectic taste in music, he also had a broad knowledge of comedians and comedy. He liked *Blackadder*, I'm sure, or that type of comedy, which not everyone was into. He had a dry sense of humour.'

At a crucial point in Adam's development he suffered a major setback. When he was about sixteen, he spent a lot of time off school. Lee McQueen remembers the time when Adam was absent for a long period. 'That was kind of strange,' he recalled. 'We were just told by our guidance teacher that he wouldn't be back. We were wondering if he was all right. We were told it was nothing really serious, it was just that he had to take time off. Then our guidance teacher explained to the class that he was coming back and explained that he could be a wee bit tired. When he came back, we didn't notice any real change. He seemed the same.'

Although Adam has not gone into detail about anything that might have afflicted him as a teenager, he has spoken about having a 'weak immune system', which might have made him vulnerable to illness when younger.

Lee and Adam picked up their friendship from where they left off and stepped up their music practice together. Lee said, 'Sometimes we'd meet up after school, but we were at different ends of the town and didn't have the transport. But at weekends we'd meet up, out in the town or at music gigs, in the same group.'

By then Lee was accustomed to playing live with his accordion, but when he heard about a forty-eight-hour music marathon in aid of Children in Need at the Birkhill Hotel in Dumfries, he thought it was a good opportunity for him, Adam and another friend, Michael, to make their live debut together: 'Every year they had a twenty-four-hour music marathon, but this year it was going to last for forty-eight hours because it was for Children in Need. It was to be a non-stop showcase of live music, with all types of musicians playing all the way through.'

Adam liked the idea of taking part, but back then the idea of playing live terrified him. Lee recalled, 'Michael and I asked Adam to come, but he didn't like to play in front of people. We thought we could get him up and he could play bass and Michael play guitar. We also spoke to guys who were a couple of years older than us. They were in bands and they were really good.'

Eventually Adam relented, but when he got to the hotel he saw a way of fulfilling his obligations for the charity event while still remaining in the background. Lee said, 'He agreed to come up with us, but he still didn't play in front of people! I can't remember what time we played at. There was a room with a stage area. As you looked up the room you could see everyone, if you kept more to the right of the stage, but Adam, when he was playing, he was at the exit to the toilets, so if you were looking up at the stage you couldn't see him. We kept saying to him, "Come over this way so people can see you," but he wouldn't do it.'

It's hard to think of Calvin Harris, either in his oversized 'fly eye' shades, front and centre onstage, or as a DJ, controlling a room in Las Vegas, and imagine that cripplingly shy teenager.

The charity event out of the way, Adam resumed his jamming sessions with Lee every Thursday, but he drew the line at playing live again. Lee said, 'I was starting to play out with different things, but if he didn't like playing in front of people it wasn't a thing I'd have made him do.'

He might not have wanted to take part in the live performances, but Adam's expertise with music continued to impress Lee – even if it seemed he wasn't quite sure what he was doing! 'We did Higher music and later on we had practice sessions. Once you had done your music module you had time to practise. Sometimes we practised, sometimes we just mucked about. He could go on the piano and played all these jazz chords, but he didn't have a clue what he was playing. I would hear something and say, "Wow, what is that?" He would say, "I haven't a clue, but it's great, isn't it?"

'I was learning chords and I found it strange that he was playing something that he didn't know. His ear was there, and it was impressive because I had watched jazz bands and I couldn't have even thought to work out these chords, but it came intuitively to him.'

In those practice sessions, Lee saw the first glimpses of the technical skills that would turn Adam Wiles into a worldwide pop phenomenon. 'During our Higher music we had music software on the computer,' Lee said, 'and there were two people I noticed were good at it. I never had a PC so these things never made sense to me.

But Adam and the other guy would go on the computer and they knew their way about it. I used to watch them and wonder, "How do they know this stuff?" He knew how to loop pieces of music even then.

'You had to write a piece of music for your Standard Grade and Higher music. They could add chords and synthesiser and loop things, while I just wrote a piece and played it. He was quite clever in that sense because he knew how to do that and make it sound great. He was chopping and changing sounds and rhythms – pretty in-depth stuff. Not everybody was on the computer. Only a handful of people were doing bits and bobs and he was definitely at the top in terms of knowing what to do.'

Adam was clearly enjoying experimenting on the computer but at that stage did not voice any ambitions to take it further. Lee said, 'Adam seemed quite happy to do his own thing – he didn't seem set on becoming a professional. He didn't seem keen on going down that route. He was obviously very talented, but he seemed quite happy to do his thing as a bit of fun, really.'

Adam was able to turn his hand to many different musical styles because he was open to the potential of all genres. His parents had raised him on the music of the sixties and seventies, his older siblings the eighties and early nineties, and he was willing to give anything an ear – even styles he might have at first thought were alien to him.

One example of this was when he heard Missy Elliott's 'Get Ur Freak On' for the first time. 'I was totally uninterested in hip hop until this came out,' he said. 'But as soon as I heard the killer opening, I wanted to investigate further, and when I did I quickly found out that there are about a million hip-hop and soul records out there that absolutely everyone should own. My love of hip hop grew from there. When I listen to it now, it makes me astonished that an entire genre passed me by for so many years.'

Dance music, however, was what he focused on creating. During Adam's teenage years, the popularity of house music was at an all-time high. 'I got into house music at its peak, when the songs by people like Fatboy Slim and Daft Punk were charting in the top ten,' he recalled.

Adam's preference to work on material in the confines of his bedroom meant he was a late developer when it came to the opposite sex. 'Growing up, the part of my brain that boys used for thinking about girls all went on music. It's the same with football,' he said. But he candidly admitted, 'I think it was a mixture of my height and my personality that put girls off. During all my years at school I only had two girlfriends. It's a bit hard to find a girl when you spend all your time locked away in your bedroom making music.'

Lee confirms, 'He wasn't very good around girls at school, as I remember. He was tall and thin and lanky but still quite shy.'

While Lee left school during sixth year, Adam stayed on to complete his last term. Although he might have given the impression that he was only playing at his musical hobby, behind closed doors he was deadly serious.

He became more fashion-conscious and started wearing a chain – 'the kind of look you find in a small town like Dumfries', he said. After school he would head down to Barnstorm Records, a small independent music store hidden away on one of the back streets of the town centre, where owner Gordon Maxwell remembers a lad keen to expand his collection of dance remixes. Maxwell said, 'With his DJ bag slung over his shoulder, Calvin, or Adam as I used to know him, used to come in and flick through the 12-inch singles. He was such a nice boy, quiet, and he'd often come in on his own. From an early age, he was always into his dance music.'

Mark Irving, another school friend, who first met Adam when he was sixteen and who would go on to play alongside him when he became Calvin Harris, said he was always looking to broaden his musical education. 'Calvin was into eighties music like David Bowie and Prince. I doubt it comes from his parents – he probably just liked them because it was interesting music production,' Mark recalled.

Adam had his room painted orange and from there, with his headphones on, he imagined he was in the studio and plotted his assault on the charts, firmly believing that one day he would have a hit single of his own. 'I was well into the charts as a boy, but in all honesty I didn't think that being number one was something completely unattainable,' he said of that time. 'Right from a young age I had a cockiness that I kept hidden. I'd hear a hit record and think, "I can do that." Sometimes I thought, "I can do better." From the age of fourteen, I thought I was incredible.'

Convinced success was out there waiting for him, Adam sent out demos of his tracks to record companies. 'I fired off loads of demos,' he said. 'I got two replies from my two favourite record labels at the time, which were Defected and Zoo. The bosses of both of them sent me very nice handwritten letters with a few free bits of vinyl, saying it was good for a fifteen-year-old, which was great. The thing that kind of spurred me on [to] not go to university or anything like that was those letters.'

But as more rejection letters came in, he started a folder. Scrawling 'Music' on the front with his Sharpie marker pen, he catalogued his setbacks.

Undeterred, he returned to the Amiga, worked on a fresher sound and plotted a new assault on the record industry. Perhaps success was not out there waiting. If he was going to forge a career in music, he had to try harder. He had to raise his game.

3

London Calling

MANY creative geniuses have to suffer for their art. Painter Toulouse-Lautrec drowned himself in absinthe to ward off the effects of syphilis and genetic malformations; Russian author Dostoyevsky spent years in Siberian exile; while Tennessee Williams produced some of his finest work while suffering from mental and physical anguish from the stress of depression and repressed homosexuality.

What none of these artistic greats had to endure was rising at 3.30 a.m. to catch a bus an hour later to Annan, a small town on the Solway Firth, to start work at 5.30 a.m. and slog it out for eight hours in a fish factory before heading home again, reeking like a trawlerman!

Yet that was the job Adam found himself doing at seventeen. When he left school, he weighed up his options. He thought about going to college to study music but decided he would receive a better education in that field by working in the industry. 'When I first left school I wanted to do music, but I didn't particularly want to go on a training course for music because I was seventeen and thought I knew everything already,' he said.

In addition, he'd had to give back the equipment he'd borrowed from school. 'My studio suddenly looked very empty,' he explained. 'I suppose that's when I decided that I wasn't going to university. If I went to uni, I'd have no money and that meant I couldn't buy more gear. So I got a job. Just to earn money to buy more equipment.'

Jobs were a bit thin on the ground, but Pinney's, the local seafood-processing plant, hired him as a seasonal worker to help with the huge demand in the lead-up to Christmas, when the workforce nearly doubled in size. The money was good, although Adam found the early starts 'shocking'. His first role at Pinneys was on the smoked side, processing salmon that would eventually end up on the shelves of Marks & Spencer. 'I had to take hot fillets off a production line, put them on baking trays, put the trays in a big rack and put the big rack in an oven,' he explained.

However, as former colleague Colin Wells recalled, Adam encountered an unforeseen occupational hazard. 'He was too tall for the tables and had to be moved,' said Colin, who knew Adam through his brother Kevin, who had been in a band with Mark Irving. 'He was tall,' Colin said. 'That's what I remember about him. And he was quiet but self-assured.'

Pinneys is a traditional local employer, with many workers having devoted their entire career to the firm. Inside the factory it is a friendly, bustling atmosphere, and with strict and necessary controls and hygiene procedures the job requires dedicated and efficient workers. Adam's time there might have been limited, but he struggled with some aspects of the job.

'The 3.30 a.m. starts took their toll,' he recalled. 'I got treated badly, as I was one of the young people there, saying, "I can't wait to get out of here," whereas the older people had worked there for years and climbed through the ranks.'

Adam might have found a kindred spirit in the shape of his bus driver, who ferried workers to and from Dumfries. Ki Creighton hailed from Annan and every morning drove around the region, picking up the workers for the factory. Like Adam, he was a huge dance music aficionado who harboured dreams of forging a career in the business and was honing his skills as a DJ and live act.

Although Adam was now working full time, his parents decided not to charge him 'digs' money or rent, hoping that the wages he saved would pay dividends in the long run. Adam squirrelled away his cash and spent seven months in the factory. He was moved to the 'Wet Fish Packing' department and, because he was desperate to work as much as possible to earn cash, he sacrificed his already limited social life. 'The worst part was on Saturday nights,' he said. 'I'd be walking to work in the town in my stinky clothes and everyone else would be on nights out, having fun.'

Adam might have found the hours long, but they were necessary if he was to take his musical ambition to the next level. His position at Pinneys was only seasonal, but if he stuck at it long enough he could buy the mixing desk he needed to make his tracks sound more professional. Then he might have a better chance of attracting interest from a major label. He worked right through Christmas and New Year, but with unfortunate timing was told on 17 January 2002 that because business traditionally dropped off after New Year his services were no longer required. They were letting him go. 'I got laid off on my birthday,' he confirmed. 'It wasn't the best birthday present, as jobs aren't really that plentiful in Dumfries.'

Adam wasn't out of work for long, managing to land a role stacking shelves in the Safeway supermarket in Dumfries. Compared with Pinneys, Safeway was 'less smelly but worse paid', and he joked he was the perfect build, with 'very long arms and torso', for reaching the high shelves. But the good news was that his early starts at the fish factory had not been in vain – he had enough money to start building his own recording studio.

'The music thing had really got me . . . I suppose it's fair to say that I was obsessed,' he said. 'I didn't go out. I didn't really have many mates. I didn't watch telly or go to clubs. I just listened to music and made my own tunes. It was probably all a bit unhealthy, but locking myself away like that meant I could really concentrate on the music.

'I remember going totally over the top with the Akai S950 [a sampler] – I managed to get it off this bloke in Carlisle for two hundred quid. I knew every button and every switch. Knew how to get the best out of it. I was mad about trying to get the drums to sound punchy. Chopping and tightening as much as I could. Eventually, I realised I needed some sort of compression too, so I put in loads of overtime at work and bought eight Alesis 3630 compressors! Not one . . . eight of the buggers! And I stuck one on every output of the S950.

'I listen back to some of the tunes I made at the time and they just sound weird. Compressed all over the place, pumping and ducking and sounding terrible. What the fuck was I thinking?'

He is grateful to have understanding parents who must have wondered what their son was doing when all these packages started arriving to their house. In all, he spent £1,000 on his studio.

'They knew what was going on when I was building the studio,' he said. 'They just let me get on with it. I'd come home from school and Mum would go, "A dude came round with a delivery for you," although she wouldn't use the word "dude". And it would be the mixing desk. We live in a detached house, so being too noisy for the neighbours wasn't really an issue either.

'I built a vocal booth out of MDF and industrial foam next to my bed. It's quite a small room for the amount of stuff in it, dominated by a massive mixing desk and the Amiga computer.'

Adam's songs still had an eighties vibe about them. To him, the tunes were banging, but something was missing – a killer vocal. He had a double-edged problem: in a small town like Dumfries it was unlikely there were too many people who shared his love of dance music and would be able to give him the sound he was after. And even if there were, he was too shy to broadcast his need for one.

'To most people, I was the guy who worked on the bread counter at Safeway,' he said. 'I never talked about my music because that wasn't the sort of thing you did.'

Although by his own admission he wasn't putting himself out there, Adam, it seemed, had written off Dumfries as a musical mecca.

Speaking years later, he was quite withering about the musical tastes of his fellow townsfolk. If a poll had been taken during the high-profile 'Battle of Britpop', when Oasis vied with rivals Blur for chart dominance in 1995, Adam was sure which band Dumfries would have voted for. 'Where I was from, it was Oasis. Blur were far too southern to be accepted. So it was Oasis and, later on, the View and bands like this.'

It seems a little sweeping to suggest small towns can't provide an environment for the avant-garde to flourish. After all, Bill

Drummond, who with the Timelords made a mint from the number one record 'Doctorin' the Tardis' and then even more with acid house pioneers the KLF in 1990, was raised in Newton Stewart, a much smaller town in Dumfries and Galloway, and where, incidentally, the cult horror *The Wicker Man* was filmed and premiered. Yet Adam certainly felt as though he was ploughing a lonely furrow.

'It was me in my bedroom trying to produce, trying to write tracks and make instruments sound good and turn them into songs that might sound like they would appear on the radio,' he said. 'I liked soul and disco and stuff like that. In the late nineties it was disco/house that was the big thing in dance music, so it would be house records with big obvious disco samples, or not so obvious in the case of Daft Punk, so I got into that. I liked basslines and chords. So it was hard to find someone who had that understanding of soul but also modern dance music.

'I'm from a small town in Scotland and I think I was the only guy who liked dance music or understood how I wanted a vocal to be delivered. Everyone was more into indie bands.'

So in the end, Adam decided: 'I had to try and figure out how to make me sound good on a record singing, which, as I'm not a singer, was quite hard. Singing was just because I couldn't find anyone to sing on the tracks.'

Adam defined his style as 'getting by with a limited range': 'When I started making music, I never sang. When I was making house tunes, there would be a search to find featured vocalists. But it soon became apparent I wasn't going to find anyone, so I built the tunes and the lyrics around my limited range, which is either really low or a ridiculous falsetto.'

Adam continued to send his music out to record companies but only succeeded in fattening his 'Music' folder with rejection letters. However, a small break came when he received a response that wasn't negative. The small independent label Prima Facie liked two of his instrumentals enough to release a 12-inch single, in October 2002. The two that had made the grade were 'Da Bongos', a fast and funky drum-heavy beat, and 'Brighter Days', a stop-start calypso-themed track.

Adam must have scarcely believed it. Five years after first tinkering about on his brother's Amiga, here was a company willing to take a chance on him.

He decided not to release records under his own name; instead, he came up with a new moniker and drew inspiration from his favourite comedian, Harry Hill, whose madcap show was then airing on Channel 4. Hill's sidekick was a blue rubber hand-puppet cat called Stouffer, whose catchphrases included 'He got a big face' and 'Sorted – respect due'. As his old schoolmate Lee had recalled, comedy played a big part in Adam's life, and so Stouffer would be his house alter ego, for now anyway.

The cover featured an image of Antonio Canova's statue *The Three Graces* – the mythological daughters of Zeus said to represent beauty, charm and joy.

The single circulated in clubs around the country. Adam's music was finally getting an airing beyond his own bedroom. However, although the tracks were slightly reminiscent of the Mighty Dub Katz – Norman Cook's incarnation before he reinvented himself as Fatboy Slim – they failed to make an impact beyond clubland.

Frustrated, Adam stepped up his attempts to circulate his music, handing in demos to record shops. He travelled down to London in late 2002 and, with enough tracks to make an album, left CDs in specialist dance shops there.

One of the shops he visited was Uptown Records in Soho. A popular haunt for music makers and dance fans alike, it was a great source of new music and undiscovered talent. Working behind the counter on the day that Adam walked in was a bubbly Iranian girl called Ayah Marar. It might take him years to appreciate it, but the fact she was there and not anyone else might be one of the most significant moments of his career.

Ayah recalled the moment she first set eyes on Adam Wiles. 'He walked in, this tall Scottish lad,' she said. 'He came in with a demo and then he walked out. People used to bring white labels and quite a few of the Radio 1 DJs used to come in and buy their records – and people like Craig David and Richard Blackwood.'

Adam returned to Scotland more in hope than expectation that his attempts to widen his audience would bear fruit. What he didn't know was that back in Soho Ayah wasn't just chucking his CD into a pile of demos. She actually listened to it. And she liked what she heard.

'I put it on,' she said. 'He had that really analogue sound. I was amazed. I thought he was incredible. I emailed him and said, "Who are you? What's all this about?" He said, "I'm from Scotland and I'd love to live in London but I have nowhere to stay."'

It just so happened that Ayah had a spare room in her flat in North London.

'So I asked him if he wanted to move in. He said yes.'

It was an incredible twist of fate. Not only had he met someone who liked his music but Ayah was also giving him a chance to pursue his dream in London.

He weighed up his options. He could stay in Dumfries and keep sending out his music in the hope that someone would pick it up, or he could head down south and give it a real crack. It was now or never. Maybe it was time to get out of this town.

'Dumfries was a nice place to grow up,' he said, 'but, like any small town, if you have any aspirations you have to get out or end up working for the council . . . or for Marks & Spencer.'

His former school friend Lee McQueen recalled a conversation with Adam at the time. Since leaving Dumfries High, Lee had been working in a bar and playing music live. He had an idea of opening a music café in Dumfries, somewhere that people of all musical tastes could hang out. He remembers Adam talking about going to London. Surely in a city of eight million people he could find singers to front his tracks and a label willing to release them.

Lee recalled, 'He was talking about moving to London, possibly to do a course on sound management or recording or different things. Before he went away I spoke to him. I must have spoken to him about my plan to have my own business, opening a music café or something that involved music. I was going to Business Gateway. It helps people start their own businesses and gives you training. He seemed quite intrigued by this.'

Adam was nineteen and the money he had saved from stacking shelves would give him some security to move down south. And at least he had a place to stay. It was impulsive and perhaps risky, but

Ayah seemed like a cool girl and what was the worst that could happen?

As he formulated his plan he must have ditched the idea of a music course, preferring instead to find work to pay bills while using his spare time to progress his musical ambitions. He got his parents' blessing and in early 2003 prepared to transport his entire home-made studio down south. He hired a Ford Transit van and, with his dad's help, loaded it up with all his worldly belongings.

'I thought that would get me signed,' he said. 'I moved my whole studio down there in a big Transit van. My dad drove me down.'

He was taking a gamble but knew he would only get ahead if he stuck his neck out. For a boy who had lived in Dumfries his whole life and only been to London on a day trip, it was a huge step.

He was off to seek his fortune. Would he find the streets were paved with gold?

4

Creating Calvin

ADAM could always tell when it was about to happen. It was the sheer audacity that got to him. The brazen disregard for authority or rule of law.

It was going to happen again, and as he looked around the chilled-foods section, he realised he was the only member of staff around.

He watched as the man strode over to the meat section. They always knew where to come – where the prime cuts were stacked. As he approached the steaks, the man produced a large Lidl bag from his pocket. These people were so wide he didn't even try to disguise his crime with an M&S bag. Casual as you like, the man lifted as many packets of meat as his hand would carry and dumped them into the carrier bag. Then he reached for another.

Adam looked round again. No one.

The security guard was not on for another half an hour. They knew this, of course. It was why they came so early.

The man cleaned out the shelf, scrunched up the top of his bag, turned and headed to the exit.

This was not in Adam's job description. He was paid only to ensure the shelves were kept stocked with food.

The man was nearly at the door. Someone had to do something.

Adam stepped forward.

'Excuse me,' he said. 'Where are you going with that?'

The man stopped. He looked at Adam with dead eyes. One hand was inside his coat. He opened it wide enough for Adam to catch the glint of metal. *As you were.*

Adam stood back.

The man grunted. It was as if he was thinking, *How dare someone challenge me?* He strode off in the direction of the pub down the road. In a few minutes those steaks would be sold on for a fraction of the price Marks & Spencer were selling them for. Recalling this much later, Adam said, 'They did it every day.'

Adam shrugged and went back to the food hall. Those chicken fillets wouldn't stack themselves.

Tackling knife-wielding thieves was not what Adam had had in mind when he'd moved to London. The irony of his situation was not lost on him. He had left Dumfries to try to make a name for himself so he didn't have to work in a supermarket. Yet here he was, stacking shelves in the food hall of M&S Clapham South.

And his hours were scarily reminiscent of his fish-factory days. He had to catch two buses to get from North London to Clapham to start his early shift.

Ayah Marar recalled, 'He used to get two night buses to get to work in the morning. I'd be coming home from clubbing and he'd be going to work.'

Despite the long hours, and even though he had only been in London for a few months, there was no escaping harsh economic reality. Even with a job, the rent for his small flat was three times what he was earning. His savings were dwindling fast.

The only upside was Ayah. Meeting her was the most positive thing that could have happened.

They were from wildly different backgrounds. Four years Adam's senior, she was born in Jordan to a Czech-Bulgarian mum and Jordanian dad and had attended an international school alongside members of Jordan's royal family. Musically, she had a different education to Adam. While he was still into football, Ayah had been listening to everything from Elton John, Boney M. and Freddie Mercury to the Beatles, Deep Purple and Thin Lizzy. At school she'd got into hip hop and something had clicked. She'd found her groove.

Yet despite being raised on different continents, Ayah and Adam did share some startling similarities. As a teenager she too had felt a desire to leave home and seek adventure elsewhere, but had left home at a younger age, at just seventeen.

'I love the Middle East,' she said. 'I loved growing up there and the values it instilled in me, but there was a distinct lack of support for my trade. As a young woman wanting to do something in music, there was a bit of a fight and it took me a while to convince people, including my father and family, that it was the right thing for me to do.'

Ayah hails from a prominent family in Jordan, where the majority of the population live below the poverty line, and for her to want to pursue a career in music was frowned upon by her parents, who had high aspirations for her, something to which Adam, as the son of a biochemist, might have been able to relate. She said, 'I told my dad I was leaving and there was nothing he could do about it. I just stormed off. I was cut off for a few years and just came to the UK. It just seemed natural; it felt like home to me. I knew that I couldn't do what I wanted to do musically in Jordan. I came to the UK with the mindset, "I need to prove it to myself, hang out with the big boys."'

Initially she attended Warwick University, reading history of art, and lived in Coventry. She had harboured a love for London after holidaying there, and after two years she moved to the city. 'London is the place where anybody can come to start their lives, to be who they want to be,' she said, and one can imagine her selling the city to a sceptical Adam as such. 'You can come from anywhere, from any background, any education, political views, it's still one of the few places in the world where you can do that.'

However, the fact that she was still in the city and was able to give Adam a helping hand was down to her own quirk of fate. Due to a problem with her visa she had had to return to Jordan. At the time Ayah wasn't even known as a singer, yet producers Loxy & Ink, who had met her while she was in London, were looking for someone to front a drum and bass track and called her while she was back home.

'Loxy & Ink gave me my first break on a record,' she said. 'I couldn't stay in the country and I went back and I remember one of them calling me and saying, "We've got this track and we know you're not really a singer but we know that you like music. Would you like to give it go?" I said, "Yeah," and that was what started it all.'

She came back to the UK, recorded the track, worked at Uptown Records and started to make music a full-time occupation, turning her hand to all sorts of genres and roles. She started a funk band and went on to launch a drum and bass record label, promote club nights and become a touring MC.

Much of this was still to come, as she offered Adam and his recording equipment space in her flat, but she was set on the path to music and experimenting as a singer. Her first single was released in 2001 on Metalheadz and when Adam discovered she could hold a tune it seemed they were destined to work together.

He had come to London to find singers and had found one in the next room. He surely could not have believed his luck. And Ayah was not just any singer. Although she had come to soul and funk relatively late, her voice was rich, deep and husky, with terrific range and sparkling with personality. Not content with singing other people's words, she was a committed lyricist too, and it must have been refreshing for Adam – after years of feeling he was on his own musically in Dumfries – to have someone to spark off.

Ayah has also said that she too found solace in music when things got tough. 'Music was there for me when people weren't,' she has said.

Ayah seems to possess a God-given knack for recognising talent when she sees it. She would later spot the future star in a young Ed Sheeran, and she knew from the moment she listened to Adam's demos that he possessed something special. 'I don't know if it's something that I've got or whether I have a knack for it, but I think that anything that comes from a true place, a place of love and honesty, the technicalities don't really matter, the performance doesn't matter – [but] if the performance is real, you'll know, you'll feel it. And I felt that with [Adam],' she said.

'There are other people that I saw that in, like Ed Sheeran. He used to support me when I played an acoustic night in North London. I remember telling people about him and they were like,

"No, that young boy has a long way to go," but I was like, "No, no, no, there's something about this kid." There's something about true grit that shines through.'

When Adam and Ayah started working together, they found they clicked. 'We've written a lot of tracks together,' Ayah said. 'We did a track called "Let Me Know" when we were living together, also on his Amiga. It took ages. You have to record the vocal, burn it onto a CD, load it on the deck. There's no Auto-Tune, there's no tracking, none of that.'

They recorded it all at her place, on Adam's equipment, which, once it was all in his room, hardly left space for a bed. 'He brought a vocal booth, which took up most of his room. He had his desk there,' Ayah said.

Now that he was recording with an actual singer, Adam figured he needed a new name with which to relaunch his career. Stouffer was a handy stopgap, but he must have felt it wasn't a name on which to base a serious assault on the industry. When it came to devising a new name – one that could provide a completely new persona – he wanted something that was ethnically neutral.

For inspiration he looked to gangsta rapper Snoop Dogg, whose real name was Calvin Cordozar Broadus. As pal Mark Irving added, 'When he went to London, I don't think he thought Adam Wiles sounded very cool, so he chose the name Calvin. It came from the rapper Snoop Dogg – that's his real name – but I have no idea where Harris comes from.'

Adam has said, 'My first single was more of a soul track, and I thought Calvin Harris sounded a bit more racially ambiguous. I thought people might not know if I was black or not. After that, I was stuck with it.'

And so Calvin Harris was born. It was a name he would grow into. He had the pop star persona, but not the life.

Although his time in London had been successful inasmuch as he had found a singer, his battle to keep his head above water was proving less so.

Ayah's place was in Golders Green, in North London, and even though the name promised Dick Whittington-style riches he always knew it was going to be tough to make ends meet.

31

The long schlep he had to endure to work meant that the staff discount was about the only bonus from his working life: 'The best thing about working at Marks & Spencer? The 20 per cent discount: take that off a packet of Percy Pigs, that's 79p. Amazing.'

As money got tighter, however, even the staff discount didn't cut it: 'I used to steal Percy Pigs from the M&S food hall, sometimes even the cows and sheep if I was feeling particularly ballsy. I'd devour them on my lunch break.'

This wasn't how it was supposed to be. He had been under no illusions, but he had hoped that gradually his music would take over from the day job. He was discovering the hard way that he was a very small fish in one of the world's largest and most competitive ponds. As it was, songwriting sessions with Ayah aside, his recording equipment was sitting in his room, unused.

'I was too busy lining up chicken fillets in Marks & Spencer and stopping people nicking big beef joints and selling them in the pub down the road,' he said. 'Just working constantly and not making tunes.'

The demos he did send out got the usual response. 'It was always the same letter,' he said. 'In fact, one label that I sent numerous tapes to sent me back more than one identical rejection letter, each with the same spelling mistake. I don't think they even listened to the tape.'

He tried to delay the inevitable but eventually had to admit defeat: 'It was the worst year in the world. I would work, sleep and cook my dinner. It was a bit of a disaster. I felt I had failed.'

By early 2004, his adventure in London was coming to an end. He spoke to his bosses at M&S and asked about the possibility of a transfer to Dumfries. At least if he moved back in with his parents he could regroup, save some cash and work out his next move.

'So eventually I ran out of money in London,' he said, 'moved back to Dumfries and transferred to M&S there.'

5

Fly Eyes on the Prize

MOST viewers who watched the vivid technicolor splendour of T. Rex only focused on one thing – the gyrating genius of glam-rock god Marc Bolan, who the camera seemed to love to the exclusion of all other band members.

But one pair of eyes studying an old BBC clip from the seventies was drawn to Steve Peregrin Took, sitting at a keyboard, looking effortlessly cool in a set of oversized 'fly' shades with dozens of what looked like diamonds dotted all over each lens. The eyes belonged to Adam Wiles. And he knew he had to have shades just like them. However, sourcing them would be the hard part.

'I was watching *The Old Grey Whistle Test* on BBC2,' he said, 'and they were showing T. Rex. The keyboard player had those sunglasses on and I just thought they were amazing.'

Back in Dumfries he found the town had little in the way of shades for the aspiring pop star, so he did what any resourceful guy would do – he made his own, using diamante sequins instead of diamonds. They were practically impossible to see through but provided exactly the look he wanted. 'I searched everywhere for a pair, but when I couldn't find them I decided to make my own. I just made a pair out of cardboard and bubble wrap. It took me a couple of days. I took a picture of myself with them on, turned up the contrast, made it black and white and that became my logo.'

He had the new name, the songs, the look. All he needed now was the record deal.

Although he considered his time in London a disaster, it had not been a complete failure. Manchester house pioneers Justin Crawford

33

and Luke Cowdrey, who operated under the nom de plume Unabombers, selected 'Let Me Know', the song Adam had recorded with Ayah in his bedroom, for their 2004 live-mix CD *Electric Soul Vol. 2*.

It was a small ripple on a gigantic pond. Despite the small appreciation of his talents, Adam was feeling disillusioned; after years of feeling invincible, of being convinced that he had something to offer the music industry, it was beginning to feel like it would never happen.

Dance music expert Tim Barr, author of *Brighter Daze: The Dance Music Revolution* and *The Mini Rough Guide to Techno Music*, recalled some impressive influences on those early releases but said the records struggled to make an impact because the scene was in a state of flux at the time.

'If you go back to his earliest releases,' Tim said, 'the Stouffer tracks or the track with Ayah, for instance, they betray the influence of some very forward-thinking New York records – releases by Masters at Work and Todd Terry, obviously, but also David Morales and Eric Kupper. By the time he released those records, however, that strand of house music was experiencing something of a reversal of fortunes commercially. Sales were significantly down, and for a new artist it was a tough market to crack. So it's not difficult to see why he'd have begun to recalculate his approach and rework his sound. Particularly by the time of the Ayah record, there are some important developments that, I think, go a long way to explaining how that might have happened.'

Adam continued to send out the demos, but each rejection felt like a body blow – his dream dying from a thousand cuts.

'From the age of fourteen to twenty, I thought I was incredible,' he said. 'Then, when I was twenty, I had my confidence battered and I thought I was rubbish. Labels saying no, all the dance tunes I was making, they were like, "Nah, bit weird." So I thought, "Wow, I'm actually not good enough. That sucks."

'I was more or less on the verge of giving up. By the time I was twenty-one or twenty-two, I was getting pretty jaded. No one seemed to be that interested in what I was doing.

'I was getting nowhere. I stopped making house records.'

As hard as it was to accept, he had to admit his aspirations were on hold. He started to resign himself to the fact that the music he was making might have to be for his benefit only.

'I just started making dance tunes I wanted to hear and it became a hobby again. I was doing it for a laugh, but I started to enjoy it more. I started messing about, listening to nothing but good hip hop and making beats for myself.

'My M&S salary didn't really stretch to sophisticated gear, so I was forced to use fairly basic stuff. It was actually pretty beneficial because I had to work extra hard to make it sound any good. I didn't have the option of just pressing a button to create a drum sound.'

After a couple of months back in Dumfries he settled into a routine and started to think like an average employee for a big company. 'I decided to try to become a normal person and see how far I could get working for M&S,' he said. 'I even bought a family car, a Vectra, and made music just for fun.'

He got on well with his M&S colleagues and even started socialising, joining them for after-work drinks on Friday nights in the Globe Inn, across from the supermarket. Adam enjoyed drinking in there and it's easy to see why. The pub, one of the oldest in Scotland, dating back to 1610, and the favourite 'howff' or haunt of Robert Burns when he frequented the town, has an atmosphere all of its own.

Burns was so enamoured of the place that he wrote of the kindness of the then owners, William and Meg Hyslop, who gave him a room in which to sleep – which is still there today. Also preserved are two poems that Burns etched into the windows during his time there, one an ode to barmaid Polly Stewart. When Burns drank in the Globe, he was working as either a farmer or, later, an exciseman, while writing his poetry when he could, something Adam might well have related to.

'I'm very fond of the Globe Inn in Dumfries,' Adam said, 'where Rabbie used to go drinking and is even purported to have scribbled some of his poetry on the wall. Burns was a trailblazer, a true visionary. And the fact that he was a bit of a rock star in his day makes me like him even more.'

Working in the Globe was Adam's old school friend Lee McQueen, who was still trying to pursue his own dream of opening a music café in the town. Although Adam might have been trying to progress within Marks & Spencer, he was also keeping his options open and was clearly still desperate to do something music-related. Lee remembers Adam calling him up when he moved back to Dumfries.

Lee was impressed that Adam had remembered the idea. But he was further surprised when Adam offered him a proposition – how would he feel about going into business together, as partners?

Lee recalled, 'He said he was back in Dumfries and asked if I was still doing something along those lines: "How far did you get with your idea?"

'It was quite a surprise when he called and wanted to be part of it,' Lee recalled. 'He had remembered what I [had] said about trying to start my own business and he wanted to make it work. I said I was still going to Business Gateway but I hadn't got that far. Although the agency helped you start your own business, you still had to provide your own money, which was the big downfall in my plan so far.'

'He asked if I fancied joining up. We went for a pint and discussed it. We weren't sure what we wanted to do, but we knew it would be around music.'

Although he had not been back in Dumfries for long, Adam's feet were getting itchy. While he enjoyed the security his job with Marks & Spencer offered, Adam could not suppress the desire to make music. The urge to get involved in the music scene once again took hold and he started DJ'ing. It provided some money on the side but also gave Adam the opportunity to get out of his bedroom and perform, albeit still behind the decks. If the café idea got off the ground, he could develop his skills there too.

Lee was delighted to have a partner on board, but they had one small problem – cash flow. Lee recalled, 'He was DJ'ing at that point so we had a wide scope. He could DJ and I could play. We wanted it to be a place for youngsters, but we had to get the money to do it. We had the idea of playing individually to raise the money to put into the business. We approached the manager of a nightclub in the town, the Venue, about hosting nights there and the money would go back into the business.'

With Adam on board, Lee's idea started to take shape. 'We both started going to Business Gateway and went to the bank, opened an account,' Lee said. 'Adam set that up. It cost a tenner and he asked if I was happy with that. He set up the name of the company. We needed an account for the business and trade status. We had everything – except the money.'

Although the lads were performing live – Lee with his accordion and traditional musicians; Adam with his DJ set – it was going to be a slow process generating the kind of cash needed to launch their own venture.

Adam seemed to grow impatient at the speed of progress and looked at other ways to generate funds.

'We were down at Business Gateway one day,' Lee recalled, 'and the receptionist told us that the town was about to be rejuvenated and redeveloped over the next ten years. One of the streets earmarked for transformation was Friars Vennel, leading down to the river.'

When Adam heard this, his ears pricked up. 'Why don't we go down and have a look at the Vennel?' he asked Lee. 'We could buy a place, then wait until it gets redeveloped and sell it and make the money to put into the business.'

The scale of Adam's ambition took Lee aback. 'It was quite a big jump,' he said. 'People our age weren't even thinking about buying houses then, let alone buying property to make a profit.'

Adam wasn't to be deterred, however. A short time later he called Lee and told him he had something he wanted to show him: 'He took me down to this building in the Vennel. It was just a shell. He said, "What do you think?"'

Lee surveyed the building; it was like a bomb had hit it.

'I looked at it and said, "It hasn't even got a f*cking roof!"

'"I know," Adam said, "but it's the potential. Forget about the building or what is left of it."

'I said, "How is it going to work?"

'He said, 'Think about the space. We wouldn't be doing anything with the building."'

Adam talked enthusiastically about the site's potential.

'He talked me round,' said Lee, 'and I could see what he was saying.'

The next stumbling block, however, was raising the cash to buy the derelict building. Lee said, 'I had a flat in the town and he was staying with his parents, so we didn't have that sort of money. We were both looking to people we knew to help us out.'

Adam's plan seemed viable, but until they had the funds it was as much a pipe dream as anything. The two friends decided they would continue playing their own styles of music, and saving the cash with a view to buying the building. Adam told Lee he had landed some gigs in Glasgow – at King Tut's Wah Wah Hut, the venue where Oasis were famously discovered.

Lee was impressed but admitted he was ignorant about what exactly Adam was doing. The naturally shy man wasn't giving too much away. 'I knew he was going out DJ'ing, but I never asked much about it,' said Lee. 'I didn't know that much about it, so I didn't ask. I assumed he was doing parties and the like. Then I heard he was doing King Tut's in Glasgow. I just took it that it was a pub. He said he was going up to do his first gig up there. That didn't mean that much to me because I didn't go out that much in Glasgow.

'I remember mentioning it to a mate, who asked what exactly it was Adam was doing there. "It's quite a big venue," he said. "Is he supporting someone else or is it a fun night, because they get quite a lot of big acts." I didn't know. He was getting more gigs at this place on a regular basis.'

Lee left Adam to get on with his thing, while he kept up his end of the bargain by working and playing out live. He said, 'I was doing my own thing, so we agreed we'd work on our own things and rather than meeting up on a regular basis we'd meet about every month and take it from there and see how we were getting on.

'After a few months he was doing nights under his own name. By then I was thinking about buying a house. We agreed while he was getting these gigs and I was buying my house to leave it until we could see what was going to happen. We never set a time. Even though I was trying to buy a house and that might have affected how much I could borrow for anything else, it might also have helped us by improving my credit rating. The mortgage might help us.'

Although the mates were working on their own things, they remained focused on their shared goals – or so Lee thought.

He hadn't heard from Adam in some time when one night he walked into the Globe Inn to start his shift behind the bar. His attention was drawn to the TV screen. Lee stared in disbelief. He recognised the man on the screen, dancing and gyrating around like a bona fide pop star.

It couldn't be, could it? Was that really the shy young lad who hadn't ventured out onstage for the charity music marathon all those years ago? Was that him there, on the screen, singing about life in the 1980s? Lee was baffled. He really should have paid more attention to what Adam Wiles had been up to.

Clearly a lot had happened in the previous couple of months. A lot indeed.

6

Merrymaking at Myspace

'ABOUT bloody time.'

As the champagne popped all around him and people were celebrating the signing of a hot new musical talent, one man remained unfazed. After all, he was the overnight sensation who it had taken seven years to discover.

By then Adam had grown into a 'cynical b*****d'. But now he had his chance. And he wasn't going to blow it.

He had finally made the breakthrough – after the disappointment of London, and at a time when he had told Lee he was going to concentrate on his music purely to raise money for their joint café venture. Yet when it happened it was down as much to fate as any grand design.

In early 2006 Myspace was the fastest growing social-networking site (before social networking was even a recognised term); it had become so popular that Rupert Murdoch's News Corporation saw fit to shell out $580 million for its acquisition. However, the idea that it was a platform from which budding young musicians could launch an assault on the world was yet to be established. Back then it was simply a space on the worldwide web that people called their own – a mini site on which to write a blog, post pictures and put up your favourite songs. Its simplicity and usability was the key to its success. Quickly, word spread. People could customise their pages and experiment with their online personas. In addition, and most crucially, the infancy of the web meant that everyone – musicians, celebrities, and the movers and shakers – was in the same boat. It offered the kind of access to important people that had previously been unthinkable.

Adam knew little about the site when a pal suggested they set up their own pages. His friend had been the first of the two to become switched on to the benefits of the site, of its suitability for posting tunes and building contacts. Furthermore, a run-in with the law – for a 'minor offence' – had resulted in Adam's friend having to wear an electronic tag monitoring his movements, with the proviso that he could not leave the house after 6 p.m. for six months.

By day Adam was still stacking shelves at Marks & Spencer, gaining recognition in the produce department and working out how to better raise the cash that could get the café idea off the ground.

At night, with nothing better to do, he was Calvin Harris, posting tunes online that he had written over several years in the hope that someone significant would listen.

When his friend challenged him to see who would be the first to gain 1,000 connections on the site, Adam rose to it.

As he later recalled, 'My friend had an electronic tag. He'd done something bad, which in fairness wasn't really his fault, a minor offence. Basically he couldn't leave the house after 6 p.m. for six months.' He went on: 'I put the tracks up on Myspace to give myself something to do in the evenings. We had a race to see who could get a thousand Myspace friends first.'

He added that it was 'probably the most pathetic thing I've ever entered into'.

The friends started adding anyone in order to boost their profiles, but Adam soon developed a strategy, targeting fellow musicians or people in the industry, like A&R guys – the 'artists and repertoire' specialists whose job it was to source new talent for the record labels. The beauty of Myspace, particularly back in the innocent days of 2006, was that few people set their pages to private, so linking between friends was ridiculously easy.

In terms of their private competition, his friend hit the target far quicker. 'He won, obviously,' Adam admitted. 'He had a lot more time on his hands.'

He had posted four songs online but had already enjoyed a significant boost before then – one that says a lot about how dedicated he was to his craft. Adam had delivered a demo to legendary Radio 1 dance DJ Pete Tong, a man so famous his name had entered the language as rhyming slang for anything that ends up shaped like a pear. Pete liked what he'd heard, particularly one track called 'The Girls'. On it, tongue very definitely in cheek, Calvin Harris had sung boastfully about getting all the girls, somewhat ironically, given that Adam had not had a meaningful girlfriend for years.

Tong recalled, 'He came to me at a festival years ago with a CD and handed it to me. He was this tall, shy kid and it was a year before he blew up with his first album.'

Adam was delighted his song was played, but, listening to it in the context of a dance show amid several other more polished dance beats, he realised it had shortcomings. Adam recalled: 'When Pete Tong played an early mix of "The Girls" on the radio, it didn't sound too good, so I went back and worked on it and produced the final version. I wasn't aware at the time, but a lot of interest came from that.'

He posted the new version on his Myspace page, along with a track called 'Acceptable in the 80s', another song that on the surface didn't take itself too seriously but beneath the retro sound and light-hearted lyrics had a killer hook.

'I had a system,' he Adam said. 'I found, say, one person who was maybe a songwriter or an A&R or someone like that. I'd look at their top friends and then I'd click on each of the top friends – the ones that weren't private, I'd see what they did. So maybe one of them would be an A&R for EMI publishing, maybe one would be management, something like that. I added all of them and said, "Hey, check out my songs," like every other person.' By the time Adam's pal made his 1,000th friend, the Calvin Harris page was sitting at 960, but when it came to useful connections it was Adam's page that was making a far bigger impact.

While Adam had been clicking from person to person, keeping an eye on his 'friends' total, he spotted a name he recognised.

Felix Howard was a relatively new name on Myspace but an established one in the industry – and his introduction to the music business could not have contrasted more with Adam's. As a child model in the UK, he was plucked from obscurity and thrust into the worldwide spotlight by Madonna after she cast him in the video for 'Open Your Heart'. The thirteen-year-old melted the hearts of girls and was the envy of teenage boys around the globe, as he charmed Madonna's exotic dancer in the elaborate promo video. He was due to accompany the pop superstar on her subsequent Who's That Girl? world tour but couldn't get a work visa. His connection to the music business was born and he went on to become a songwriter.

Adam recognised Felix Howard's name but had no idea that he had just started in a new role – as an A&R man for EMI – and he was just the type of guy he should be getting to know.

'I happened to add this guy that just started his job at EMI publishing. I didn't know he was working for EMI, but I recognised him because he wrote a Sugababes song – the Sugababes being a British girl band who were cool back then,' he said. 'He wrote their first song, "Overload", which was a kind of moody, breakbeat song. I added him because he seemed like the kind of dude I might want to know via the Internet. He listened to the tracks because he was switching into A&R mode.'

To Adam's surprise, Felix got in touch, desperate to hear more. 'I got a big long message with the address and all sorts, saying, "Send me everything that you've done in a nice shiny package to this address," which I did.'

As if that wasn't enough, Adam was to receive two other slices of luck, as he recalled: 'At the time I added this other guy who said he wanted to act as my manager, which sounds kind of dodgy, but he had a lot of good connections.

'It all happened in the same week. Then there was another A&R man as well who worked for a completely separate company called CR2, which is just dance music, and then apparently the story goes they all played the CD to one guy at EMI – the boss. They all came in one week and they all played different tracks by me. And then when [the boss] realised that it was all by the same guy he was all, "Oh, we need to sign him."'

Among the other industry players who'd suddenly switched on to this dance-influenced pop producer was Tommie Sunshine, a Chicago-born producer and DJ who was starting to make a name for himself remixing American rock acts such as Fall Out Boy and

Good Charlotte. The company interested in managing Calvin Harris was Three Six Zero Group, founded by Mark Gillespie, a talent booker for festival organisers Global Gathering, and Dean Wilson, who'd honed his skills for talent representation at 24 Management. Calvin Harris would officially become their first signing under their joint venture.

Looking back, Adam appreciates to how much he owes that astonishing run of good fortune for launching the career he's had as Calvin Harris. 'I wasn't like an Internet [sensation],' he admitted. 'I wasn't known. It was just that I added the right guys.'

And, in terms of timing, it couldn't have happened at a more crucial moment.

'By the time I was twenty-one or twenty-two, I was getting pretty jaded,' he said. 'No one seemed to be that interested in what I was doing. That was when I joined Myspace. Back then it was a god-send. It was a way of getting my tunes out there. Adding loads of DJs and record labels to my list of "friends". My music landed in the hands of the right people at the right time . . . purely by chance. I was *this close* to giving up!'

He added, 'Had those three people not sent the track at the same time, I'd probably still be Nobby No-Mates, pissing around in my bedroom. That was my one bit of luck and it allowed me to get my foot in the door . . . I don't know why I bothered trying to get people to listen to my CDs because all it took was joining Myspace.'

Regarding Felix Howard in particular, he said, 'I'd recognised his name and wondered if he wanted to write a song with me. Nowadays, there are so many bands he doesn't have the time to listen to them but, because he had just joined back then, he listened to my songs and liked them. That's how it began.'

As interest in Calvin grew, a meeting was scheduled in London to discuss how to take his career forward. Yet, as exciting as it was to finally achieve some recognition for his music, Adam was still a dedicated worker for M&S.

'We had a meeting in London, he recalled, 'and it escalated from there. I remember going to a record-label meeting and thinking, "I can't stay. I've got to get back to M&S because I work there."'

His would-be managers and collaborators were keen to tie the artist known as Calvin Harris down to a publishing deal. What had attracted their attention was the fact that this Harris guy wrote, produced and performed every note of his infectiously catchy songs himself. In addition, he had fourteen songs that could effectively make up his debut album. When you think about it, signing Harris was a no-brainer – a one-man operation with an ear for pop melodies. It's a wonder he hadn't been snapped up sooner.

But when Howard and Sunshine found out just how Adam had been producing the tunes that gave birth to his alter ego, they were shocked. 'I showed producers what I had been using and they just laughed and said, "What do you really use?" It was Stone Age compared to what everyone else had and what I'm using now. It was ridiculous.'

Regardless of how he did it, EMI wanted to sign him up to a publishing deal. Calvin Harris the pop star was edging closer to becoming a reality. However, a publishing deal does not necessarily lead to a record deal. For the time being, that did not matter to Adam. The publishing deal at least allowed him to work as a producer and writer – and get paid for it. He was on his way into the music business and he couldn't wait to call time on his other career.

Ironically, at M&S, while his music ambitions had been stalling, he had been progressing up the promotion ladder. His days as a shelf-stacker were behind him. The management in the Dumfries store had spotted his potential. 'I'd been working in the fruit-and-veg section in Marks & Spencer and they wanted to promote me to head of the department,' he said of the period just before the publishing deal was finalised. 'I went to a fruit conference with the heads of all the other Scottish stores and got to taste some delicious mangoes, so I thought, "This isn't all bad."'

When he finally put pen to paper on the publishing deal, he knew what he had to do. 'My publishing [deal] came through and I left,' he explained, calling the day on which he handed in his notice 'probably one of the happiest days of my life'. The news didn't go down well, however. 'My boss was really angry,' he said. 'She goes, "Where will I get a new fruit-and-veg man?"'

45

Adam was now officially Calvin Harris and he wasn't caring. 'Within that month I'd signed the deal and I'd stacked my last chicken breast on the shelf,' he said.

An exciting new chapter was beginning. After all the hard knocks he was on the cusp of something great. Yet he refused to get carried away. His bitter experiences so far had taught him not to get ahead of himself. 'When I finally got signed, I wasn't blown away. My attitude was: About bloody time.'

'It's turned me into a cynical b*****d,' he candidly admitted. 'Even when I was literally signing my deal and people were having champagne, I was like, "Aye, but the record's not actually out yet – it could bomb."'

He was itching to release his own music, but his new management had other ideas. Even though he did not have a hit single to his name, they were lining him up to work with one of the biggest names in the pop world.

How would he like to work with Kylie Minogue?

Calvin Harris needed a stiff drink!

7

I Should Be So Lucky

WHAT do you do when you're due to meet pop royalty – and not just to shake hands in passing, but to help relaunch the career of someone who had dominated the charts for seventeen years?

You hit the Jack Daniel's.

That's what Calvin Harris did ahead of his first studio meeting with Kylie Minogue. In fact, he downed three measures of the bourbon – curiously, mixed with orange juice.

It was September 2006 and the Australian pop princess was working on her tenth studio album, X. It was her first after she had been diagnosed, at thirty-six, with breast cancer in May 2005 – an announcement that had shocked the music world and forced her to cancel her Showgirl world tour and take an eighteen-month hiatus.

By the time she was ready to go back in the studio she was due to shortly resume that world tour and hopefully pick up her career from where she had left off. Already something of an institution, Kylie had retained a special place in the hearts of the British public since she first appeared on television screens. There was even greater sympathy for her since her successful battle against cancer. However, there would be no charity from her critics if her latest incarnation fell short of the mark. The singer had enjoyed a hugely successful career, constantly seeming to defy trends with the kind of dogged determination normally associated with Madonna. It was with the pop queen that Kylie was most commonly compared and, like Madonna, her success had been down to the company she kept.

Her collaborations with SAW launched her career, but, although they had brought chart success, artistically she had felt stifled. A high-profile relationship with INXS singer Michael Hutchence signalled an edgier public persona but also a new sound and marked a period where she claimed greater control over her musical choices. Although her ratings in the charts dipped, the change allowed her some freedom.

Her work with Steve Anderson, a writer and producer who has been with her since 1992, resulted in some of her finest work, starting with the single 'Confide in Me'. Yet she nearly blew it in 1997 when an experiment with Manic Street Preachers' James Dean Bradfield and Sean Moore led to accusations she was trying to ditch her pop background and forge a more indie sound.

It was only when she recaptured her signature style with the ridiculously danceable 'Spinning Around' that she returned to a firmer footing and to the top of the charts. Since then she'd stuck to safer ground, but in 2006 the goal was to bring her back into the public eye with a strong new sound, while not betraying her disco-dance roots.

Who better to team her up with, then, than a precocious new kid whose own reputation had yet to be formed?

For Calvin, it was a whirlwind introduction to the music world, especially as he was someone who was wary about collaborating with another singer. When it was a singer who had sold more than 70 million records worldwide, however, it was a different story. 'I didn't need to think about it twice,' Calvin said. 'I mean, it's Kylie!'

He explained how it came about: 'I had a publishing deal with EMI, they were sending out demo CDs of my stuff, and one got to Kylie's A&R man.'

That man was Jamie Nelson. Immediately he was sufficiently impressed to think Calvin could be a good match for Kylie, but in the first instance he wanted to try Harris out with something a little more straightforward. Nelson also looked after All Saints, the girl band who enjoyed great success in the mid to late nineties with a string of hits, including 'Never Ever', which sold over 1.2 million copies, 770,000 of which came before it reached number one, earning it a place in the Guinness World Records. The band split in

2001 but reformed five years later when subsequent solo and spin-off projects were less successful, suggesting the girls together were more than the sum of their parts. 'Rock Steady', with a November 2006 release date, was to be their comeback single, and Nelson thought a remix by a promising new producer might give them even fresher appeal.

Calvin said, '[Jamie Nelson] heard my stuff and he said, "Oh, that's good, would you like to remix All Saints?" So I said OK and I did that.'

Nelson must have been suitably pleased with the result because once that was delivered he had another project in mind.

Calvin went on: 'After that, he said, "That was good, would you like to work with Kylie?" So I said, "Well, yes!" So we did that and before I knew it I was in the studio with her, writing a song.'

Nelson's interest had initially gone beyond hooking up Calvin with Kylie – he had wanted the talented Scot for himself. Calvin explained: 'I think he briefly wanted to sign me, but I'd already just about signed with Sony, so he asked me how I'd feel about producing for [Kylie]. That was it. Two weeks later, I was in the studio with her.'

Originally Calvin worked with singer Róisín Murphy, who wanted to develop a sophisticated dance sound after splitting from Moloko to go solo. However, his tracks did not make her album, so by the time he was due to meet Kylie the pressure was on and it was by no means assured that they would hit it off.

That's when he turned to the JD and orange for a confidence booster.

'It was scary being in a little room with Kylie,' Calvin said. 'I needed a shot of Jack Daniel's to calm my nerves. That wasn't a very good idea. It was early in the morning and I ended up a bit drunk, but just as nervous.'

Calvin travelled from Scotland well prepared, with a number of tracks for her to choose from. He explained, 'I went down with eight instrumentals and she picked the ones she wanted to work on.'

It was an odd pairing – in more ways than one. At 6 ft 5¾ in., Calvin towers above most people, but to the pop pixie, who stands at just under five foot, he must have seemed like the giant he had always wanted to be. Calvin acknowledged it was a noticeable difference. 'She's a funny height,' he said later, pointing to just above his belly button. 'She came up to here on me.'

Calvin wasn't the only writer Kylie was working with. The fact that Biff Stannard, who wrote for the Spice Girls and had a wealth of experience, was in the studio with him helped bridge the gap between this raw Scots talent and that of one of the doyennes of the pop scene.

Calvin said, 'There were no nerves, as she is so down to earth.' On Stannard, he added, 'He helped break the ice.'

It's hard to imagine that Kylie is anything other than as sweet and wholesome as her image and reputation suggest and, if anything, Calvin was relieved to find her even lovelier in the flesh than he imagined. 'She has a strange, mystical aura,' he said. 'Everyone said, "You'll love Kylie, she even makes the tea, blah blah blah." That's what media people say. But she did. She let me stroke her hair as well. It's soft, like a little lamb.'

He added, 'Kylie is the loveliest person. She's awesome. I've never met anyone who had a bad word to say about her. And she's ridiculously nice too. She brought carrot cake to the studio.'

The fact that she was keen to put him at ease was clearly something Calvin appreciated, but when they got down to the business of making music he was equally impressed by how much she got involved. 'Kylie was amazing,' he said. 'I didn't realise just how much she contributed musically. She was lovely to work with. Really fantastic.' He added, 'She writes the songs! I wasn't expecting that at all. I came with a backing track, but then it was her who was coming up with most of the ideas. She's a really, really good writer.'

'She was very energetic and proactive,' he gushed.

He was relieved it was going quite smoothly, but it seems he was always aware of his place – and was never entirely comfortable, understandably, in those early first sessions.

'I just talked to her like I'd talk to anybody else,' he revealed. 'I tried not to offend her, but I tended to keep myself to myself. There's almost always another writer in the room with me. During a lot of the sessions I did with Kylie, and with Róisín too, I said very, very little and just nodded when I thought it was a good time to nod, or went to the toilet when I needed to, and that was it.

'Although I had lots of ideas, I found it hard to articulate them and didn't like to ask if she'd mind trying them out. That was one of my first writing sessions, so it wasn't great. I didn't really know what to do. What do you do when you're in a room with Kylie? She says, "Shall I do this?" and I'd panic and say, "I don't know, ask him," pointing to the other writer.'

He went on: 'I ramble as well. I remember on occasion seeing Kylie Minogue's eyes glaze over when I was talking to her. And that image fills me with regret.'

On the whole, though, his time in the studio with Kyle was an incredible experience. After all, she could have had her pick of many of the world's finest writers and producers and chose a shelf-stacker from Dumfries.

Although he cringes at some aspects, other memories have lived with him. 'Kylie was bouncing about to my music, she said she loved it,' he recalled. 'She even put a photo of us recording in Australia's *Vogue* magazine, which she guest-edited.'

In all, he was living his dream. 'That was one of those things I dreamt of doing as a boy. I love making songs with different people and it was great, as she was just a normal girl.'

The end result of their collaboration was 'my music with her singing on it – dirtier than the usual Kylie song' – 'but quite poppy', he added.

They recorded five or six tracks, but Calvin had no idea how many – if any at all – would make it on to her album. He obviously hoped his would be in contention.

He was delighted with the way things had gone with Kylie, but their collaboration wasn't going to soften his view on working with other singers. He said, 'It was just kind of forced upon me and you can't say no if someone asks if you want to work with Kylie. But I never really have the time to work with other people because I'm very controlling and precious about my music and I find it very hard collaborating. Which is good, because I went down with backing tracks for that particular session so it was strictly lyrics and melody, which is fine, but just don't mess with my bassline!'

One of the first radio DJs to discover Calvin Harris on Myspace was Radio 1's Vic Galloway – and he was in no doubt about what would have attracted Kylie to Harris. 'I'm sure Kylie would have been blown away when she heard his music,' Vic said. 'It's often the case that big stars such as her and Madonna look to relatively unknown producers to inject something new into their music. Calvin is really innovative.'

The collaboration caused such a stir that Kylie's people came out at the time to confirm: 'Kylie has been working on some tracks with Calvin. She heard some stuff he'd done before and liked it. Things are going well in the studio.'

That Kylie had chosen to work with such an unknown talent did wonders for Calvin's reputation. He became a go-to guy for A&R people and was next remixing a track for childhood heroes Jamiroquai.

Crucially, however, it also sparked interest in his own music. From the time he signed his publishing deal to working with Kylie, he had contemplated the kind of musician he wanted to become. Being a producer and writer behind the scenes was one thing, but once there was interest from labels in developing him as an artist in his own right he had other factors to consider.

Initially he had been against becoming a pop star, particularly the playing live element. Deep down he must have remembered his experience at the hotel charity event with Lee. The idea of putting himself out there still terrified him. But the more the labels wanted him, the more it became clear that he would have re-evaluate those opinions.

Regarding playing live, he said, 'I was dead against it. People who are solely producers suffer, even if they're making really good tunes. But then it became apparent that I was only going to get signed if I did live shows.'

Luckily, he didn't have to look too far from home for musicians who could join him on his pop-star adventure – old school friends Mark Irving on bass and guitar and Sean McCole on keyboards were willing to lend a hand. Sean was six months older than Calvin and shared his pal's deep passion for the technical side of music, learning his craft by playing live from an early age with a number of bands and developing his knowledge by studying music and audio technology at Stow College in Glasgow. He was an invaluable addition to Calvin's live act, as he could draw on wide musical influences, including folk, alternative rock and electronic beats, and as well as being proficient on the keyboards and guitar he understood the drum machine and could even chip in with backing vocals. Mark was one of the first people to tell people about Myspace, so his inclusion in the band was in small part a reward for helping him to discover the site that led to his record deal. Calvin said, 'I put him in my band as compensation: "You did well . . . you can play guitar."'

With his band in place, he embarked on some gigs to build his confidence. The dates at King Tut's that Lee McQueen thought were part of his old pal's DJ'ing attempts were likely early performances. Calvin said of those early gigs, 'I can't DJ! I've never DJ'd because of that. I do have a band, there's five of us inclusive, and I am the front man. My job is to occasionally "sing", that's in inverted commas, and basically dance about to the other members of the band, who are actually musicians.'

Playing live and being in front of a mic, centre stage, showed how much he was willing to make his dream a reality. And once he made the decision to do whatever it took to make it, the interest grew.

'It quickly escalated into a minor bidding war between these two labels,' he said. 'I had a publishing deal and then the publishers put me in with Kylie Minogue. At the time Kylie Minogue was a huge, huge, huge pop star, like at the peak of her career in the UK and Australia. So they were like, "Who's this twenty-two-year-old who we've never heard of producing for one of the biggest pop stars of our generation?", so that got labels interested.'

As there was interest from more than one party, Calvin's position was strengthened. He could insist on all sorts of conditions and he was keen to limit the control from outside producers or writers. He had come this far on his own talent; he didn't want to sign to a major label just to hand over that control to someone else. Columbia Records, the label most keen to secure Calvin Harris, were only too happy to agree. Calvin said, 'You can put all sorts of things in the contract [and] the A&R will not change anything. He's [Calvin Harris] mixing it himself, he's producing it himself, which is fair enough, kind of.'

Calvin Harris signed to Sony's Columbia Records in late 2006. His album – the thing he had dreamed about as a young teenager – was about to become a reality. Once he had the assurances he wanted, he had no hesitation in signing for a major label. Perhaps in an ideal world he would have loved to have hit the big time with a smaller label, but as he said, 'I tried to do the indie route, but, [with] the sort of music I was making, it was hard to know where to pitch it. As soon as there was a chance to sign with a major, I was like, "Yeah, definitely."'

Once signed, Calvin was ready to go. He already had a complete album of songs – and he wasn't that keen on changing anything. His A&R man at his new label was Mike Pickering, a man who you would think was a perfect fit for Calvin. Pickering was a resident DJ at the legendary Haçienda club in Manchester, the birthplace of the Madchester music scene, which fused dance and alternative rock, and led to the Second Summer of Love and the rise of acid house, which had so captivated the young Adam Wiles. During Pickering's time at Factory Records – home of Joy Division and New Order – he signed the Happy Mondays and James, and enjoyed staggering success in his own right with the band he founded, wrote for and produced, and which even bore his initials: M People. With a Mercury Music Prize under his belt for the album *Elegant Slumming*, which spawned a number of monster hits such as 'One Night in Heaven' and 'Moving on Up', Pickering knew a thing or two about what it took to produce a hit record.

When asked how instrumental this relationship had been in producing the sound for his first album, Calvin revealed Pickering 'has no influence at all', adding, 'It's a good relationship to have in a music business where so many people try to push you this way and that.'

He also further explained his newfound belief in his own talent. 'When you first get signed, you think that you're amazing. So I thought I was doing well. I didn't really try very hard on the whole first album because I thought it would do, which is an amazing attitude to have, as someone who was barely signed and was so precariously hanging on to his record deal. "Nah, that'll do, that's fine." It was crazy.

'I figured that because I was responsible for this record, it was like, "I could make it better if I wanted to, but I just don't want to." It was good enough. It ended up really [as] this raw album.'

As 2007 began, he knew it could be the year that changed his life forever. It was time to launch Calvin Harris on an unsuspecting public.

8

Acceptable at Last

BUDDING musicians only have to walk into the hallowed subterranean corridors of the BBC's Maida Vale Studios to feel the weight of history bearing down on them. For many, simply the sight of a plaque with the words 'The Beatles recorded here' is enough to give them the jitters. It's a sign you've entered the big league.

Calvin could have been forgiven for feeling like a footballer about to walk under the 'This is Anfield' sign for the first time. Yet he took it all in his stride.

In March 2007, he and his five-piece band were in Maida Vale to perform a live session for Pete Tong's Radio 1 show. In another studio an orchestra were in full swing. Gone were the days when all Calvin saw of London were dark skies and city lights from buses to and from work. Now the city was opening up its secrets to him.

That he was being asked to perform a live session ahead of the official release date of his debut signal was testimony to not just the potential of this new dance star but also the power of Myspace to create an underground hit before the physical format was in the shops. The song creating the buzz was 'Acceptable in the 80s', one of the tracks from his Myspace page and the obvious choice with which to launch his career.

Calvin sang about having love for people born in the eighties, in the voice he was always keen to replace. Although the lyrics suggested he had a specific age limit for prospective dates – in 2007 that would mean seventeen to twenty-seven-year-olds – he was quick to point out that it was 'just a song'.

'Yeah I've got a good little target market there, don't I?' he said. 'It's just a coincidence, though. I wasn't writing it to get signed. I just did it for jokes. Everyone can listen to it, young and old.'

Calvin explained, 'I liked the culture in the eighties. People would say I like your shoes or what you've done with your hair. In the last ten years until lately everyone has tried to look the same and daren't step out, or do anything crazy.'

It often happens that the styles of one decade are rejected by the next, and so it was that the ideas and fashions that identified the period were universally rejected in the nineties, as people yearned for a simpler look that was then more retro. By the early noughties, fashion had become so sterile that it was only natural that the eighties enjoyed a partial revival. Calvin's timing was perfect. 'I thought the eighties would be a good idea,' he said. 'I wanted a loose eighties theme, so I just stuck it all in that song.'

The video for the single showed Calvin celebrating some of what was dodgy about the decade that taste forgot. He was dressed in bright clashing colours and oversized green headphones, dancing, somewhat bizarrely, with a stuffed otter.

In the song, Calvin sings in the falsetto he was keen to replace, referring to anything from big hair and fashion disasters to animal testing, which was still legal then. A surgeon is shown pulling all sorts of matter from the same otter, which then ends up in hair-styling products and Asian cuisine – a serious statement cleverly wrapped up in a would-be disposable pop video.

'The video is quite comical, I guess,' Calvin said, 'but it's just on the right side of comedy. My music isn't about invoking [sic] deep thought. I'm just happy if people want to dance to it.'

We were witnessing a raw but bona fide pop star, one that was comfortable with his sound. His hair was black – it was not until much later that he admitted he dyed it, modelling himself on avant-garde comedian Noel Fielding, who had built a cult following thanks to his performance as Vince Noir in the brilliantly bonkers BBC3 series *The Mighty Boosh*.

Calvin later admitted the realisation that he would be perform-ing in front of a camera led to a change in his attitude when it came to his image. 'The second I got my record deal I joined a gym,' he said. 'I thought, "Oh God, people are going to take pictures of me now, I'd better look fit and remotely like a star." But it didn't really work out for me, as I find working out in the gym too monotonous.'

The *Daily Telegraph* described the initial Calvin Harris look as 'endearingly student-y'. A fashion appraisal of his style said, 'He liked bright hoodies and clashing colours, and tweezers were, if not quite strangers, certainly the friends his eyebrows hadn't met. He didn't seem to be cultivating designer stubble – but maybe he'd mislaid the Gillette gift set he was given for Christmas and hadn't got round to finding another razor. The general, pleasing impression was "this is a handsome, scruffy man in his twenties who loves his work, lives in clubs, likes a party and probably still has a Burton suit that his mum bought him hanging in his wardrobe".'

Even though the act of performing must have been alien to him, he looked comfortable in his skin, something that wasn't always the case when he was a teenager. It had taken him a long time to get used to his larger-than-average height. As he said, looking back over this period in 2009, 'It's only in the last five years that I have come to terms with the fact that I am a big tall b**tard.'

'Acceptable in the 80s' was so catchy it veered towards novelty record or one-hit wonder but stayed on the right side of the line and suggested there was hidden depth to this curious new talent.

One of Scotland's biggest-selling tabloids, the *Daily Record*, named 'Acceptable in the 80s' its single of the week, proclaimed Calvin as 'a new Scot on the block' and became the first to make the comparison between him and the country's established dance star, Mylo. Like Calvin, Mylo – whose real name is Myles MacInnes – comes from a small town. In his case it is Broadford on the Isle of Skye, where it must have felt he was the only person into electronic dance music. Like Harris, Mylo produced his first album – the provocatively titled *Destroy Rock & Roll* – on a computer in his bedroom. Unlike Calvin, however, Mylo had not taken a punt on music from the moment he left school, preferring to continue his education, first at Edinburgh before being accepted to study at Oxford, where he graduated from Brasenose College with a first in psychology, philosophy and physiology. Yet when it came to making a breakthrough, Mylo's work, like Calvin's, was first seen through his remixes of established stars' works. Coincidentally, it was a remix of Kylie's 'I Believe in You' that gave Mylo his first taste of chart success.

Dance expert Tim Barr said that the comparisons with Mylo cannot be ignored. 'The parallels with Calvin are obvious,' he said. 'For me, Mylo is almost a prototype for Calvin's early career. Though he was based a little further north, Myles was the first Scottish dance music producer at that point to achieve success by distilling a potent, commercially viable sound from a set of fairly underground influences. In fact, the label that supported Mylo and helped him to shape his sound initially was called Glasgow Underground – a very credible independent label releasing very sophisticated club records. Effectively, they provided A&R support as he moved from making embryonic grooves on a second-hand Apple Mac to developing something that was pretty close to the fully realised sound of his debut album, *Destroy Rock & Roll*. With that support, he was able to catapult himself beyond the boundaries of club culture and onto the Radio 1 playlist. It went so mainstream that Elton John publicly declared himself a fan and Kylie Minogue wanted to collaborate. Mylo wasn't shy about harnessing dance music grooves to fairly cheesy pop hooks, and the techniques he was using – mashing together different drum samples, for example, or tweaking synthesiser patches to recreate the sound of vintage analogue machines – were very similar to the approach that Calvin used to develop his own sound.'

The *Daily Record* agreed that 'Acceptable in the 80s' also wasn't ashamed of some cheesy pop hooks. It said, 'Calvin Harris's blend of basstastic beats and high energy fun is more Mel & Kim than Mylo, but has a chart-friendly melody.'

Comparisons with Stock, Aitken and Waterman duos aside, Calvin was garnering acclaim across the media spectrum. Vic Galloway was an instant fan. 'He's a very talented young man and I love his tongue-in-cheek, cranked-up, funky, punky disco music,' he said. 'What's really great about him is his sense of humour. His music is brilliantly produced and has real crossover potential in terms of turning him from a cult phenomenon to someone who could score highly in the charts. What is important in pop music is word of mouth and the Internet multiplies that a millionfold. It allows a buzz to spread globally very quickly and brings new music to the attention of music fans rapidly.'

Before the single hit record stores, Calvin paid a visit to another shop – Marks & Spencer in Dumfries, where former colleagues were amazed to hear what he had been up to since he quit his job. Speaking at the time, he said: 'I went back to M&S before the single came out to say hello. There was a big circle of people around me, but it feels weird going back without having to put bread out. I feel like I should be helping. I feel like an escapee, but they did treat me well. If you asked them, they'd say I'm really quiet or the tall quiet one. There was an element of sulking and not being bothered, all the classic teenager emotions.'

Calvin had no reason to sulk over the single's chart performance. The track commanded a lot of airplay and rose to number ten in the UK singles chart, a remarkable achievement for his first record.

Further comparisons were now being made with the London new rave-pop band Klaxons, who, after struggling to make the breakthrough on independent labels, had created an Internet buzz and had also been given a chance by a Radio 1 DJ. Steve Lamacq had invited them into Maida Vale to perform a live session before their album *Myths of the Near Future* was released to widespread acclaim in January 2007.

Yet as Calvin sat in those same famous studios he told *The Times*, who had joined him for his session, that he was keen to play down the significance of Myspace as a route to success, acknowledging then that it had already become a bit of a cliché. 'It's a bit embarrassing,' he said, '"online community" and all that stuff. Bit sh*t, isn't it?'

And regarding Klaxons, who were being heralded for combining dance music with the live experience of rock'n'roll, he wasn't afraid to speak his mind. Branding them 'really contrived', he said, 'I don't know why people can't see that that's not what they're like when they're chatting to their mum.'

Ironically, it was at that time that Calvin, too, was about to test out his fusion of dance and rock on a wider audience, as he prepared for his first tour, supporting mainstream dance act Faithless.

To open for such a recognised act was a massive endorsement for a bloke who only had one single to his name. Faithless's best days might have been behind them – their biggest hit, 'Insomnia', had been released twelve years previously – but they had a loyal following, evidenced by the fact that they were still able to play London's Wembley Arena. Faithless founder Rollo Armstrong, whose production of sister Dido's albums helped propel her to worldwide fame, was generous in support of new dance talent (indeed, their final tour dates, in 2011, would be called Passing the Baton) and Dutch DJ Tiësto and English singer Example are among those who cite the band as an influence.

Amazingly, for someone who had only recently got used to the idea of being a frontman – and by then was said to be 'belting out vocals and punching synths with abandon' at live gigs – the prospect of playing in front of 12,000 people at Wembley, the arena where the Beatles, Bowie, the Rolling Stones, U2 and Bob Dylan had all sold out, did not seem to faze him all that much. 'It'll be hilarious,' he told *The Times*.

Describing the other venues in which he would be playing as 'some of the biggest arenas I've ever seen', he did say the experience would be 'exciting and daunting', but he added, 'I don't know, I'm not really feeling either of them at the moment. I'm on a strange sort of plateau of nonchalance.'

One aspect of touring that would take a bit of getting used to was life on the tour bus. Outsiders might think it's all singalongs and groupies, as depicted in Cameron Crowe's film *Almost Famous*, but the reality is somewhat different. 'I don't like the tour bus, I must admit. I don't like it,' Calvin said later. 'It was not a pleasant experience for me. I didn't get any sleep. I was laid on the floor bunk, literally rolled on the carpet into my bunk and then realised I had about a centimetre of space above my head when I was lying down. It was like a coffin! And it was also lined in red, which lent itself to the coffin effect.' He added, 'I'm pretty sure I slept under the gearbox too, because every time they changed gear, my head would bang on the ceiling. It wasn't a pleasant experience.'

Despite the downsides of touring, as summer 2007 approached Calvin had a top ten single and a tour under his belt. He could not have hoped for a much better launch to his music career and Sony had belief that their new acquisition would become an even bigger success. 'Despite his crude equipment, Harris is causing a sensation on the UK music scene for his talent to reinvent disco,' said Marina Plentl, of Sony BMG. 'He is going to be massive. There is such a buzz about his music. Everyone's talking about it. The reaction speaks volumes. It's absolutely phenomenal the amount of offers he's had from people who want to collaborate.'

The buzz around him was building. He was said to have stolen the show at a recording of *Transmission with T-Mobile* at the Corn Exchange in Edinburgh, outshining Macy Gray, the Shins and Fall Out Boy. In addition to 'Acceptable in the 80s', Calvin showcased the song that was set to be his second single. 'The Girls' had been the other standout track on his Myspace page and the one given airplay by Pete Tong. The song would be released in June, with his debut album following a week later. He was on the verge of the big time and he was loving every minute.

'It's a bit of fun basically,' he told *The Times* at Maida Vale. 'I never expected to be signed to a major label. It's hilarious.' That fun was clearly coming out in his music. 'People don't seem to realise that most really good music has loads of humour in it.'

As interest in him grew, journalists wanted to know what it was like working with Kylie. However, although Calvin was happy to talk about how nice the Antipodean pop princess was, he maintained a hard-line stance on future collaborations. 'I am really bad at working with other people and avoid it – unless I get an offer I can't refuse, like Kylie,' he said in one interview. 'If anyone messes with my music I get upset and precious. If they mess with my drum sound, I tell them to f*ck off – especially if it is another producer. So I won't be one of these serial collaborators. The idea of doing an album with loads of great guests is appealing, but usually that stuff ends up sh*t anyway. It's always better when it all comes from one person. When twenty producers and eighteen vocalists work on a tune, it sounds terrible.'

Calvin might have thought his days of slogging around the clock to make his dream a reality were behind him now he'd left Marks & Spencer, but back then he got his first taste of how hard he would have to continue to work to sustain his early promise. Weeks and months of mixing, recording, playing live and promoting took their toll and he was forced to cancel a gig in the Czech Republic supporting Faithless because of flu. Gutted at having to announce he would not be performing, he said, 'I have flu symptoms, but I've had to cancel a gig tonight for the first time and I feel like a big f*cking loser.'

He needed to recharge his batteries because, with the release of his album, the next few months would prove to be more hectic than ever.

He refused to look back and was already making plans for what he would do next: 'Out of Dumfries first, and then, I don't know, the world? No, I don't think I can be bothered with the world. The UK is fine, then I'd maybe like to disappear. I don't particularly want to be a pop star, but if it is forced upon me then perhaps I'll just become a hermit and retreat back to Dumfries.

'Music has always been my life but now it's what I do all the time, which is an incredible feeling,' he said. 'It's definitely better than aligning lettuces in a supermarket.'

Calvin still sounded like someone caught between two places – not wanting to consider going back to his own life but reticent about what changes fame and fortune might make to his situation.

That was all to come, however. In the immediate present he had a new complication to endure – his first sex scandal.

9

Getting the Girl?

IT'S a sign that you've made it when the country's biggest tabloid starts taking an interest in your love life.

Calvin Harris might have been surprised that it was happening to him, as he had only just released his first single. He would have been even more surprised when he read what he was supposed to have been getting up to.

The *News of the World*'s showbiz editor Rav Singh, whose column was read by nearly nine million people every Sunday, reported in April 2007 that Calvin's relationship with Kylie Minogue had gone beyond that of co-writer. 'Enjoying a Highland fling' was the rather clichéd take on her alleged romance with someone with a Scottish connection. Rav doubted the suggestion that Kylie and Calvin were simply working together. After all, why had she plucked him from obscurity to have him work on her album? And she was single after parting from her previous partner, the French actor Olivier Martinez.

According to Rav, a close pal had told him that Kylie and Calvin had 'spent loads of time together working on the album'. He reported, 'They've struck up a very close friendship and are now an item. Kylie's had a tough time but has finally found happiness with Calvin.' The source went on: 'She's excited about the new album, but meeting Calvin was the icing on the cake. He always makes her laugh and they're a lovely couple.'

On the surface it looked a good tabloid story: she was thirty-eight and unlucky in love; he was twenty-three, a hot new kid on the block – the only trouble was that it wasn't true. It was the ideal example of that old newspaper adage about not letting facts get in the way of a good story.

Calvin couldn't believe it when he saw the article. 'I was on a train coming back to Glasgow from my sister's wedding when that story broke and I just burst out laughing,' he said. Once he told his mum there was no truth to the story, even she saw the funny side. 'My mum's cut out the stories to collect,' he said. 'They're hilarious. They aren't true, unfortunately.'

What really was unfortunate for Calvin was that he had to go back into the studio with Kylie again that week, but fears of any awkwardness between them were soon proved unfounded. Calvin said, 'The funniest thing was that literally two days later I was seeing her in the studio. It had been scheduled for ages. But when that came out I hadn't even seen her for four months. I did say to her, "By the way, did you see that?" And she was like, "Don't worry about it, it happens all the time to me. Let's just carry on and make music."'

In the showbiz world there is a theory that one should 'never complain, never explain' about the tittle-tattle that appears in tabloids and magazines. It's a rule that supermodel Kate Moss lives by after advice from Johnny Depp. By denying a claim, however spurious, one only draws more attention.

Calvin was new to the game and, when asked, he just had to deny it – to him, the idea of him and Kylie as an item was simply ridiculous. He admitted that before he had met her he had failed to see what the fuss was about. That soon changed, however. 'I never got the Kylie thing before,' he said. 'I never fancied her and she wasn't my type. But when she walked into the studio I thought, "You've been a fool" – she was beautiful.'

In terms of them becoming a couple, however? 'She's Kylie Minogue,' he said. 'There are a million reasons that was never going to happen. I don't know which one to pick. My height? We'd have been an odd couple. It'd have been like C3PO going out on a date with R2D2.' He added, 'That and the fact that she's gorgeous and I'm this tall, lanky, skinny Scot.'

Like his mum, he held on to the article. 'I cut [it] out and kept it,' he said. 'That was the highlight of 2007. I blatantly didn't go out with her, it's so obvious.'

The attention was something Calvin would have to get used to and being linked to someone like Kylie might not be a bad thing.

In his new song fans would hear him sing how he got 'all the girls', and while the reality was perhaps still wide of the mark, he joked about how he always 'wanted to be a sex symbol!'

Attention regarding women was one thing, but as media interest continued to grow, Calvin became irked about the other person with whom he was constantly linked – Mylo. 'I'm getting a bit bored of that,' he told one interviewer after repeatedly being asked about his fellow Scot. Calvin saw himself as having a completely separate development to Mylo, with different influences and styles.

As summer 2007 approached it seemed everyone wanted a piece of Calvin, or some reflected glory. US singer R. Kelly was seen sporting a pair of shades that looked suspiciously like Calvin's trademark 'fly-eye' glasses. Even though it was hard to imagine the former basketball star fashioning his own pair out of cardboard and bubble wrap, like Calvin had, the Scot still wasn't happy that his look was being hijacked. 'Have a look at the new R. Kelly video,' he said, 'and you will see the man is brazenly wearing fly-eye spectacles. I think this means I am some kind of fashionable trendsetter.'

There was no denying the man was in demand, though. Radio 1 asked him to open the main stage for the One Big Weekend event in Preston in May. Another notable appearance on the bill that day was Rihanna, who at the time was enjoying a lengthy run at number one in the UK singles chart with 'Umbrella', a song that would go on to spend ten weeks at the top – and spawn the so-called 'Rihanna Curse', whereby the UK experienced a spell of inclement weather for the duration of the song's dominance of the charts. It would be up to Calvin to ensure that spirits wouldn't be dampened should the rain start falling at Moor Park, something he was well up for.

It was at the Radio 1 event that he began to see what impact his music was having – not to mention his sense of style. His 'fly-eyes' caused such a stir it seemed everyone wanted a pair. He persuaded other stars to try them on and videoed the result for an online blog he had started. Calvin said, 'I did a stunt during One Big Weekend where I got as many celebs wearing them as possible and describing what they could see. Mika saw elephants. Dizzee Rascal was hilarious. I tried to get Kelly Jones from the Stereophonics and he just said, "What are these?" He didn't get the joke.'

Jones must have later caught on, for he said, 'Anyone wants a pair of these, get some bubblewrap and Pritt Stick, and Bob's your uncle.'

Also on the bill for Saturday was a London rapper who revealed himself to be a fan of Calvin's. Dizzee Rascal had built up a solid following, had two gold albums and was credited with taking grime into the mainstream. Dizzee – real name Dylan Mills – was about to release his third album, *Maths + English*, that summer, but he was deliberately aiming for a more commercial sound and so far had come up short. When he heard the catchy sounds of this new Scots dance star, Dizzee wondered if he could be the man to help him achieve his dream.

Dizzee said, 'I set myself a challenge to get a number one record. But I'm not going to lie to you – I'd tried to write pop-influenced songs before and it was a disaster. That's when I thought of Calvin Harris. We met at Radio 1's Big Weekend and swapped numbers because I liked "Acceptable in the 80s". So I asked him to come up with a beat.'

As a pioneer of grime and an expert at mashing different styles together, Dizzee was conscious that his move to make a deliberate pop song could be viewed by some as a sign that he had abandoned his principles or turned his back on his roots in East London. But the rapper said, 'Experimenting with dance music is a good way for British rappers to get on the radio and into the charts. Some people might see this as me selling out, but no way. Every track I write I try to make different from the last, and as my profile has risen with all the festivals and live shows I've done, I've wanted to experiment more. My audience has got more diverse, which I love. I've even started seeing teenyboppers in the front rows.'

Calvin confirmed, 'I met him at Radio 1's Big Weekend. We exchanged numbers and later he asked me if I could come up with some music for him.'

So began an unlikely relationship. How they worked together was similar to the Elton John/Bernie Taupin arrangement. In the same way that Elton John came up with the music to fit lyrics provided by Taupin, so Calvin had to come up with some beats to match Dizzee's rapping. Their very modern arrangement meant they did not actually record together, as Calvin explained: 'I've never actually been in the studio with Dizzee. We've both been too busy, so he sent me an a cappella of his rap over email.'

Over the next few weeks Calvin got to work coming up with some beats for him. Dizzee seemed delighted with the result. 'When I sent him the finished track, he called me at 2 a.m. to say it was amazing,' Calvin said. 'So I knew it was good.'

It wasn't just Dizzee that wanted to work with Calvin. R'n'B star Kelis made her name professing that her 'milkshake' brought 'all the boys to the yard' and the Harlem singer hoped her charms would now work on the in-demand songwriter. Although she'd been producing records since 1998, 'Milkshake', which spent four weeks at number two in the UK and became a worldwide smash in 2003, remained her high point. No stranger to collaborations, she hooked up with Calvin while he was in London and sounded him out about working together.

Kelis said, 'I did meet Calvin in London and he was just lovely – he is very sweet. So yes, we are looking at doing something together. It is a bit too early to say how much will happen or when. At the moment I am just looking at ideas and getting everything ready. I won't be starting work on the record for a while.'

Like everyone, it seemed, Kelis was impressed by the way Calvin operated. 'Calvin was great and I am a big fan of his music,' she said. 'He is very creative and exciting and I can see why Kylie wanted to work with him and why there is such a buzz about him. He is very, very talented.'

Calvin was equally effusive about Kelis, who'd returned to the charts with the single 'Lil Star' featuring CeeLo Green. 'I met Kelis and she was putting the feelers out to meet a lot of producers because she is working on her next album,' Calvin said. 'I shared a bowl of fruit with her and the main thing I found out was that she doesn't like melon. She's an incredibly funny and normal person. I hope I can work with her. It would be incredible. She is probably number one on my list of people I'd like to work with. It's a very short list. "Lil Star" is brilliant.'

For someone who had been anti-collaborations just a few weeks previously, he was now having a host of top names beating a path to his door.

However, not everyone was a fan. Some artists who'd only recently burst on to the scene themselves were wary not to give the new boy too much credit. The monster hit 'Grace Kelly' might have announced Mika's arrival, but the Lebanese/British song-writer wasn't about to anoint Calvin with his endorsement. In fact, he went out of his way to take a pop at 'Acceptable in the 80s' and damned his perceived rival by seemingly forgetting his name.

In the summer of 2007 Mika was mindful to accept that his career might be a flash in the pan, with 'Grace Kelly' remembered as noth-ing more than a one-hit wonder. But, speaking of his pop hate, he said, 'I can't remember the name of it, Calvin Harris? I'm a bit tired of that one, although I suppose only in the same way that people might be sick of my first one.' Whether Calvin was even aware of the slight is debatable, but if he looked back on both their careers he would be the one forgiven for asking, 'Who?'

As the release date of Calvin's album approached it didn't seem like he had much to be upset about, but, with only one hit single to his name to date, he was conscious that in some quarters he was still better known for the Kylie factor than as a genuine artist in his own right. He let rip: 'Honestly, the world of pop music – I don't like it at all. Most people are idiots. But it's amazing and unusual when you meet people who are lovely and normal – Groove Armada, Kylie and Biff [Kylie's songwriter]. I'd just like it if people knew that I sometimes work with people who aren't Kylie. I'm not her little production bitch.'

Calvin also didn't mince his words when asked about his link-up with former Moloko singer Róisín Murphy. She was going for an edgy dance sound to launch her solo career, and you would have thought being hooked up with Calvin Harris and established hit-maker Cathy Dennis – the songwriter behind Kylie's 'Can't Get You

Out of My Head' and Britney Spears' 'Toxic', among many others – would have been a match made in heaven. Word had got out that Calvin had submitted songs for consideration for her album but ultimately they weren't used. Calvin fumed, 'Róisín's an idiot. They were really good songs, masterclasses in pop music.' He went on: 'She must be crazy because the songs are really good and Cathy Dennis is obviously legendary. That was a disappointment.' And he revealed, 'I ended up losing money, cos the lawyer's fee for doing the contract balanced out my [writer's] fee.'

Calvin's honesty was as refreshing as it was surprising. Here was a new talent publicly deriding another singer for her song choices. Some observers might have thought he was getting a bit big for his boots, but they would later learn he just liked to call it as he saw it.

He could still toss out a nice line in self-deprecation when need be and was only too quick to show respect when it was due. Asked ahead of the Isle of Skye Music Festival about what would happen if he was due onstage at the same time as his more established 'rival' Mylo, he replied, 'I hope I'm not on at the same time as Mylo because I'll lose.'

At the festival he admitted it was another new experience for him. 'I'm a festival virgin,' he said. 'They are quite expensive. Growing up, I always ended up spending my money on other things. I was never that into live music until I started playing it. I was all about the recorded sound.'

And although his newfound fame meant that a lot more women had joined his Myspace page, he said most of them were left disappointed if they ever met him in the flesh. 'There's not enough Scottish girls on the Myspace page,' he said. 'Everyone knows Scottish girls are the best-looking. If I've become a sex symbol, then I'm an unlikely one. As soon as girls meet me, all their hopes and dreams are quashed. They think, "Who is this big lanky fool who stands before me? Calvin Harris? Oh, never mind. On to the next one."'

As his diary filled up, it was announced that he would be performing at a number of Beck's Fusions events around the UK that September, a unique concept that challenged leading musical and artistic talent to unite to create original and inspiring performances, presented with the Institute of Contemporary Art. Calvin would be appearing with dance revolutionaries the Chemical Brothers and, if that wasn't exciting enough, the show would be in 3D.

'Beck's Fusions is a crazy music and arts lovefest,' he said. 'It includes a show at Trafalgar Square with the Chemical Brothers. It's going to be a huge experience. People will be wearing 3D specs, so it's going to be crazy.'

In the more immediate future, however, he had more gigs for which to prepare. He was building up to the album's release with a string of dates in his homeland, including an emotional return to King Tut's Wah Wah Hut in Glasgow, where he had first played live. 'I can't wait to go back to King Tut's,' he said. 'It's sold out and should be a lot of fun. It's quite nice to go back there because that was the first gig we played. It's a great place with a good vibe.'

As Calvin looked back on a manic couple of months, he paused to appreciate how much his life had changed. 'I have to say this just doesn't feel like a job,' he said. 'It's hectic, but it is a lot more fun than what I used to do. The shelf-stacking wasn't the best job in the world really.'

But then it was to the future he looked – and hopefully more success and opportunity.

Before the album would be the single 'The Girls', but Calvin was desperate to see another dream realised. 'I've not heard "Girls" being played once yet, even though I hear it's getting lots of radio play,' He said, adding, 'I can't wait to see the album on the shelves – it's what I've always wanted.'

He wouldn't have long to wait.

10

Disco Maker

IF only he had known it was that easy . . . sing about getting all the girls and watch them flock to you.

That was what happened to Calvin on the release of his second single 'The Girls'. With tongue still firmly in his cheek, he sang about liking tall girls, short girls, big girls and even those girls that carried a little bit of weight.

In the intro he seemed to be endeavouring to be as inclusive as possible, listing black, white, Asian, mixed race, Spanish, Italian, French and Scandinavian girls as among his favourites. This wasn't a musical first, of course. The Beach Boys tried something similar with 'California Girls', while the Beastie Boys paid their homage to the fairer sex with 'To All the Girls'.

Calvin tried to explain it: 'I'd find it hard to write lyrics if I was being serious. I wouldn't know what to write about. Serious lyrics just wouldn't fit my music.'

The benefit of such a lyric was that Calvin could adapt it to suit any audience. Yet what about Scottish girls, particularly those in his home town? Success might have brought him to the attention of girls who'd previously snubbed him, but it also brought new problems.

He returned home for a night out with bandmates Sean and Mark in the summer of 2007 and was taken aback by the reaction: 'I know I shouldn't slag off my home town, but I couldn't find any girl that I could relate to when I was growing up. It's bizarre, because I was down there at the weekend for the first time in four months with Sean and Mark from my backing band. I just got absolutely molested. It was so bizarre. There were girls I recognised from school coming up and going, "Oh, wow, you are amazing," and I was like, "Well, you didn't even speak to me at school." I ended up having to go home because I couldn't even get a quiet drink. Everybody just wanted pictures and it was a bit scary.'

He sang about being oversubscribed with relationships, but, before anyone should think Calvin was getting cocky about his prowess with women, pal Mark was quick to set the record straight: 'He took quite a lot of flak for "The Girls". People around Dumfries thought he was being arrogant. But in reality he wrote the track when he was working in Marks & Spencer stacking shelves and hadn't had a bird for a year. People just don't get his sense of humour.'

And Calvin admitted, 'I've never been popular with ladies until now. It's a bit hard to find a girl when you spend all your time locked away in your bedroom making music, so I find all the attention bizarre.' He added, 'I hate the groupie mentality, it's awful. I hate people fawning, it makes me really uneasy and I have to get out of the room.'

He said some women were keen to even bypass the dating ritual and go straight to the nuptials. 'Yes, there have been lots of marriage proposals,' he said. 'That's great, and it's better than people saying, "I don't like you." But there's not a chance I'd consider romancing any of them – never, ever, ever. I think it's best to meet someone through the usual channels.'

The attention was inconvenient for another reason. For the first time since he had been in the public eye, Calvin had a girlfriend. He named her only as 'Sophie', but it is understood she too worked in the music business in artist representation and publicity and, like Calvin, was a Scot so didn't take the industry too seriously. Hailing originally from Edinburgh, she now lived in Glasgow, and she seemed to be the ideal person to have by his side as his career took off.

'I'm a one-woman man, honest,' he announced in June 2007. Telling the *Scottish Sun* that he had been dating her for six months, he said, 'I've got a girlfriend, Sophie. She's a wee bit older – she's twenty-eight and perfect for me. I met her in Glasgow through a friend of a friend and we've been seeing each other since January. It was good at first because it came at a time when everyone was sort of going, "Oh, you're amazing, your music's incredible," and she was just like, "Oh, you're all right."

'A big part of our relationship is that she slates me all the time and she's helped keep me grounded since it all went nuts. I think it's important to have people around you who take the mickey. Otherwise you end up surrounded by people who always love you, no matter what, and you turn into a bit of a prat. But Sophie just laughs at everything.'

It's a good job she got Calvin's particular sense of humour – because the video for 'The Girls' might have tested the patience of a less understanding partner.

The promo – another stylised yet somehow retro offering – showed Calvin dressed in a white suit and T-shirt surrounded by near-identikit women save for a series of different-coloured wigs and Lycra. If there was one thing that Sophie could take comfort in, it was that Calvin looked distinctly uncomfortable throughout, as if searching for someone outwith the legions of girls around him.

Some fans likened it to a modern take on Madonna's 'Material Girl' video, where the pop queen strutted around amid homogenous men. While a far less polished production, it was hard to ignore the similarities.

Calvin explained the hardships of filming such a video: 'The video for "The Girls" was fun. I was stuck in a studio for eighteen hours surrounded by girls in Lycra.

'I was texting Sophie pictures and she wasn't impressed. But it was the director's idea and the director was a woman. Sophie is very understanding.'

She would need to be because Calvin took the theme from the video on the road, packing a double decker bus with a host of attractive women – dressed in the same wigs and outfits – in a stunt to promote the single.

Starting at Rock Ness in Inverness, the idea was to tour the summer's UK music festivals on the special Myspace bus, on which fans would be able to hear the new album ahead of its release.

He explained the thinking behind the exercise: 'I'm sending the Myspace bus back to Scotland with all these lovely girls as a thanks to all the Scottish fans for buying my single. Hopefully any fans who haven't bought it yet can help get me my first number one.'

Whether the stunt translated into that many extra sales was debatable, but the resulting publicity did help 'The Girls' eclipse the success of 'Acceptable in the 80s', peaking at number three.

Yet, despite a second successive single, Calvin was feeling the strain of constant performing and promoting for the near-imminent release of his album.

'Everyone on tour, including me, is poorly,' he said. 'We've been working so hard over the past few weeks that we're all coming down with colds and bugs.'

He had gone from supporting Faithless to gigs with Groove Armada, the electro pop duo Andy Cato and Tom Findlay, who were on their fifth album.

Being on the road had resulted in one health benefit, however: forcing him to quit boozing.

'I don't do anything fun any more' was the way he described it. 'During the Faithless tour we got a lot of Jack Daniel's laid on and we would drink quite a lot. But we just ended up really ill because we're always on the move and you have no recovery time. I haven't even had a drink since just before the Groove Armada tour two months ago. As a result they think I'm the most boring man on the planet. I used to do a lot of drinking but now I realise I don't need to do it any more.'

That proclamation would have been music to his mum's ears.

'My mum doesn't come on the tour bus with me but she worries whether I'm eating healthily when I'm away,' he said.

On top of feeling poorly, it seemed the attention he was receiving was getting to him; the initial buzz of being a pop star and the front man of a band was wearing off.

As always with Calvin, it wasn't clear if he was being sarcastic or speaking honesty, but he said: 'I find myself in a position where I'm a pop artist and that wasn't the plan. I'm here making tunes that are going to number three and at some point it's just got to stop.

'I'm slightly uneasy. I'm an uneasy person generally. My label have made it clear they're very excited. The hype machine has got me really uneasy.'

Just a week away from his album's release, he said: 'This record's not going to be on a par with "Purple Rain",' referring to Prince's classic. 'It's only my first one. If this album goes top ten and I come up with a second album and it hasn't got any pop hooks, then I'm f*cked. I'm dropped. I'm sh*t.

'There's been a few occasions when I've found myself going: "Oh, for f*ck's sake, how did I get into this situation?"'

On 15 June 2007, the waiting was over. *I Created Disco*, the debut album by Calvin Harris, hit the shops. It was a dream realised, something he'd wished for since he'd started making tunes in his room aged fourteen. The album was homage to that time in many ways. The studio, where disco was created indeed, was credited to 'Calvinharrisbeats in Dumfries', i.e. his bedroom.

It was one of the most eagerly anticipated releases of the year, and immediately critics and fans raised eyebrows at the title. He created disco? Really?

Of course Calvin Harris wasn't meaning that. He meant he created his own brand of disco in his bedroom on the Amiga but subtlety is not something found in abundance in the music industry.

'It's not actually a very disco-y record, which is just the way it goes,' he admitted. 'It's just the title for one of the tracks on the album which involves a man telling everyone how he created disco just before the First World War. Which is, of course, all nonsense. So I thought that would be a good album title.'

He said: 'I called it *I Created Disco* basically to get a reaction, as people will say, "No, you didn't!" I thought it was a funny title, as I listen to nothing but hip hop and R'n'B. I don't even listen to dance music!

'But it's a hard line to tread between a bit of humour and a comedy song. No one wants to be the next Goldie Lookin' Chain and when "Acceptable in the 80s" first came out there were some critics who questioned whether I was a one-hit novelty wonder.'

He added: 'It's just a bit of fun. I'm not professing to have actually created disco – it's a chronological impossibility – but hopefully it gets people talking.'

The title aside, the album did not contain any radical change of direction from what had been suggested by the two hit singles. Any listener expecting the disco of Chic would have been sorely disappointed. The groove created by Calvin was a more industrial affair, with stark synths and Daft Punk-style bass beats, something that dance music expert Tim Barr recognised.

'I know Calvin acknowledges the importance of Daft Punk, and for anyone involved in dance music in Scotland they cast a long shadow – since they'd been discovered by Soma Records, perhaps the country's most important dance music label,' Tim said. 'Thomas and Guy's [Guy-Manuel de Homen-Christo being the other half of Daft Punk] career offered an important lesson for young producers like Mylo and Calvin because they proved that an act could come out of the underground and achieve really extraordinary success (and those first Daft Punk releases were very deep indeed, a kind of cross between DJ Pierre's Wild Pitch house style and the hard, uncompromising techno of Underground Resistance).

'But around the time of the third Daft Punk album, *Human After All*, pop music was going through a really flamboyant, technicolor phase. If you think about releases by Scissor Sisters and The Killers, at that time, there was an obvious attempt to go for primary colours in terms of the sonic palette and to build in very commercial supersize hooks. I think that period may have helped Calvin define the ideas that came to fruition on the first album.'

Tim highlighted some other key influences. 'Disco, of course, was a key element of the New York house records that influenced him – and that comes through again and again in Calvin's own records,' he said. 'But I don't think you can discount the importance of the underground electro scene in helping him to define his sound. Electro has consistently fed into the underground club scene, from the early 1980s releases of Morgan Khan's Street Sounds label onwards. There have been periodic upsurges ever since and, in the mid to late 1990s, there was a really strong electro seam being mined in Detroit. The music of Keith Tucker and Aux 88, in particular, helped kickstart a resurgence of interest in the form in Europe's most techno-centric cities (Berlin, London, Frankfurt, Eindhoven and Glasgow). Around the time Calvin was first getting into music, the tune "Doidy Dawg" by the British duo LA Synthesis [vs Johnny

Astro] was a big underground electro hit so it's not out of the question he'd have picked up on that – it's exactly the kind of electronic music that might have grabbed him at that point because it's amped-up, quite gritty and really syncopated. The bass frequencies have to be spot-on in electro and that has clearly had an impact on Calvin, not only in terms of his writing style but in the attention he devotes to bottom-end detail in his productions.'

Of the tracks on that first album, 'Vegas' had already been released as a limited edition vinyl, but the standout tune was the opener, 'Merrymaking at My Place', a clever, catchy rap where Calvin alternated between deep soul voice in the verses and falsetto for the choruses, singing about the vast numbers of people he had invited to his house, largely to take drugs.

The song would be a sure-fire hit with clubbers and stoners alike, but Calvin revealed he had to make sure his mum knew he was not drawing on personal experience for inspiration.

He said: 'I know a lot of my songs talk about boozing, girls, and partying but it's not necessarily autobiographical. My parents had never heard any of my tunes because I'm a secretive sod.

'But once I realised it was going to come out I just sat my mum down and said to her, "You do realise these are fictional tales." So she's fine with it.'

'This Is the Industry' was a pop at the music business that for so long had shunned him.

Harris described it as 'a song about the insular, horrible world of the media and music' but admitted it wasn't really a song, 'just lots of repetitive vocals'.

He said: 'Now I've had two top ten hits things are a bit better but, before, I was treated like some kid. I think the more success you have, the easier it gets.

'I've not changed, it's just the mentality that's changed.'

He added: 'It's basically about people who know nothing about music talking about music – and deciding what's good about music.'

Elsewhere it was hard to find real meaning in his songs.

'Most of my songs don't mean anything,' he said. 'Most pop songs don't. In my experience, there's not much agony in writing. I write by coming up with sheets of song titles – then I get round to constructing lyrics out of funny catchphrases.'

Tim Barr feels that even from his earliest records Calvin was doing something few other electronic artists were attempting: fusing pop and dance back together.

'Of course, pop and dance music aren't entirely alien to one another – the earliest house music to make it out of Chicago clubs like The Warehouse and The Music Box was pretty commercial too,' Tim said. 'All those records by the likes of Steve "Silk" Hurley and Farley "Jackmaster" Funk – or, an even better example from Detroit, Inner City's "Good Life" – were big commercial hits. But by the time Calvin was beginning his career, those two strands had separated. Club music was seen as an underground phenomenon and pop music was something for pre-teens and squares. What set Calvin apart was that he deliberately set out to reunite those two distinct elements.'

As far as the critics were concerned the album was on the whole warmly received but reading through the reviews at the time gave the impression that in some quarters it was viewed like musical Marmite. Some raved while others ranted. Colin Somerville in *Scotland on Sunday* wrote that Calvin was 'destined to be one of the acts of the year'. He wrote: 'The 23-year-old from Dumfries is a musical phenomenon in the truest sense, as thrillingly real and genuine a product of his generation as the *X Factor* culture is flimsy and pathetically phoney. This is old school electronica, contrived on an all but redundant Amiga home computer, and managing to produce a humanity and warmth all too often lost in state-of-the-art digital studios.'

The Herald hailed it as a 'pretty fantastic offering of novelty-sounding electro pop and self-proclaimed future-disko [*sic*]'; *Billboard* magazine said it possessed 'unique sonic heft'; *The Sun*, meanwhile, said it was full of non-stop floor-filler tracks, suggesting that the listener hadn't paid too much attention to the eight-second 'Vault Character' or the fifty-four-second fuzz fest 'Traffic Cops'.

However, *The Times*, while acknowledging the 'brilliant title', found the debut 'less than satisfying, though not uninteresting' and

The Guardian, in giving the album only one star out of five, called the lyrics 'stupid'.

James Delingpole in the *Sunday Telegraph* seemed to hit the nail on the head, though, when he said that while on the surface the sound is 'cheap and dated', at the same time it is 'sophisticated, knowing and cool'.

'Try as you might to hate it,' he continued, 'it does start to get under your skin.'

Calvin didn't seem to be paying too much attention to reviews, good or bad. His concern was that music buyers loved it.

'It's all about chart positions for me, so what's the point of lying?' he said. 'I don't care what people think of me saying that I like the fact I've had two top ten singles. I think it sounds good and I'm proud of it, though I thought "Acceptable in the 80s" should have done better than number ten.'

He was keeping his fingers crossed for similar success.

'I'd be chuffed with top ten for the album – anything less and I'll sulk for the rest of the year.'

He had little to be worried about. The album entered the charts at number eight. Not bad for a record banged out on your childhood computer.

Calvin seemed to relax after the album charted respectfully.

'Very happy – I would say almost ecstatic,' he said when asked about it, but still found time to joke: 'I'm just having a laugh. Just a bit of fun, isn't it? Charts and stuff, CDs coming out, all that.'

But while he was enjoying himself, one person was looking on stunned at the success of his old friend. Lee McQueen had not heard from Adam – or Calvin, as everyone was calling him around the town – since the first single had been released.

Lee was amazed at how well Harris had done in such a short time – and seemingly from nothing.

Lee said: 'I was shocked and my mates were shocked because we hadn't really known this. The papers were interested in him because the angle was, *here's this guy from Marks & Spencer who's in the charts*. I didn't know about the Myspace thing.'

Looking back, Lee can remember when Calvin introduced him to the people who would join his band, but at the time he had thought nothing of it.

'One night we had been in a pub and he introduced me to two people who were musicians but I hadn't asked any more about it. I just really enjoyed having a few pints and general chatting,' Lee said. 'The first thing I saw was the video in here [the Globe Inn]. He was on TV. It was quite a big shock. He looked confident, totally different. It was for "Acceptable in the 80s". I couldn't believe he had done this. I felt quite proud but it took me quite a while to understand because I had no idea how he had done this.

'After that he just went really big.'

At first Lee paid little attention to the fact that Adam had adopted a new name for his pop career – but as the months went on it was the new name that took over.

Lee said: 'That was the first time I'd heard of him performing as Calvin Harris. It didn't really make much difference because I knew people who changed their names for performing. So even though it was Calvin Harris it didn't really stick, it was still Adam.

'Every time people said Calvin Harris, I said, "It's not Calvin, it's Adam," but for people who didn't know him they would say, "I see Calvin Harris is from Dumfries." It was weird hearing people in the bar talking about my mate. It was crazy.'

Lee got another shock when he caught a Calvin Harris live performance on television; he could scarcely believe he was watching the same man who, as a kid, had hidden offstage.

'First time I saw him live was on the T4 Festival,' Lee said. 'He came on and walked around this triangle stage . . . I kept going back to that time and thought how is he managing to do this? That's not even a wee jump – that's a huge jump.'

Lee met Calvin Harris, pop star, for the first time in Dumfries town centre.

'I met him after he got his first hit up the town,' he said. 'We had a wee chat. He said he was still busy. He said he had played at Wembley. He might have been supporting somebody and he said how many there was at Wembley Arena. I said I had been playing to a slightly smaller audience at a wee place in Mouswald, a wee village with about twenty people. We had a wee laugh about that.'

Lee gives a touching insight into Calvin's mindset at the time, when even though he was enjoying chart success he still had quite humble aspirations.

'He'd just got his first big cheque and he was away to buy his mum a new Hoover,' Lee revealed. 'I went away thinking, surely you go and buy yourself something first, but it says something about him that that was his first thought.'

Lee and Calvin parted, promising to catch up properly over a pint sometime, but that drink never happened.

'He was that busy,' Lee said. 'We probably left it that we would get a pint sometime but it didn't seem like a necessity – but simply when we both had time to catch up really.'

One thing that was resolved was their music café idea. It was probably no surprise, as both friends had gone their separate ways, but Calvin told Lee he had dissolved the company he had set up for the pair of them.

Lee accepted the news.

'He had got a lot further than I got,' he said. 'He then told me that he had dissolved it, as we were on different paths now, which made sense to me as well.'

Lee admitted it was difficult to rekindle their friendship after that, as new people tried to claim a piece of Dumfries's new pop sensation.

'After that day I didn't really speak to him, as he was so busy and never in the town,' Lee said. 'When he was getting bigger, I watched people who didn't really know him now trying to be his friend, so I was wary of contacting him now he was bigger. I just thought when the time was right I would get in contact, when all the excitement calmed down.'

Lee wished his friend success and predicted a big future for him, but even he could not have imagined just how big.

11

On the Move

CALVIN was lost in the groove. The beats were thumping and the crowd was up for it, the room energised. It was always tricky with an early set time, but even though outside the rain lashed down, here in the Green Room tent it was dark and sticky, all sense of time momentarily forgotten.

His band, after several months of constant touring, was as tight as it could be and the way a thousand revellers bounced before him made a mockery of his seemingly lowly status on the bill for Oxegen, Ireland's biggest music festival.

Just then he caught sight of something in his peripheral vision. An object was coming hurtling out of the darkness. He focused just in time to see what it was – a banana heading straight for his head. Instinctively, he stuck out a hand, caught the piece of fruit with the aplomb of a midwicket fielder, his lightning reactions drawing a cheer from the fans.

In mid-flow he peeled the skin, took a bite, then threw it back into the crowd, watching it disappear into the gloom before he picked up the tune where he had left it and to loud roars returned to the beat.

Calvin was one of the first acts onstage at Oxegen at Punchestown Racecourse near Naas in County Kildare, but it was a significant moment in the early career of the dance man.

'I was miles away,' he recalled, 'but I caught this banana and took a bite out of in, then I threw it back into the crowd.

'It was one of the defining moments of my life, when I knew that I had just smashed it.'

From there he launched into a thumping version of 'The Girls' and when he slipped in a mention for 'them Irish girls' a thousand people were eating out of his hand.

Smashing it he most certainly was. From Oxegen to the daddy of all the festivals, Glastonbury, to T in the Park, Loch Lomond and even far-flung Ullapool on home soil, Calvin Harris was everywhere that summer, justifying his status among many in the business as the saviour of dance music.

Certainly he felt a responsibility to shake the genre up and wake it from a slumber he believed it had been in since the late nineties.

'I don't really listen to dance music any more,' he said, in a damning indictment of the scene.

He went on: 'For me, the low point for dance hasn't really ended. I still listen to 1990s dance and think it is so much better.

'I'm into the proper Ibiza anthems – because it's so throwaway. They worked two hours on a tune and if it was good, it was good. But then everyone started trying too hard.'

Instead of dance acts, the artists he was finding interesting included Klaxons, Sri Lankan rapper M.I.A., Smashing Pumpkins and Bat For Lashes.

Calvin had never been short of confidence in his own abilities, but now his chart success had confirmed it.

'I'm not even remotely concerned that I can't prove myself,' he said. 'I'm good at making tunes.'

This was a view shared by others, who recognised his worth to the industry.

Clubland publisher and artist manager Ben Turner said, 'After twenty years of dance culture, it's worrying that we're still falling back on the old stadium-dance acts. Harris is a breath of fresh air. It's refreshing that people his age are setting themselves up as performing acts.'

It seemed everyone was lining up to be associated with him. Blondie's Debbie Harry announced she was a fan, while Pete Tong asked Calvin to fill in for him on his Radio 1 show. The pair were sharing the bill at Loch Lomond in August and Pete was so thrilled that one of his early tips had made the breakthrough in such a textbook fashion that universities should use it as a case study.

'I've always liked his stuff,' Pete said. 'He had a very rare situation with Sony BMG where they seemed to clear the decks and just break him. It doesn't always go that smoothly – usually the achievements of the artist aren't enough for the record company, who want number ones overnight. I take my hat off to them. It should be a case study at uni on how to get it right in the music industry.'

A sign of his popularity and the penetration of his biggest hit came when up-and-coming electropoppers Dragonette planned to perform a cover of 'The Girls' at Loch Lomond, but rename it 'The Boys'.

Singer Martina Sorbara hoped their version wouldn't ruffle Calvin's feathers.

She said: 'The song came from nowhere – we did it as a fun thing for Gay Pride in the middle of our song "I Get Around", then recorded it just for a laugh. We never expected it to go this far and I hope Calvin is OK with it – I think he is.'

Calvin didn't know what to make of it. He had history with the band so could be forgiven for being suspicious of their motives.

'Dragonette weren't very nice to me,' he revealed. 'I did a remix of their single and they asked me to change everything about it.'

Their attitude prompted one of his choicest comments, regarding the fickleness of the industry: 'Honestly, the world of pop music – I don't like it at all,' he said. 'I'm not doing remixes any more.'

So regarding their version of 'The Girls', he said: 'I heard twenty seconds or so of it on the radio but I don't really know how to take it. Is it meant as a dig? There is a bit of history between us as I did a remix for them and their A&R turned it down – he came back wanting me to change things so I told him I was too busy.

'I'm not sure if it is a response to that but I don't think so. It will be interesting seeing them.'

Calvin was riding a wave, but playing nearly every festival on the circuit took its toll.

'I'm f*cked,' he said, before the run was over. 'Always ill, and in sharp decline. I survived the Faithless tour but it's been downhill from there. I gave up drink. I couldn't carry on the way I was going. I'm meant to be the heir to the dance music throne but all I do is read now. People will say I'm the world's most boring bloke.'

When he did venture out, it ended in mishap.

Arriving in Glasgow ahead of Loch Lomond he caught the Mitchell Brothers' gig at the city's ABC venue. Calvin had produced their single 'Michael Jackson' as an antidote to the pop stuff he was used to working and he'd had a great time.

'I needed to balance out the Kylie thing so I've produced the new Mitchell Brothers single,' he said. 'I love it. I'm farting about in the video as well.'

As a show of gratitude, the Ghanaian rappers presented him with a T-shirt at the Glasgow gig. But when Calvin headed into town with friends for a late-night meal afterwards things went awry.

'I had a really bad dinner,' he said. 'Don't ask me why, but I thought crab claws were a good idea. It was a really, really bad idea.'

Despite his upset stomach, he stayed out and caught a gig by Ben Westbeech at the Classic Grand before heading back to Sophie's flat in the West End.

She wasn't best pleased and he had to crash at a musician mate's house instead. Posting on his Myspace page, he said: 'I got locked out of my girlfriend's flat and had to stay at Rikki Stixxx's place, which turned out to be a lot of fun as I got to sleep on an airbed.'

Calvin enjoyed a triumphant debut at Scotland's largest festival, T in the Park, and rated the experience on a par with Oxegen. He was left enamoured by Glastonbury, while Loch Lomond he described as 'dodgy'.

This might have had something to do with the fact that Scotland's newest festival ended up being a mudbath after some terrible weather. Calvin then became embroiled in an argument with one fan who thought it hilarious to fling chunks of mud at him onstage.

'You're my biggest enemy,' Calvin told the wag. 'I'm going to hunt you down and shoot you!'

Still, it could have been worse. Former reality star turned DJ Kate Lawler played to an empty big top when organisers were late opening the gates and revellers missed the start of her set.

At each festival it seemed journalists viewed Calvin as the go-to guy for soundbites, and because he invariably gave good copy they were desperate for a line from him. However, sometimes it felt he was sharing a little too much information.

In one chat he revealed that recently he had found himself crying at the slightest thing.

'I cry at anything. I'm an emotional guy,' he said. 'It's embarrassing because I cry at films and stuff. Even films like *Finding Nemo* – that's a tear-jerker. And TV shows get me. It's a real problem. I almost started crying during [an] interview the other day and I've no idea why. Maybe I'm just overwhelmed by the emotion of success and all I can do is cry.'

He was still taking time to get used to the attention he was receiving and even though he was still promoting his album he indulged thoughts about stepping back from the limelight.

'I'm tempted to have a little break and just do production for a while,' he said. 'I never really wanted to be in the limelight. I don't really like being the centre of attention.'

The peculiarities of the music business continued to frustrate him – and it was easy to see why. *I Created Disco* had pushed past the 100,000 sales mark – and some observers suggested its success could single-handedly halt his publisher EMI's plunging share price.

Yet Sony BMG, his label, had held off releasing the record in Europe – despite getting heavy airplay in countries such as France, Spain and Italy.

'The album is out in Australia and doing amazing in Japan, but I could quite as easily rant about Sony BMG in Europe at this point,' he said. 'There is no point in touring there because the record isn't out in Europe. It's strange and annoying. It's getting played on the radio over there but nobody can buy it. From where I'm sitting it's laziness on a grand scale. If they have plans to release it, it's too late now because I'm going to have my second album out in the summer. It's not going to work. They may have to have an amalgamation of the first two albums but, whatever they do, I'm sure in their wisdom it will sell ten copies. At the minute it is doing my head in. I'd be quicker going over there in a van and selling it in service stations myself.'

Doing it himself was something Calvin was well used to and he came up with a novel idea to promote new single 'Merrymaking at

My House'. The plan was to unite Britain's other 'merrymakers' with an attempt to break the record for the most house parties happening simultaneously across the country on 18 August, with the single released two days later.

He vowed to travel the land, visiting as many of the house parties as he could, while one lucky winner of a competition would receive £1,500, plus have Calvin and some mates come to perform live in their living room.

Launching the competition, he sounded like someone who was in training for the party-fest. Although he had proclaimed to have given up the booze during the summer, he'd fallen off the wagon.

'I have been partying far too much for my own good recently,' he said. 'I gave up drinking a couple of months ago but then succumbed to a mojito about two weeks ago and since then it's been full-on carnage.'

To qualify for the special gig, fans had to host their own party and the winner would be the most outlandish and most 'C-themed'. However, the call came after a series of house parties had left homeowners with tens of thousands of pounds of damage. Just the month before, teenage gatecrashers had caused damage valued at £15,000 during a party at a house in Harrogate, North Yorkshire, when the owners were away, while in April about 200 youngsters wrecked a house in Country Durham to the tune of £230,000 after the party was advertised on Myspace.

Perhaps fearful that fans might take the challenge too seriously, Calvin urged a note of caution: 'Don't bring fireworks, as I'm not a fan of people losing limbs or faces . . . But I don't see any problem with elephants or dancing girls. Dancing bears are a no-no, however.'

And regarding his own house calls, he promised fans: 'I will be at your disposal until you chuck me out.'

Not that Calvin had any experience of house parties, of course.

'It's hilarious,' he said. 'I've never thrown a party in my life. Never ever. I wasn't even allowed to have house parties.'

The prospect of thousands of house parties being held across the country caused some parents' groups to react in dismay amid fears that houses could be trashed and police would be overstretched.

In Glasgow, *The Herald*'s headline warned: 'Why parents should stay home on the 18th'. The paper reported that police feared the majority of the parties would likely to be held in 'the time-honoured teenage tradition of unsupervised excessive underage drinking sresulting in damaged property'.

It went on: 'It may be a great publicity stunt for Harris but the cost will undoubtedly be borne by homeowners across Scotland.'

Sony BMG's lawyers must have been alerted to the possible repercussions because the company issued a statement of terms and conditions, excluding it from all liability for 'damages (whether direct or indirect), tangible property damage, losses or injuries' incurred during parties.

The entry form also issued some general guidelines:

> Please ensure that you have all necessary permissions to hold your house party, and the use of the venue of your choice. We strongly recommend that you do not invite strangers or advertise the party as open to all – or else you will be responsible for the consequences. Remember that both you and your guests must be over eighteen years old if you are planning to serve them alcohol.

Such was the concern that Calvin was then forced to record an announcement to teach fans how to party responsibly. A video clip showed him driving around, saying, 'They think it is going to encourage you to trash your mum and dad's house. So invite your friends only. Point two, only drink if you are over eighteen.'

The farce continued, with Calvin saying to the camera: 'Can't do this seriously. I've been coerced into doing [it].'

Amid the furore ITV breakfast show *GMTV* invited him on to quiz him about his irresponsible request, but his record company stepped in to stop it.

Calvin said: '*GMTV* wanted me to answer various probing mumsy questions. But the label thought I would be unable to cope with Ben Shephard's tough line of questioning.'

Despite the controversy surrounding the competition, when 'Merrymaking' was released its performance was disappointing, failing to make the top 40, peaking at 43. Given fans already had the album it was perhaps optimistic to think Calvin would score a third top-ten hit, but after the publicity surrounding the house parties and its catchy lyric it was reasonable to think it should have done better. Perhaps the fuss over the parties had a negative effect and the references to drug-taking could have played a factor in airplay on radio stations.

Over 1,000 people entered and the lucky winner of the competition, with her Charlie Chaplin-inspired bash, was seventeen-year-old Myspace fan Christie Hollstrom, who had the pleasure of her favourite singer's company at her parents' house in Kidlington, Oxfordshire.

Calvin was possibly relieved that the stunt had passed without the major drama predicted but put the fuss down to media hype.

'Certain people think ill of the youth but I like the controversy,' he said. 'As long as it's based around something that's not going to happen I think it is hilarious. This is fun, like me apparently "going out" with Kylie – things like that I absolutely relish. As for being a hate figure for parents – my mum and dad love me very much.

'Tonight is the ideal house party, as mum and dad are here and enjoying it.'

They say never meet your heroes, and Christie admitted she had been a little apprehensive about what Calvin would be like in the flesh, but she was pleasantly surprised – particularly when he turned up with his mum and dad in tow.

'We were worried what he would be like, but he was such a nice bloke,' she said.

Christie wasn't the only person to have her expectations challenged – it seemed to be a regular occurrence for people when they met Calvin.

'I'm a sad bastard,' he said with his trademark self-deprecation. 'People ask me if the music is my alter ego. To be honest, there's not even that much thought been put into it.'

While privately people might not know how to take him, professionally he was more relaxed when being compared to other more established artists.

'At first when I was getting compared to Mylo, I was a bit unsure,' he said. 'I don't really think I sound that much like him. But now I'm fine with it. It's pretty fabulous, actually.'

What he was growing tired with was the constant questions about Kylie. He understood journalists were keen to know how he found her when he first burst onto the scene, but after several months of answering the same questions he was beginning to lose patience.

'I'd just like it if people knew that I sometimes work with people who aren't Kylie,' he told one interviewer.

To another who asked what she was like to work with, he bluntly replied: 'I've exhausted my "working with Kylie" quotes. I can only say it was lovely and she was really nice. Just google it; I've only got two anecdotes and I've done them to death. There's nothing I can say about that which is even remotely interesting.'

It wasn't that he was getting sick of Kylie. He helped her out with a cover of Roxy Music's 'Love Is the Drug' for an album to celebrate forty years of Radio 1. Some of the leading current chart stars were asked to choose a classic track they would like to perform. Kaiser Chiefs decided to cover the first song ever played on Radio 1 back in 1967 – 'Flowers in the Rain' by The Move. As Kylie's collaboration with Calvin was yet to see the light of day, the version of 'Love Is the Drug' was credited as her first recorded track since recovering from breast cancer. Many of the songs resulted from 'Live Lounge' sessions, which DJ Jo Whiley had cultivated on her daytime show, and were rerecorded especially for the album. Calvin Harris was also asked to contribute, choosing to cover a classic from his childhood, 'Stillness in Time' by Jamiroquai from 1995.

As Calvin waited to hear which, if any, of his songs had made the final cut of Kylie's album, he did continue to have fond memories of their work together, particularly when asked about who he would consider producing in future.

'After working with Kylie, everyone's difficult. She is a sweetheart,' he said.

One person you would not have thought he would be rushing into the studio with again was Róisín Murphy, who he had so publicly reprimanded for rejecting one of his songs. She revealed they had bumped into each other but any awkwardness was quickly dispelled when he apologised for his comments. And she also disclosed that the aforementioned song might yet breathe again.

'I saw him recently, he apologised profusely,' she said. Of the offending song, she added: 'It didn't fit with the rest of the record. I decided not to use it and he got upset. I can't hold that against him.'

But Róisín added: 'Now Sophie Ellis-Bextor has recorded that song to release as a single, so it hasn't gone to waste. If it makes a global number one, obviously I'll be a little p***** off but I knew it didn't suit me. I wouldn't rule out working with Calvin in the future, though.'

Calvin, to his credit, held his hands up.

'We hugged and I apologised,' he said. 'It was emotional.'

He confirmed the tie-up with singer Sophie, whose career was in need of a fresh injection of creativity after she'd taken a break to raise her first son, following the early success of 'Groovejet' and 'Murder on the Dancefloor'.

Calvin posted on his Myspace blog: 'I've been in the studio with the lovely Sophie Ellis-Bextor . . . we're making very beautiful music. Something should be coming out soon, so I'll keep you informed.'

At least he was able to enjoy working with another pop star and now he could look back on that session with Róisín – his first with a recognised star – with an element of perspective.

'It was a difficult session, and it was my first one,' he recalled. 'It wasn't much fun.'

Questions were always being asked about whom he would be working with next and top of his list was Beyoncé. The R'n'B queen had soared to new heights after putting her band Destiny's Child on hold to focus on a solo career. 'Crazy in Love', the debut single she co-wrote with rapper Jay-Z, with its fusion of funk, hip hop and soul, not to mention an explosive sample of the Chi-Lites' 1970 hit 'Are You My Woman (Tell Me So)', had cemented her place as the hottest female star on the planet.

Calvin recognised her talent but wasn't a fan of everything she released and felt he could do her justice.

'She's easily one of the best singers of her generation and they keep giving her really poor songs to sing,' he said. 'It's annoying. She could be doing amazing stuff.'

Another group going places who could expect Calvin's support was one closer to his heart. His home town football club Queen of the South had apparently asked the chart star to write them an upbeat new club anthem in a bid to inject a 'feel good' factor around Palmerston Park. Whether Calvin took them up on their offer is doubtful but as it turned out the team might not have needed it, as they started to string together some good results.

At the time Calvin was busy helping another community initiative, adding his backing to a charity which spotlighted mounting suicide rates among young men.

Those critics who were quick to condemn him for being irresponsible regarding his house party competition might have been rethinking their opinions after Calvin agreed to appear for free at Koko in Camden Town, London, for the night for Wasted Youth.

'It's the first charity gig I've done this year,' he said ahead of the gig, which also featured his new pals the Mitchell Brothers, Boy Kill Boy and Alan Donohoe from the Rakes. 'I'm really looking forward to doing something,' Calvin said, 'as it's such a great cause.'

The charity had been set up by journalist Daniel Fulvio, whose brother Steven had taken his own life on Christmas Eve, aged just twenty-two. Fulvio hoped the event would help send out the message to young men everywhere that staying silent about their problems wasn't a sign of being strong.

Calvin was happy to lend a hand to causes he deemed worthwhile but there was one act who wouldn't be benefitting from his philanthropy: Girls Aloud, the female five-piece who had won the battle of the bands resulting from the reality TV show *Popstars: The Rivals*. Although the band had managed to some degree to shake off their manufactured tag to create some credible records, they had hit a stale patch.

Calvin, however, wasn't impressed and did not see himself as the man to turn around their fortunes.

'God, no,' he said. 'Those people I'd never work with. I know they can all sing but it wouldn't be an enjoyable experience at all.

'They really need to change their sound. It's getting extremely boring now – but it's not for me.'

Calvin also had his own problems with which to contend. Hope of playing his first dates in the States were dealt a blow when there was a problem with his passport and visa. The American authorities were struggling to accept that humble Adam Wiles, as his passport said, was really this rising chart star Calvin Harris.

His publicity people told journalists: 'We have to send press clippings over to the American Embassy to prove he is actually Calvin Harris. Passports don't work.'

For the time being, he would have to be content with gigs at home and they continued to throw up incidents to keep him on his toes.

When the Wasted Youth event got underway, he was stunned to find his stage stormed by overexcited moshers who unceremoniously pulled down his trousers!

Then, at the Beck's Fusion gig at Glasgow's Fruitmarket, he thought he was under attack again when a man climbed up onstage and threw his mobile phone towards him. Calvin was nearing the end of his set and had just finished a rousing rendition of 'The Girls', but as security closed in to eject the fan, Calvin read a message on the mobile, which said: 'I want to propose to my girlfriend tonight.'

Calvin invited amorous Andoni Graham onstage and handed over the microphone so the twenty-two-year-old could pop the question to his shocked girlfriend, Amy McGaury.

The rest of the audience stood equally stunned as Andoni said, 'Amy, Amy . . . I want to ask you something . . . I know I am fat but I'll go to the gym. Will you marry me?'

As Amy, twenty-one, said 'Yes' to a relieved Andoni, Calvin told him: 'You're the man, congratulations Andoni.'

Turning to address his crowd, he said, 'Bringing people together under one roof, that is class. He's not my mate, by the way.'

Calvin then dedicated his last song, 'Vegas', to the happy couple, as the rest of the crowd raised the roof.

Calvin was getting used to the oddities of performing live and by playing at festivals, and in mid-sized venues and small clubs he was proving he was adaptable to all arenas – even those that threw up issues he wouldn't have planned for.

'I played a gig in Cardiff and a beam obscured my face for the whole gig,' he said. 'The crowd were seeing the band and this headless body singing. I had to duck down to say hello. People were laughing and pointing. It wasn't very nice.'

It's worth remembering that before he performed onstage Calvin hadn't attended that many gigs. Given his height you might think he had an advantage over other revellers but everything came at a price.

'On the positive side, you can see stuff in a crowd,' he said, before adding, 'The drawback is you get small women having a go at you at gigs.'

He went on: 'It's always a short woman who'd be short anyway, never mind compared with me. She'll have a hang-up about being short and have a go. I'd just played the support slot on a Faithless gig and went out to watch them. I got prodded in the back and thought, "Oh, not another autograph-hunter," and it was an angry, short woman shouting, "Oi! I was f*cking watching that!" I was like, "Sorry. Love you, by the way."'

With each gig, Calvin was gaining momentum in terms of his style and its eighties eccentricity. He was finding the more attention he paid to his onstage get-up, the cooler the stuff he was finding.

'Tracking down highly dangerous eighties shell suits has become an obsession,' he said. 'These things are 100 per cent synthetic, extremely flammable and as cool as hell. I found a £5 Michael Jackson History tour commemorative jacket in a vintage shop the other week. On the back it says "King Of Pop". I haven't worn it onstage yet because I'm waiting for the ideal moment. It has to be the perfect gig – you can only wear something that cool once.'

Calvin also seemed to be developing an obsession for trainers.

'At the moment I'm really into classic Adidas trainers,' he said. 'I'd say certain Nike trainers are cooler but they have too much height in the sole for me. So I can't wear Nike trainers, just like I can't wear top hats. I'd look daft.'

The style he was adopting seemed more accidental than designer, but being a fashion icon was something he was struggling to get his head round.

'I wouldn't regard myself as fashionable. My style just happens,' he said. 'One time I bought a cheap black-and-white hoodie from H&M and put a picture of me wearing it on Myspace. Then at my next gig there were six people wearing the same H&M hoodie. It freaked me out.'

One way to stop the copycats is to splash out on real designer clobber.

'Because of my height, I've always had trouble finding decent suits that fit. But then someone told me that designer Ozwald Boateng is also really tall and he makes clothes for freaks like me. So I went down to his shop and it was just beautiful. Within half an hour I bought the absolutely perfect suit for £2,000. It looks amazing.'

The revelation that there were designers out there catering for his needs was life enhancing. From the rough, oversized-kid look we saw on 'Acceptable', Calvin was now going for a more sophisticated style.

He said: 'I'm very pro male grooming. OK, I look a total scruffbag at times, but it takes ages for me to look this messy. I spend too long in front of the mirror every morning. My hair takes a full ten minutes, which surprises a lot of people, considering the way it looks.'

There were some things, however, at which he would draw the line.

'Who would go through waxing?' he said. 'I totally respect men who have got the guts to do it but that's one thing I'd never try. Where would you even start? It must be the most horrific of experiences. That's why I'm pro metrosexual men – it's hard to wax, so respect to them.'

Having adopted a philosophy of being prudent when he received his early cheques, Calvin was now enjoying spending some money on himself. He ditched his practical Vectra for a sleeker Alpha Romeo 147.

And he was finding there were advantages to being famous.

'Backstage at festivals there is often a "free stuff" tent,' he revealed. 'If you are playing at the festival, you can walk in there and take what you want. At one, the Adidas stall had these amazing gold shades. The bloke said, "They're 24-carat gold," so I took them. I own the world's most bling pair of sunglasses.'

And he added: 'My bassist wanted the same leather jacket as me – but I beat him to it. It's made by Superdry. My bassist had seen it first but he couldn't afford it so I was really mean and bought it for myself while he was saving up. He was absolutely gutted but it's far too cool for a bassist. So it's just tough on him, really.'

Calvin was happy to give fans an insight into the labels and products that worked for him. His favourite items included a Storm watch – 'It was given to me at a festival'; Diesel jeans – 'they're so comfortable'; white H&M T-shirts – 'the most essential item in my wardrobe'; an Apple MacBook Pro – 'I couldn't live without it'; and Charles Worthington hair gel – 'this is the only product that works for my hair'.

He also gave an insight into life on the road, but admitted it wasn't as healthy an existence as he would have liked.

'English breakfasts keep me going on the road,' he said. 'I probably eat five a week. When I'm not on tour I'm much healthier, but when I'm with the band I can't get enough bacon, beans and scrambled eggs down my throat. I'm an expert on them now. The best breakfast in the world is at the Marriott hotel in Glasgow.'

Yet even though he was enjoying the high life he was quick to show he hadn't lost touch with real issues. Among his bugbears were potholes.

'It's a huge issue where I live,' he said. 'They can damage your car and the wildlife.'

And for all the opportunities he had to eat at top restaurants and hang out at the most exclusive clubs, his ideal night out was 'an incredibly quiet meal out with my girlfriend, maybe go to a trouble-free gig and then home'.

And he revealed there were times when he just liked to get away from it all. 'When I'm a bit sad, I often go for a drive in the country, quite fast, with my music up. Where I live – it's a small town surrounded by countryside . . . after ten minutes you're properly out there and it's very scenic.'

It's hard to tell what might have been making Calvin sad but, as he started to think about what he would do to follow up his hit debut album, he would have to do it without his trusted Amiga, as the computer that launched his career had finally given up the ghost the moment *I Created Disco* was complete.

That moment must have been a particularly poignant one for him. He owed that Amiga so much, but he remained philosophical: 'I've consigned the Amiga to the dustbin. It only lasted a week once I'd completed the album. It was almost as if the effort proved too much for it. But I can't complain – it served me well.'

It had been his brother Ed's, of course, but he was delighted at how far the outdated hardware had taken his younger sibling. Calvin recalled, 'Ed is the most pleased out of all my family. He knows how long it's taken and how much effort I've put into it to get this far. He's absolutely over the moon with it all.'

The challenge was to find the right equipment to make the next step in his musical journey. Now he had money to spend, his options were greater, but cash didn't always equate with success. After much deliberation he plumped for an Apple Logic EXS24 sampler and studio, and an Apple Mac. The technical advance must have been considerable.

'The Amiga did a great job! Even after things started to take off, I did my best to carry on working with it. We were a team,' he said. 'Sadly, I realised it was probably time to give the studio a bit of a spruce-up. The Amiga – God bless it – was put on the shelf, replaced by Logic, with all the bells and whistles, and a Mac. That first jump to Logic is pretty spectacular. There I am, in my bedroom, with my trusty Amiga. All of a sudden, you've got a studio set-up that's as big as your budget and your imagination will allow.'

Showing the same prudence that Lee McQueen witnessed over the new vacuum cleaner for his mum, Calvin admitted he was wary about blowing all his earnings on fancy equipment.

'I was quite wary of that jump to Logic-World. Wary of suddenly having money and endless toys to spend it on. I've heard stories of bands that spend all their advance on gear, then the album tanks and they're left with loads of gear and no cash. I was careful. I only bought the things that I really needed, but I didn't go crazy. I didn't need to. I was having enough trouble getting my head around Logic and trying to start work on the second album.'

Calvin was refusing to rest on his laurels and immediately set to work on new tunes, but barely a month after his first album had gone top ten he doubted whether he would make a second!

'I'm already doing stuff that sounds different. I'm making tunes all the time,' he said, but added, 'I'm not sure if there's gonna be a second album. It depends on whether I think anyone's gonna buy it. I'd rather put something out that people will like, rather than just, "Oh, here's the bloody second album." I want something that's good. I don't want to do something pointless.'

He did, however, provide some insight into the music he was listening to – and there weren't a lot of current dance acts floating his boat.

'I don't really pay attention to genres, and I couldn't even tell you what's happening in the Scottish electro scene right now,' he said. 'I'm listening a lot to the View right now and Kings of Leon. But I've got lots of D'Angelo and an Enrique Iglesias CD in my collection too.'

He also told how he found inspiration in some unusual places.

'I listen out for good beats and sounds all the time. Ping-pong balls, bleeps, clicks. Not the microwave, though – that's just an annoying sound.'

But he was quick to add: 'I'm not one of those weirdie Brian Eno types who carries a Dictaphone on him all the time. You know, just in case he hears a rare bird and wants to sample it into a keyboard.'

He had a big summer of live shows to get through but he revealed there were still times onstage when he wondered why he was putting himself through it.

'The live stuff's good when it goes well, but when it doesn't I just think, "I could've been sat at home making up some songs." Which is a lot more fun.'

Aside from the touring, he was spending more time in London – but the city still held unhappy memories for him.

'London is just so bloody miserable,' he said. 'Full of miserable people. I spend a lot of time doing things there that seem really shit and pointless.'

Although not everything was rosy, he had to remind himself how far he had come in such a short time.

'The overriding feeling is just: "I'm so lucky." Even if I'm not always having fun, I'm like, "This is going to end up in me having real fun." Not just "go out and get pissed on a Saturday night and have fun in Dumfries" fun.'

He wasn't quite done promoting *I Created Disco* yet and, even though 'Merrymaking at My Place' didn't do as well as he had hoped, there were still plans to release a fourth single.

There should have been no controversy surrounding 'Colours', the second track on the album, but two decisions by his label, Columbia – who refused to let him record a video, then allowed it to be used on an advert for a furniture shop – left him fuming.

In protest, he posted a home-made joke video clip for the track, but that's where his enthusiasm for supporting it ended. Calvin took to Myspace to register his disgust, posting a sarcastic video in which he answered a phone call from his mum and said, 'Ah. You've got the new chart position. 127. Amazing. Yeah, it was on the DFS advert. Tell me about it. I didn't even get a f*cking sofa.'

Calvin explained that the song was 'about a man who doesn't like girls who wear dark clothes because he's a bit of a fascist'. This led the *Metro* to jokingly insinuate that he was in danger of alienating at least one sector of the music-buying public with his new song. Did he have it in for goths?

'No, I love goths,' he insisted. 'They're my favourite type of people. It's nice to be part of a team like that.'

Next it was suggested that the song could become an anthem for goth-haters.

'Possibly,' Calvin said, 'but there's little chance of this becoming an anthem for anyone. It's the fourth single and I'm thinking about other things.'

The single eventually only appeared on MP3 and 12-inch format, and barely registered on the chart.

The modest chart showings of his latest releases might have helped provide Calvin with a reality check. His album had contained songs created long before he hit the big time. Any new material would have to reflect his progression since then and he appeared to appreciate this when he said he would start work in earnest before the end of the year.

'I'm starting [to write music] properly in December,' he said, 'because I want to have it done by next summer. I want some new tunes for the festivals.'

As well as moving on from the Amiga, he would be moving on from Calvinharrisbeats Studio, or at least taking it with him. He was moving into a flat in the West End of Glasgow. It made sense for him to relocate to the city 'because it's easier to get places from here rather than Dumfries', he said. 'If I need to get down to London, I can get straight on a plane.'

Even though he was moving out, he still wanted to be remembered in his home town. He cheekily put forward the suggestion that the town could erect a statue in his honour – after the local council sounded him out about whether he would like to open a new £17 million leisure centre.

'I'm gunning for the next town centre statue to be erected in my honour,' he said. 'Dumfries hasn't had many famous sons so it's about time really. Robert Burns has a statue but he wasn't even born in Dumfries and only lived there.

'I'm struggling to think of anyone else famous from our area. So I think there should be a campaign for me to be honoured, and a big bronze statue of me is something I have always dreamed of.'

With tongue once again in cheek, he went on, 'Maybe after my second album the town council will decide to commemorate me with a statue. It would also need spikes all over it so that people can't climb up and put a traffic cone on my head.'

Being serious, he was genuinely chuffed to be asked to open the leisure centre, which had been something the town had been crying out for.

'It is the biggest thing Dumfries has ever seen. It holds about 1,200 people,' he said. 'It's one of my big regrets that I've not had a chance to play my home town yet.'

Dumfries would have to wait, however. After his passport problems were sorted out, he got his first taste of life in America and was eager for more.

'I've changed my mind now about cracking America,' he said. 'You have to take on board that this business is a learning curve and half the things I said earlier in the year, I was talking total b******s.

Actually going over to the US opened my eyes and I'd be daft to say I didn't want a piece of it.'

And it looked like he would be ending a remarkable year with another boost: two of his tracks had made it on to Kylie's new album.

'I'm relieved rather than thrilled because there was a point after all the hype that I thought it wasn't going to happen,' he said.

And he joked: 'The fact I'm on it can only strengthen my campaign for a statue in Dumfries.'

Unfortunately, however, his presence on Kylie's album couldn't save it from some negative reviews when it was released in November 2007. The songs Calvin co-wrote – 'In My Arms' and 'Heart Beat Rock' – were largely praised for their fresh production. Scotland's *Daily Record* loyally said 'In My Arms' saved *X* 'from the bargain bins', adding that the 'Calvin-style happy synths . . . is what joy is all about'.

On the whole, though, *X* was seen less as a comeback and more as a clash of styles and themes, the real pop hooks that had made Kylie famous being seemingly absent.

Not long after moving to Glasgow, Calvin revealed he was flitting again – to a flat that was still in the West End, just off Great Western Road, and handily placed for the hangouts popular with other musicians, artists and actors. This flat seemed to be short of basic amenities – so was this a suggestion that all was not well between him and Sophie? When he moved to Glasgow, it appeared as if he was hoping to build on their relationship. For a time they had lived together and it seemed to be the start of an exciting time for them both.

Yet out of the blue came two suggestions that their relationship had floundered.

When asked what he was after for Christmas that year, he replied: 'I really want an ironing board and an iron. That's top of my list. I have just moved flats so I don't have them at the moment. I don't have a washing machine either; it's a bit of a problem. I'm fed up of having to go to the launderette all the time.'

Then, while talking about a pair of Adidas trainers that he had fallen in love with, he happened to add: 'I'm starting to think they're unlucky, though. Bad things started happening after I first wore them. My girlfriend split up with me, my tonsils swelled to double their size and we played a sh*t gig.'

He was booked to end the year in style, playing to thousands of revellers at Scotland's premier Hogmanay party in Edinburgh's Princes Street Gardens, and he would have been hoping the unlucky Adidas wouldn't take the shine off a remarkable few months.

Publicly he said no more about his relationship status, preferring instead to reflect on a 'ridiculous' year that had seen him go from obscurity to being one of the country's hottest stars.

The self-assuredness that had marked his comments in the summer were tempered slightly as he looked ahead to the New Year bash and his slot, following indie favourites Kasabian after midnight.

'I'm very apprehensive about how it's going to go down,' he said. 'Just generally whether people are going to leave after the bells. I don't know. They've already seen Kasabian, what's the point?

'I don't know if I'm as well known as what some people think I am, so I don't know if people are going to stick around or not. I dearly hope they do. I think if they do they'll have a really nice time because we're actually quite good.'

Looking back on 2007, he found his swagger once more: 'I like to think that I conquered Britain,' he said, one of the highlights being that he had almost become a walking gazetteer of the UK. 'I'd never been to Cardiff before,' he said, 'but this year I played there five times. Norwich and Southampton used to be places on road signs; I played them too. When folk ask me, "What's Nottingham like?" I can tell them, "It's got trams."'

He added: 'This year we've been predominantly playing the UK. We've done a few in Europe as well, but the record was slow coming out there, so we decided to stay here, rather than go over and tour for nobody. It was pretty much the same circuit each time, or the same cities in various-sized venues, at least. We supported Faithless, then Groove Armada, then did our own tour.

'It's quite good, going to places in the UK where I'd never have been otherwise, though. Why would you go to Southampton if you live in Dumfries, unless you've got relatives there? But I've been to

Southampton, and it's quite nice. All I'm saying is, it's good to go around the UK in a bus sometimes. I recommend it to anyone. You don't even need to play gigs, you know; it's just quite good to see your own country.'

His extensive travelling meant he was now an expert on the best places in the UK: 'Leeds has the best Xmas lights; Glasgow is the greatest place on Earth; Newcastle bought the most hotpants; Nottingham has the most glowsticks; Sheffield throws the most glowsticks.'

As he looked to 2008, he knew the pressure was on to create something new, to show that he was more than just a one-trick pony who could turn out an annoyingly catchy tune. He seemed to be in two minds about whether to go down the collaboration route or continue on his own. His only rule appeared to be that it didn't matter, so long as it was good.

'I'm trying to make the best music I possibly can and it helps that I'm working with nobody but myself. When I made *I Created Disco*, I wasn't making a proper album, it was just a collection of songs that I had anyway. So it doesn't feel like an album to me, it feels almost . . . I don't know, just a bit rushed? This time I know it's going to come out on CD, so in order to put my name to it I've got to make sure it's amazing.'

He was wary about releasing something that wasn't up to the standard he had set himself. 'I think that would be a bit embarrassing for everyone involved, particularly me. The difference between me and certain other artists – bands, specifically – is that I can sit by myself and write a complete song from start to finish on my laptop, because I'm a producer. It's different from sitting writing a song on guitar, then taking it to some big-name producer to record. I know what I want things to sound like, so it's just a question of sitting down and working as hard as I possibly can to make it sound like . . . well, just what it sounds like in my head.'

Once he had the sound he wanted, the next decision was whether to sing it himself or do as fellow producer Mark Ronson had done so spectacularly and bring in guest vocalists.

'I think the most obvious thing for me to do would be to get a fourteen-song album with fourteen featured vocalists,' he said.

'That'd make me relatively happy, but having said that I've noticed that the use of vocoders is on the increase. I reckon I might get in on that.'

He was clearly in two minds, but had to get his next move right – be it on his own or with other people. He had made such a huge impact on the music scene, it seemed unthinkable that Calvin Harris could just be a flash in the pan? Or could he?

12

Luck Runs Out

IT'S 1 January 2008. Calvin, fresh from a storming set in Edinburgh, gets an email. It's another request to work with a budding starlet keen to link up with the hot young producer in the hope that it will further her career.

Had the request mentioned the singer's real name – Stefani Germanotta – might Calvin have given it more attention? And if it had mentioned how much making it as singer, songwriter and artist meant to this young woman, how her love of music and her odyssey to get noticed in many ways mirrored his own, would he have replied more favourably?

Who knows?

All we know is that Calvin took one look at the name of the singer, thought it ridiculous and sent a reply saying he wasn't interested.

As it transpired, that particular artist did not need Calvin or anyone else's help. She was Lady Gaga and one year on from that email was on her way to world domination.

Calvin only realised his error of judgement in August 2009 when Lady Gaga was everywhere, but he wasn't about to let it get to him.

'Her name rang a bell,' he recalled, 'so I checked my emails and it turns out that on 1 January 2008, I got an email asking to work with her. I thought, Lady Gaga, what sort of name is that? So I replied saying, "Nah, I'm not into that."'

Today it is hard to imagine Lady Gaga, or any of her representatives, feeling she needed a leg-up in the industry, but back in 2008 she was struggling to make the breakthrough. Born and bred in New York, at the age of twenty-two she took a gamble to head to

Los Angeles in a desperate attempt to make it, leaving her old life behind. Sound familiar?

'I was in such a dark space in New York,' she said in one interview. 'I was so depressed, always in a bar. I got on a plane to LA to do my music and was given one shot to write the song that would change my life – and I did. I never went back. I left behind my boyfriend, my apartment.'

Even by Calvin's own standards, Lady Gaga's rise to prominence moved at glacial pace. The song she wrote in LA was 'Just Dance', a happy mix of R'n'B and straight-down-the-line pop that, lyrically, dealt with a topic Calvin might have related to – getting out of it in a club.

The song was eventually released in April 2008 and redefined the concept of a 'sleeper hit', first becoming a hit on the club scene before finally scraping into the Billboard Hot 100 chart in America in August that year. Over the next five months it snowballed, gathering fans as it climbed the charts. It eventually hit number one in January 2009, twenty-two weeks after first charting. It grew into a monster hit, with nearly seven million digital downloads in the United States, becoming the ninth best-selling digital single of all time in America. In the UK, she found success a little quicker, the song taking just two weeks to hit the top spot. By the time January 2009 was out, Lady Gaga had found hits were like buses, as she scored her second with 'Poker Face'.

Calvin later reiterated his decision to turn her down, telling BBC *Breakfast* that he 'didn't really like the songs', as well as not thinking much of her nom de plume.

This time Gaga took the bait, angrily denying that she had ever enlisted his help.

'Seems to be trendy to talk sh*t about "Lady Gaga" when your albums/singles drop,' she ranted online. 'Y'all should live off your own hustle. Never even emailed you @calvinharris I guess it's hard to believe I write + produce my music. Cuz I'm a woman I don't know about EDM [electronic dance music], right?'

That was all in the future, however. In January 2008 he had no idea he was snubbing one of the most exciting pop talents to emerge in the previous decade.

And his less-than-spectacular start to the year continued when his car was broken into. All Calvin suffered was a loss of some CDs and some pride. But he was quick to question whether it was indeed a break-in when you leave the car unlocked in the first place.

'I would say "broken into" but is it still broken into if you forget to lock it and they simply open the door? Probably not,' he said of the incident. He rued the fact that three of his current favourite albums – by American rockers Kings of Leon, hip-hop duo Outkast and rapper/hit-maker Pharrell Williams – were nicked, but he was able to view the theft wryly, based on what the thief left behind, adding: 'They chose to leave *The Best of the Isley Brothers*, which confirms my suspicion that thieves have questionable taste in music.'

His run of bad fortune continued as he was inexplicably overlooked when the nominations were announced for that year's Brits Awards. He might have expected a nod in the categories of 'Best Male', 'British Single' or at least 'British Breakthrough Act' but was snubbed in all three.

For years, the music Oscars have suffered from credibility issues, as the awards struggle to reflect a diverse music scene and battle to balance popular reality TV acts that enjoy disproportionate coverage and genuine talent that might not otherwise get the exposure it deserves. Often it feels like acts that receive five stars from *The Guardian* have a good chance of making the cut, while moderately successful yet hugely popular acts slip through the cracks.

What might have been galling for Calvin was the artists nominated ahead of him. English singer-songwriter Newton Faulkner might have scored a platinum number-one album, but he only achieved one top-ten hit; former Longpigs frontman Richard Hawley's *Lady's Bridge* was loved by critics but made little impact on the singles chart; while Bat For Lashes troubled neither the single nor album charts with *Fur and Gold*, which incidentally was released in 2006, yet funnily enough was championed by *The Guardian*.

It was worth noting that other Internet sensations such as the Arctic Monkeys and Klaxons were recognised, while Adele, a graduate of the BRIT School for Performing Arts and Technology in Croydon, was awarded a special 'Critics Choice' gong, despite only having one modest hit to her name.

Publicly Calvin laughed off the slight, saying, 'I'm going to lobby for a "Tallest Man in Dance Under 25" category next year – I reckon I'm definitely in with a shout at that one.'

The only way to get back at critics is to keep working and Calvin did just that, taking a punt on an unknown British band. He seemed to have backed the right horse when indie pop duo the Ting Tings made a huge impact with breakthrough single 'That's Not My Name'. Calvin had remixed an earlier track, 'Great DJ', and singer Katie White was grateful for his early endorsement: 'He sent us a message, saying he liked our stuff and he remixed the song. We loved it.'

It was a minor positive in a general theme of negativity, however. He had lined up a series of special 'An Audience With' gigs in the UK but in April had to cancel because of a scheduling clash.

'With a heavy heart,' he announced to fans, 'we've had to cancel our upcoming UK shows because of European commitments on my part.'

His frustration with his tour date organisers must have been considerable, as it is one thing to have to cancel because of ill health but another to call off a gig because of a diary cock-up.

Surely, things couldn't get any worse?

Given the luck he was having, it might have been best to steer clear of an accident-prone new airport terminal, but needs must when you're travelling around as much as he was. Yet he must have felt a sense of impending doom when he landed at Heathrow's new Terminal 5 in April 2008.

The Queen had opened the latest addition to London's transport hub less than a month before but already the terminal was suffering from massive teething problems. Given it had taken nineteen years to construct, at a cost of £4 billion, air passengers might have expected that the baggage reclaim system would be working properly by the time planes started landing. On the very first day, however, it was clear something was badly wrong. British Airways, who had exclusive use of the terminal then, had to cancel thirty-four flights that day and were forced to suspend baggage services. Over the next five days BA misplaced 23,000 bags and cancelled 500 flights at a loss of £16 million. MPs called the scandal a 'national humiliation' and a catalogue of errors were blamed for the fiasco. The airline suffered IT problems and a lack of testing; staff had not been trained properly and were unable to park when the car parks became too full on the day of opening. Staff security searches were delayed, and construction work on parts of the building was not finished when the airport opened. Out of 275 lifts, twenty-eight were not working, with eleven still to be fixed by the time Calvin landed there.

He was returning to the UK after spending time in the States to play some dates and work on the follow-up to *I Created Disco*. But when he got off the plane he discovered his bags hadn't made the journey with him. Like thousands of other passengers, Calvin was left fuming and frustrated. But uniquely among other travellers, he seemed to have cause to be especially furious. He claimed that among the bags that had gone missing was his laptop, complete with the only versions in existence of his new songs. It meant seven months of work was down the drain, unless BA could find his suit-case.

He explained: 'We went over to Miami last Thursday to play some gigs, and the nice people/robots at Heathrow's Terminal 5 lost ALL our bags, including my hard drive, with ALL my f*cking songs on. I have been walking in circles for a couple of days, and will continue to do so until I meet the man/robot responsible and set him/it on fire . . . I shall overcome! Once he's on fire.'

A spokeswoman for his label Columbia Records seemed to con-firm the laptop contained the only copy of the new album. '[BA] have offered about £750 in compensation,' she said. 'You can't really put a price on something like a new record. He has lost the only copy of the new album. It is a big cause for concern – months of work have gone into that.'

A British Airways spokesman said they were doing all they could to find his bag. 'As with all bags that have been delayed, we are working hard to get them back to their owners.'

As if that wasn't bad enough Calvin then had more air-related trauma when the flight on which he and fellow Brits Klaxons were travelling on to the Coachella Festival in California was hit by turbulence.

'It was the worst turbulence any of us had ever been in, it was really scary,' he said. 'Klaxons were on the same flight. I thought the crash was going to be the death of Nu Rave!'

A month later Calvin revealed BA had eventually traced his baggage, but when he got it back it was in a sorry state.

'When they found it, everything came back mouldy,' he said, making you wonder what had happened to it. 'My clothes were sodden, the music was damp, it sounded sh*t. They gave me compensation but nothing significant.'

It was several months before Calvin finally came clean: yes, he had lost his bags in the Terminal 5 fiasco, but no, his new album wasn't among the things he had lost.

He explained that Columbia had wanted a second album to come out a year after his first but that was never going to be an option. So, with his engineer Jimmy, he had hatched a plan.

'I was still touring *I Created Disco* and they said I had two months to deliver my next record. How could I do that? I was flying out to Miami to play the day Heathrow's new Terminal 5 opened, so the opportunity to get out of it presented itself, and I took it. I made up I'd lost my laptop with all my music on it,' he said.

'To be fair, they did lose some of my bags, but I didn't check my laptop in – of course, I didn't. Any sensible person knows it stays in your hand luggage.

'Anyway, I said that, and it bought me time. It wasn't about deceiving anyone, I don't get pleasure from deception, and I wasn't trying to have a joke at anyone's expense, it was just a last-ditch attempt to say, "It's not going to happen, calm down, it'll be next year."'

Had Calvin rushed out the album – and it had bombed – would the label have been so understanding?

'You just never know in this business,' he said. 'It's a very insecure [*sic*] place. It's good to sometimes take control yourself and say, "It's not going to happen, and here's why." Sometimes the reasons aren't good enough for the label to agree with you, so you have to make some up.'

Facing that kind of pressure to deliver his follow-up, it is understandable why, in spring 2008, he appeared to be in a downbeat mood. He was starting to sound like he believed everyone was out to get him. Spending time in America, where success is something to be celebrated not sneered at, had made him realise that back in the UK he felt he hadn't been getting the credit he deserved and was caught between two genres – he wasn't credible enough to be considered a bona fide dance act and wasn't successful enough to be a mainstream pop artist.

'I seem to have got this pop tag and it's great having it,' he said, 'but to have it you need to sell records, and that's not something I've really done – I've only just gone gold, which is 100,000 copies. You can't put me alongside these pop stars who sell millions.

'I'm definitely an easy target. My first two singles brought a huge amount of hype around me. Then my album came out and it wasn't really a reflection of what I wanted to do with my career. I spent many months agonising over all of this, but now I just don't care any more.

'It was a phase in my life and I can't change anything that's happened.'

Even though he was looking to the future, he couldn't seem to let go of some of the less kind reviews of his album and had clearly taken the criticism to heart.

'Most of my album reviews were pretty scathing,' he reflected. 'There were certainly a lot of unfair comments – you only have to read them to see there was bias in them. All the broadsheet journalists think that because they've been to university they're incredibly high-brow about music. They over-think things and assume my music isn't clever enough, when it probably is. That was so frustrating.'

Even though he felt annoyance at the critics' views of his debut, he was quick to point out the shortcomings of those songs that had retained the raw sound of his old Amiga and vowed his new stuff, once he got round to rerecording it, would be a lot better.

'It would be ridiculous to stick to that [early sound],' he said. Regarding his new equipment, he added: 'I've got pretty much what anyone would want at this level, so I'll be taking advantage of it. Without a doubt it's going to be a progression.'

He promised to spread the singing duties among some other

performers this time. 'I'm going to have lots of guests on it, but not the big commercial type,' he explained. 'It'll be people I think are talented, plus my mates, like Dizzee Rascal.'

He seemed to have been genuinely taken aback by the positive reception his music had received in the US. In a country not known for its subtlety, Calvin's brand of humour might not have gone down as well as he would have hoped, yet he appeared to be the toast of Hollywood, with a number of high-profile celebrities flocking to see his live shows. Movie stars Christina Ricci and Kirsten Dunst were among those who publicly declared their appreciation of his music.

'Over in America, they treated me so well,' he said. 'I didn't get anything like the slating I get here.'

It was the time of year when the festivals started finalising their line-ups and Calvin received a boost when it was announced he would be headlining Rock Ness in June. Being top of the bill at Loch Ness was recognition of what a hit he had been among festival fans the previous summer, yet Calvin still appeared to be concerned how his billing would be viewed by critics – rather than the fans that mattered.

'I'm sure a lot of people don't think my spot so far up the bill is justified,' he said, 'but they've probably not seen my live show.'

Calvin needn't have worried about what people would think about him topping Rock Ness because the announcement of another headline act that summer was causing way more controversy. Hip-hop star Jay-Z had been the surprise choice to close Saturday night's festivities at Glastonbury. Organiser Michael Eavis defended his decision, saying he hoped the rapper, who in April had married long-term partner and collaborator Beyoncé, would attract a younger audience to the event.

'He will appeal to the young people and under-25s for sure, so that's a big pull for them,' Eavis said. 'It's not like the traditional one we do, like Radiohead, Coldplay and Muse and Oasis.'

The news did not go down well, however. Ticket sales were slow and Oasis star Noel Gallagher branded the choice 'wrong'.

'Glastonbury,' he said, 'has a tradition of guitar music. If it ain't broke, don't fix it. If you start to break it, then people aren't going to go. I'm sorry, but Jay-Z? No chance. I'm not having hip hop at Glastonbury.'

But Calvin leapt to Jay-Z's defence, saying, 'After reading Noel Gallagher's disparaging comments about Jay-Z headlining Glastonbury, I'm baffled at his ignorance. I love Oasis but, seriously, which one do you prefer? I know for me it's Jay-Z.'

Mindful that his comments might invite greater scrutiny of his own live show, Calvin revealed that he had been devising a dynamic new set and promised fans he would be delivering something even better than last year.

'I worked hard at changing the set in November and since then it's just got better and better,' he said. 'It's totally different – it won't be the same for anyone who saw us last summer.'

One festival where he wouldn't be making an appearance in 2008 was T in the Park, as he explained: 'I'd do it every year if I could. It's the best festival I've played by a mile. But they tend not to book people in consecutive years unless they're huge. I'd love to do it again next year if I get an invite.'

He admitted he felt more relaxed as a live performer now but, after quitting the booze for a spell the previous year, confessed that he still needed a helping hand to quell the nerves.

'I enjoy being onstage,' he said. 'It only takes a few drinks and I'm away.'

Although his own new material was still a long way off, his talents had been showcased with the release of 'In My Arms', one of his tracks that had made the Kylie Minogue album.

It allowed Calvin to reflect on the good time he had had recording it; looking further into the future, he could see production perhaps being where his long-term career would be.

'It was a good experience,' he said of his time with Kylie. 'People seem to never stop asking me about it. I enjoyed doing it and production is where my future lies. I'll tour a lot with the new album, but it's not going to be my long-term career.'

He did joke, however, that where Kylie was concerned he shouldn't have been too quick to deny the romance rumour – because it might have made him even more popular.

Revealing that he suspected the rumour was leaked by her

public-relations team, he said, 'I denied it way too quickly. Had I been a bit more intelligent, I could have kept it going for months and all these stories could have been written about me. I would have been "Kylie's boyfriend, Calvin Harris" and I would have sold a few more albums.'

Calvin might have been considered privileged to be able to jet around the world performing at festivals, but it didn't mean things always went his way.

Queen of the South, his home-town football club, had defied the odds to make it to the Scottish Cup final for the first time in its history, to play the mighty Rangers. It was a fairy-tale achievement by a team in the second tier made possible thanks to the incredible 4–3 win over Aberdeen in the semi-final. Playing Rangers in the final meant they would automatically qualify to play in Europe the following season.

Calvin had missed out on the semi-final heroics and his work commitments would mean he would be unable to join the 18,000 fans heading to Hampden Park in Glasgow for the final. He hoped to play his part in supporting the team, however.

He said: 'I was toying with doing a Scottish Cup final song, but there wasn't enough time, as I've had to really focus on my new album. But for going into Europe next year, I'll do a song for that – that's without doubt. I'm a Dumfries boy and a big fan of the team.

'I missed the semi-final, as I had a gig in Europe, but I know the vast majority of the town went up to Glasgow for it. I just can't imagine what the invasion will be like for the actual final. The whole band is going to the final except me, as I've got to go down to London for work.

'That's just my luck – when anything major happens, I'm usually doing something else. But I'll be rooting for the boys and [will] try to see it on the TV down there – I just hope they can grab a win.'

Some fans had travelled from the other side of the world to be there and it was a day to celebrate all things Dumfries. On one bus taking supporters from the town to Glasgow, a huge cheer went up when one of Calvin's songs came on the radio.

In the final, the Doonhamers looked to be dead and buried after two goals put Rangers in control before half-time. But in two glorious minutes early in the second half two goals turned the game on its head and Queens fans were daring to dream of an unlikely upset. Rangers, however, weathered the storm and a Kris Boyd clincher saw them emerge 3–2 winners.

Calvin might not have been able to fulfil his promise of a European song – Queens' foreign adventure later in the year only lasted one round – but he hoped another collaboration might bring him some personal success.

'Dance For Me', the song he had written with Dizzee Rascal the previous year, was coming out in July. Since it had left Calvin's studio, Dizzee had given it some street cred and renamed it 'Dance Wiv Me'.

After months of mixed fortunes, could this be the track to turn his luck around?

MAY 2007 Performing at a Sony Walkman Video gig for competition winners at Neighbourhood in West London

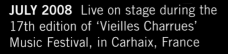

JULY 2008 Live on stage during the 17th edition of 'Vieilles Charrues' Music Festival, in Carhaix, France

AUGUST 2009 DJ set at Nokia Skate Almighty, on the South Bank, London

FEBRUARY 2009 Superfly Guy – flying the flag at the BRIT Awards at Earls Court, London

DECEMBER 2009 New Year celebrations at the Ministry of Sound Live event at the O2 Arena, London

APRIL 2012 Performing 'We Found Love' with Rihanna at the Coachella Festival, California

SEPTEMBER 2012 Collecting silverware at the 2012 MTV Video Music Awards in Los Angeles, California

JANUARY 2015 Onstage during DirecTV Super Fan Festival at Pendergast Family Farm in Glendale, Arizona

JULY 2014 On stage with Will Smith at the T in the Park music festival, Kinross, Scotland

SEPTEMBER 2014 The iTunes Festival at the Roundhouse in Camden, London

DECEMBER 2014 Home for Christmas – fan Taylor McCormick gets a selfie with Calvin on Christmas Eve in Tesco's supermarket, Dumfries, Scotland

© PRESS ASSOCIATION IMAGES

13

The Joy of Decks

WHAT was this – a rapper performing to the sound of an acoustic guitar?

No, this wasn't the moment Jay-Z answered his critics by walking on to 'Wonderwall' at Glastonbury, before launching into a blistering version of '99 Problems' mashed up with AC/DC's 'Back in Black'. Away from the Pyramid Stage it was Dizzee Rascal – who was also demonstrating the crossover appeal of hip hop by performing a stripped-down version of his new song.

And who was the tall white bloke whose groove elevated this track to that of a number one contender and who was on hand to deliver its catchy chorus?

Glastonbury 2008 was the year when genres collided: when Jay-Z confounded those who said hip hop did not have a place at a rock festival; when Dizzee Rascal and Calvin Harris combined to deliver one of the other stand-out moments.

Their impromptu acoustic performance of 'Dance Wiv Me' won an army of new fans. Glastonbury traditionally provides a commercial lift for those acts that are seen to cut it live and for this unlikely pairing it was the perfect boost.

Radio 1 DJ Jo Whiley had already made the song her 'Pet Sound' record of the week at the beginning of June. Not only was it a ringing endorsement from one of the station's most listened-to presenters but it also guaranteed it extensive airplay, working it into listeners' consciousness well ahead of release. By the time they reworked it for Glastonbury, the single was available as a digital download only. Before the week was out it was number one in the download charts and when the physical version hit the shops the week after it was favourite to claim the overall top spot.

Calvin wasn't even meant to sing on it. As the track was nearing completion the only addition was going to be from Chrome, a new R'n'B talent discovered by Dizzee.

'I loved producing the track and then they roped me into singing the hook,' Calvin said. 'But it's all good.'

Calvin also landed a cameo role in the video, starring as a barman who dryly advises the object of Dizzee's affection to get her boyfriend to hold her jar while she dances with the rapper.

'The video cost about the same as a Chomp bar wholesale and somebody inexplicably added comedy sound effects in post-production, but apart from that I think it gets the point across rather well,' Calvin said.

It's no wonder Dizzee had rung Calvin up at 2 a.m. when he first heard the track. It was complete justification in his change of musical direction and a vindication of his desire to write a killer pop tune.

Even though Dizzee had won critical acclaim – winning a 2003 Mercury Prize for best album with his debut *Boy in da Corner* when he was just seventeen – the fact that he had not enjoyed genuine chart success frustrated him, something that was brought home to him when he sang at a birthday bash for Arctic Monkeys singer Alex Turner and noticed none of his songs were on the karaoke machine.

'But now "Dance Wiv Me" is all over Radio 1 and it's getting played in pubs,' Dizzee said. 'I finally feel like a f*cking pop star, man!'

'Dance Wiv Me' was a remarkable collaboration, given the two men had never actually recorded together and, as Dizzee said, 'only met when we made the video'.

He told BBC *Newsnight*: 'Me and Calvin met and we exchanged numbers. We never actually met once to actually make the tune, we did it back and forth over the phone. It was good, we were just like over the phone, "What about changing that hook a bit?" Chrome was the only one that came in the studio, but it was good working with him because we've done a few things in the past.'

Dizzee loved the result, but when he took the track to his label, XL Recordings, they were unimpressed and refused to release it, feeling it was too commercial.

'I said, "OK, you like to be thought of as edgy, I get that, but now the person who gave you the edgiest album you've ever put out is offering you a straight-up pop track. You haven't forced me to do this, I found my way there myself: you should be pleased,"' Dizzee explained to the *Daily Telegraph*. Determined to release the song, he did so on his own, making it the first release on his Dirtee Stank Recordings label. 'It was a blessing, though,' he said, 'because I got to do it myself.'

When Dizzee and Calvin eventually hooked up for the video, they were already good friends. In the video Calvin didn't get much of a chance to show off his moves but during the Glastonbury coverage he did his best to hold his own with the rappers.

'He thinks he's a better dancer, but, come on, be serious,' Dizzee said of Calvin's hip action. 'He wishes he can dance like Michael Jackson, but I'm the one who can moonwalk.'

When the chart was confirmed, it was official – Dizzee and Calvin had scored their first number one together. To the uneducated, it might have seemed that Dizzee had just asked Calvin along to sing the chorus, but it didn't matter. Calvin was ecstatic.

'I'm slightly frustrated with those who just think I sing the hook,' he said. 'I did the beat, of course. But never mind, I'm made up that Dizzee is at number one.'

Dizzee was delighted his gamble with a more commercial style had paid off.

'It was amazing to get my first number one with "Dance Wiv Me". It was extra special because it's the first single on my label. I wanted to make a great pop record,' he said.

The song held on to the top spot for four weeks and, even though it was only July, it was clear it would be one of the biggest-selling singles of the year.

It was a tremendous boost for Calvin, coming at a time when he was the butt of jokes in one section of the music press. There was a time when *NME*, the *New Musical Express*, was considered the music industry bible and, although by 2008 it was largely an irrelevance in an increasingly digital age, for someone raised on it like Calvin it annoyed him that he wasn't being taken seriously in its pages.

The magazine had given *I Created Disco* a decent review. However, since then it had deemed it fashionable to have a pop whenever it could. Such was the regularity of the digs, Calvin said he started to object to his name being used in a publication 'that's synonymous with "sh*t" ALL the time!'

Eventually he decided to take them on at their own game and when they advertised for a new writer he sat down and, after several drinks, decided to apply for a laugh.

In an email poking fun at the mag's ropey spelling and misplaced sense of musical credentials, he wrote: 'Hiya, can I have the NME reporter job please? I think I'd be really great. My cousin once shared a bong with Petey DoCher's from Babyshambles's's.

'I love you, Calvin xxxxxx'

He explained: 'Despite a decent album review, they use my name for something that's synonymous with rubbish, like "Well, this is bad, but at least it's not as bad as that lanky cretin Calvin Harris and his s****y music." That's not a direct quote, but you get the idea. When I got home after a few shandies, I decided to try to even out the balance of opinion on my music.'

When *NME* news editor Paul Stokes received the email, he didn't know whether to take it seriously or not.

He pinged an email back, saying: 'Thank you for your application. We're processing the applications but due to festival commitments there may be a delay. We hope to be in touch in due course.'

Stokes added: 'If it was real, I thought it would be funny to keep Calvin in the running for the job. He didn't submit the ideas we asked for so he might want to send in ideas for news stories. But if he's successful, he won't be allowed to review his own records.'

Calvin might not have been getting the respect he deserved from some but he received an unexpected public endorsement from an old friend – and this one mattered far more than anything the *NME* could write about him.

Calvin had gone along to the SECC to catch Kylie Minogue on the British leg of her Kylie X 2008 European tour. One song in particular sounded familiar but it was only when she was well into 'Heart Beat Rock' that Calvin recognised it as his own!

'Watching the show and hearing my song was all a bit odd and surreal,' Calvin said, having joined Kylie after the show at her hotel, not far from his own flat in Glasgow. 'I never imagined Kylie would sing it. It was only when I was sitting there that it hit home I had written it.'

One public airing of his music was at an altogether more tragic event.

The senseless murder of sixteen-year-old student Ben Kinsella, killed in the early hours of the morning on a street in Islington, was a tipping point in public attitudes to knife crime in the capital. Just over a day after Calvin and Dizzee had been performing at Glastonbury, aspiring actor Ben – the half-brother of *EastEnders* actress Brooke Kinsella – found himself caught up in the aftermath of an altercation in which he had played no part. His attackers, a gang of three black teenage youths, stabbed him repeatedly and left him to die.

Ben's murder – the seventeenth stabbing to death of a teenager that year in London – led to protests on the streets and a government initiative aimed at tackling knife crime. Brooke's showbiz connections and the fact that a number of high-profile actors joined her and her family during the anti-knife demonstrations meant media coverage was significant, but the case became additionally poignant when it emerged that Ben had written a creative piece imagining his own death by stabbing. It was also revealed that he had written to the then Prime Minister Gordon Brown calling for more to be done to stop youths carrying weapons.

Due to the investigation into Ben's death, his family was not allowed to bury him until 18 July. They chose St John's Church in Islington, a short distance from where he had died, because it held 1,000 people, but even that wasn't large enough to accommodate all those wishing to pay their respects. Those who could not fit inside the church lined the streets outside.

Michael Jackson's song 'Ben' was played as his family carried the coffin into the church. Calvin's 'The Girls', one of Ben's favourite songs, played at the end of the funeral service.

Writing in her book published after Ben's attackers were jailed for his murder, Brooke Kinsella recalled:

> As the service ended and the coffin was lifted to be taken
> out of the church, we played our final song for him. We
> had chosen Calvin Harris's 'I Get All the Girls' [*sic*] – one
> of Ben's favourites, despite him never getting all the girls.
> The church erupted when the music began to play –
> people were laughing, crying and dancing in the aisles.

That his music was bringing some comfort to the family and offering light into the darkest of places must have meant a great deal to Calvin. While nowhere near the same scale as the tragedy that had befallen the Kinsellas, Calvin had experienced the nasty side of yob culture during a recent visit to Dumfries and revealed that he felt he could barely 'walk the streets' of his home town because of the level of grief towards him from a loutish minority.

Announcing that he only returned to the town of his birth to visit his parents, he said, 'If I ever go back home to Dumfries, I go to my mum and dad's house. I have a nice meal, sleep there and then I leave. You'll never catch me going out in Dumfries again.'

Clearly, he had suffered some serious unwelcome attention the last time he had gone out and decided the best policy was to remove himself from the situation to avoid it happening again.

'It's not a good place to be. It's one of those towns, like hundreds all over the place, with a big drinking culture,' he said. 'Though the majority of people are great, the bad ones spoil it. I have been given grief there in all sorts of ways. I wouldn't put myself in that situation again and I wouldn't want to put someone else who was with me in that situation.'

'I know folk who detest me,' Calvin said, 'and there are enough of them for me to take notice.' On one hand the lyrics of 'The Girls' made it popular with fans who got Calvin's irony. On the other it attracted flak from people who got the srong impression from the same lyrics.

Calvin spent the rest of the year working on his album but in a year when he wasn't touring or having to promote a new record to have scored one of the biggest-selling singles of the year – 'Dance Wiv Me' was the twelfth-highest bestseller – was an unexpected boost.

And he received another when the BBC announced that the once legendary chart show *Top of the Pops* would return with a special Christmas edition – and Calvin was invited to perform.

When the BBC had axed the show after forty-two years and 2,204 shows, Calvin must have thought that his chances of appearing on it were gone forever. However, thanks to a campaign by a national newspaper to revive it, the BBC performed a U-turn and agreed to bring it back, ensuring that Calvin would be the most prominent Scot to appear, probably since 1982, when Dexy's Midnight Runners performed 'Jackie Wilson Said' in front of a giant picture of popular Scots darts player Jocky Wilson.

'I will finally get to realise an ambition to pretend to DJ on the show,' Calvin said. 'I thought my chance had disappeared when the show did, but they resurrected it – so I thank the BBC for that.'

As he reflected on the year, he had every reason to be optimistic. 'Dance Wiv Me' had allowed the public to see him in a different light.

'The whole Dizzee Rascal connection made it all right to like me,' he said. 'It was kind of flattering for Dizzee to want to make a song with me. I was over the moon, it topped a lot of people's single-of-the-year polls. It was my song of the year, too. It just had one of those riffs, one that still gets stuck in my head sometimes.'

Despite that success, however, he said he was still determined to limit the number of collaborations on his next album.

'At first I was going to have loads of guests,' he said when discussing the new album he had planned for 2009, 'but I've now decided against that because people do my head in.

'There will be a couple of names though, but only when it's necessary, like when I need girl vocals.'

Although he hadn't named the new record yet, he liked the way it was shaping up.

'The next album is starting to sound like the best thing you've never heard,' he said. 'I am really looking forward to getting some new songs out.'

And as he prepared to head off to Australia to bring in the bells in Sydney, performing at the Wildlife New Year's Eve party at the Hordern Pavilion, he announced he had quit drinking once again – and was feeling all the better for it.

'I have been off the booze for three months now. I am a new man. I suggest everybody give up drinking immediately. It's no good.'

At that Sydney bash he would be performing alongside American house music producer and DJ David Morales: it was an intriguing line-up. Six months earlier Calvin had found himself invited to superclub Pasha in Ibiza – however, not as a singer or performer but as a DJ.

Although Calvin's music – and Lee McQueen's perception years earlier – had suggested otherwise, he had never spun discs in earnest. More than that, he seemed to be disparaging towards those who made a living out of it. A year earlier, when he'd been pestered by a heckler at Loch Lomond, he had shouted: 'If you don't want to see us, p*** off to the dance tent, Carl Cox is on. I'm trying to play my own music and not getting paid twenty-five grand to play someone else's.'

One of the things that irked him was when he was incorrectly labelled a DJ.

'They [the tabloids] said I'm a DJ, which I'm not,' he said. And when asked whether he would ever want to learn, he said bluntly, 'No, we get offers, but we're trying to ram the band thing home. DJ'ing doesn't look like fun – Kate Lawler does it.'

Something must have shifted, however, because at Pacha he took to the decks – but not before he'd had a trial run at the place where the world's best DJs go to test their mettle.

For nearly twenty years, Café Mambo in Ibiza's San Antonio was the place for party-goers to hang out and watch the sunset to cool house beats.

It was here – and at the more commercially savvy Café del Mar next door – where the island's DJs perfected the art of building their sets perfectly to the moment when the sun slipped behind the horizon.

And it was where owner Javier Anadon and his Scots wife

Caroline, who run the club with sons Alan and Christian, invited Calvin to come to prepare for his big night.

Speaking of Calvin's debut DJ performance, Alan said, 'I think his first-ever DJ set was here. He was a singer and Pacha booked him as a DJ, he did the pre-party here.

'He was nervous but he smashed it. He's much more confident now but even then he was fantastic. Now he's a different level. That's a nice Scottish memory.'

Calvin Harris, the DJ, was born.

14

Hitting the Heights

IN a sense it was déjà vu. Here he was packing up his things once again and moving to London. In many ways, however, it was completely different.

In 1993 he had travelled to London as unknown Adam Wiles desperate to make a name for himself but no clue how to go about it. Now he was Calvin Harris, number-one pop star, promising DJ and top-notch dance producer.

This time it must have felt as though he was doing it on his terms.

He packed up both his flat in Glasgow and his old bedroom in Dumfries. Before he vacated his West End flat he revealed he had to settle an old bill – not for himself but for the previous resident, Snow Patrol's Gary Lightbody. The Belfast singer's bank had been chasing him over a £35 debt and, fearing bailiffs would come round to claim the overdue amount, Calvin put up the cash on the front-man's behalf.

'It was pure coincidence that I ended up living in the same place Gary had stayed,' Calvin said. 'It was obviously a few years ago that he last lived in Glasgow, but he was still getting letters from a bank regarding his overdraft. I found one of them opened on my mat one day.

'I didn't fancy some burly men coming and taking my synthesisers to recover his debt, so I popped the money into the account for him.'

It seemed an unnecessary act of generosity but Calvin was sure the Northern Irishman, whose own career had rocketed since the success of albums *Final Straw* and *Eyes Open* – thanks to hit singles 'Run' and 'Chasing Cars' – was good for the money.

'I'll hopefully see him over the festival season and he can pay me back,' he said.

More poignant was the act of clearing out his old orange-painted bedroom, the original home of Calvinharrisbeats Studio. Although he had left it in some state, he unearthed some old treasures to remind him of his early days when he was struggling to make it.

'It was a tip,' he said. 'My mother wanted it as a guest bedroom, although as mums always do, she's told me I can have it back any time.'

'I found my old football tops,' he said. 'I also came across my old folder, where I kept all the rejection letters I got from labels.

'From the age of fourteen I fired off loads of demos from that orange room so it was quite symbolic being back there for the last time – just before my mum had it repainted something much less offensive.'

Calvin had accumulated so many hoodies over the years he decided sacrifices had to be made and so a local charity shop benefitted from his clearout.

'My local charity shop is about to get a whole load of my jazzy hoodies,' he said. 'Some of them are amazing but some are absolutely disgusting.'

He had found a place in Islington in which to base himself. Although this was the London borough in which Ben Kinsella had met his untimely end, largely it was a middle-class haven, with rising house prices and a bustling village feel, with the shops, restaurants and theatres of Upper Street. It was where Tony Blair's vision for New Labour was born and where the then new mayor of London Boris Johnson lived.

Although, as Calvin said, 'There's a dodgy part of Islington and a nice bit, and I'm kind of in the middle. The place is pretty pokey. Being tall, I like high ceilings.'

He seemed somewhat reluctant to be there, given his stark appraisal of London in the past, but he recognised that if he was to take his career to the next level it was where he needed to be.

'Coming from where I do, I like trees and lots of open space. But I've got to be in London for the time being if I'm serious about this, and I am,' he said.

As if to illustrate the point he was going to be in London in time for the release of his new single, 'I'm Not Alone', in April.

Recorded in his Glasgow flat in December, it represented a shift in style to a harder house sound. Anyone hearing it for the first time without knowing who it was by would have been hard pushed to recognise it as a Calvin Harris song. The slow intro almost sounds like an indie track. Lyrically, the tone is melancholy and as Calvin sang about someone replacing all that they stood for with mountains of gold, one wondered from whom and what events was he drawing his inspiration. If the pressures of building on his success or the sadness of his relationship's end had played a part, then the tone was not overtly bleak and there was an optimistic air about the chorus. And when the contemplative opening gave way to big Balearic dance chords it was a far more mature and polished sound he had created. Forget creating disco, this was a club anthem in the making.

'I like its unpredictability,' he said. 'It's about feeling too old to go clubbing – I'm twenty-five now and it does feel a lot older than when I was having my first hit aged twenty-two.' Adding, 'After the thrill of getting into a club at fifteen with a fake ID, every experience is a more and more watered-down version.'

He explained the contrasting styles.

'I wanted to make a track that sounded like "stadium dance music" – like Faithless but with a singing bit more like Snow Patrol. My main objective is to make everything louder and literally blow people away.'

He explained where the influence for the sound came from: 'It retains some of the features of the old stuff and also introduces something new. I really got into old Ibiza songs – classic euphoric dance numbers – by going on YouTube and looking up old videos. I've done stuff like that before but it just never came out.'

Even the video – shot in Norway by director Christian Holm-Glad – was a more sophisticated affair, while still retaining his customary humour. A young Calvin is seen lost in the forest with only a teddy bear for company. He loses the toy and emerges years later as a mad professor, complete with trademark 'fly-eye' glasses, experimenting on women in order to bring his old teddy back to life.

'Thing is, originally it was about something,' he said. 'And then it became a sort of bizarre. I don't even know what it is any more. But I like it. It looks like a film. It's pretty and that's all that matters to me. No videos are really about anything any more, are they? They're just people on a green screen dancing. Mine is just another one of them.'

The promo instantly ran into controversy, however – because it featured scenes with him holding a knife.

Even though there was a comical element to the imagery, music television bosses ruled the scenes had to be cut if the video was to be aired.

'My video's getting banned because I'm holding an antique knife in one of the scenes, therefore encouraging knife crime,' he said, somewhat baffled. In an attempt to appease the censors, he added: 'The only ever time I was in a fight, I fell down instantly and I believe they had only verbally challenged me to one at that stage. I fight like a girl.'

However, with tongue in cheek, he went on: 'Hopefully nobody takes the subject matter too seriously. I can assure you that I do not keep lots of women in my basement in real life. That's what the attic is for.'

A spokeswoman for Columbia Records conceded: 'Calvin doesn't actually use the knife in the video but we need to cut the scene for any TV programme that wants to show the video. Rules are stricter and a lot of artist videos get edited for TV nowadays.'

Mercifully the controversy was irrelevant where radio was concerned and unsurprisingly Pete Tong championed the track early. In October 2008, Calvin had furthered his transformation to DJ by serving up a storming two-hour set of thumping dance tunes on Tong's Essential Mix show. By further supporting Calvin's new single, Pete ensured that by the time it was released it was already a floor favourite.

However, it wasn't just the video censors who were falling foul of the producer. His favourite magazine named him 'Best Dancefloor Filler' for 'Dance Wiv Me' to be presented at the NME Awards, but then the organisers forgot to invite him. As the editor rang Calvin to apologise, blaming an administration error, the star fumed: 'What kind of awards ceremony has you winning an award and not inviting you?'

Calvin shrugged off the slight, as the song garnered even more recognition: 'Dance Wiv Me' was nominated for 'Best Contemporary Song' at the prestigious Ivor Novello Awards, which recognise songwriting, and was also nominated for best 'British Single' at the Brit Awards. Although he and Dizzee lost out to Guy Garvey of Elbow at the Ivor Novellos, at least he had not been overlooked. At the Brits he was pipped by Girls Aloud and left the ceremony to head straight to the US and his first major DJ tour.

With a hectic schedule to negotiate, the last thing he needed was anything that left him feeling below par, so he was cursing his luck when he caught a cold not long after arriving. It brought back memories of his first dates, when he had been laid low. He lasted as far as Texas and then had to throw in the towel.

'I spent two days in my hotel in Texas, just ordering room service and taking antibiotics. But in the end I had to go home, sadly,' he said, bemoaning the fact that unlike some DJs he couldn't put it down to excessive partying.

'I'm like the anti-party,' he said, confirming that for several months he'd stopped drinking alcohol. 'I don't drink at all now, I'm boring. I like going to bed early. I enjoy working and making music. Hangovers inhibit that.'

However, he added, 'The whole drink thing is hard to avoid when I DJ. It's even frowned upon if you don't drink. I also needed it for the nerves at the start. But, by the time I did the last tour, I wasn't drinking much at all. I'd have one to steady my nerves before I went on and that would be it.'

He might not have been able to enjoy it fully but he did appreciate the reception he received in the States, something that still took him aback.

'I'm surprised by everything that happens: talking to cameras, chatting to people whose records I was buying five years ago, like Kylie, playing headline shows,' he said, putting it down to the credibility that working with Dizzee had given him.

'Cool people started to like me when I worked with Dizzee, which was quite funny,' he said. He and Dizzee had already made plans to work on more tracks together, one of which Calvin hoped to have ready to come out before the festival season.

'It's a good song for the summer,' he said. 'I think it will be amazing when I finally finish it. I'm just producing it this time, so there are no featured vocals from me.'

Despite the continued collaboration with Dizzee, Calvin added, 'I haven't settled into a Timbaland-style music production line, but I've always liked songs with tunes and inevitably that's pop.'

He might not have been setting his sights on following in the footsteps of the American rapper who, since 1996, had produced a string of hit singles for Aaliyah, Missy Elliott, Jay-Z, Justin Timberlake, Madonna and Rihanna, but US star Katy Perry, who had burst onto the scene with 'I Kissed a Girl', was the latest to say she wanted to work with him – believing his skills were on a par with legendary 'Wall of Sound' producer Phil Spector.

'There are murmurings about Katy,' he said, 'but you can never tell with Americans whether it'll happen or not. She sent me a big long email comparing me to Phil Spector, which I found incredible, but you've got to laugh, haven't you? So that was great and we're possibly doing something. I'm a massive fan of hers. Huge. She wants to do a fun album, like a dance album but obviously still pop. I fit that bill, so I guess that's why she thought of me. It'd be that kind of thing.'

He did work on a remix for her single 'Waking Up in Vegas', which appeared on both the US and UK version, but he hoped it would lead to a closer working relationship.

Calvin was always flattered to be asked to collaborate but was still struggling as to when to say yes and to whom.

'It's hard because you're not sure when people are going to stop asking. It's whether working with them is good at that time,' he explained.

'Sometimes I don't like the idea and say I can't fit it in. But sometimes I am genuinely busy and they think it's an excuse. I usually make a lot of bad decisions if I'm left to myself.'

He was reminded of his earlier decision to turn down Lady Gaga. This was brought home when her first two single releases in the UK shot to number one, but he wasn't losing sleep over it.

'Fast forward a year and she's the biggest thing. But I don't regret turning her down as I didn't think the song I heard then was that good,' he said.

Calvin was also beginning to play with the idea of releasing a succession of singles ahead of an album 'bundle' later in the year, rather than the traditional model of making the focus the long player, trailed by a couple of tracks. In the digital download age songs had to stand on their own merit and the failure of 'Colours' and 'Merrymaking' had shown that releasing an album too soon could kill the commercial potential of other songs.

'I do wonder what the point of conventional albums is now that everyone downloads songs,' he said. 'There's no sense in releasing a collection that's just padded out. A great single should stand out on any playlist.'

He added: 'There's going to be a few more singles than usual. I want people to get a more rounded idea of the album before it comes out rather than put out one single then the album. Personally, I'm more into the singles market. I enjoy making tracks that I think are going to be singles.'

Calvin continued to embrace each technical advancement and while he must have been sad to watch as Myspace fell out of fashion, usurped by the trendier Facebook, he was quick to identify the potential of another social-networking phenomenon – Twitter.

The micro-blog site, where people post status updates, thoughts and musings in 140 characters or less, caught on primarily because it offers an artist a way of communicating directly with fans, without the filter of managers, agents, PRs and the media.

Calvin quickly made a name for himself, posting bizarre missives, issuing updates to his schedule and picking fights with so-called rivals.

He didn't always get the tone right, however. In one infamous tweet he revealed he was answering the call of nature in order to 'make room for' his next meal.

'I thought that was quite a good one,' he said, 'but everybody turned out to be repulsed. I don't know where the line is with Twitter. Nobody does.'

A sign of success was how many followers one could build – and Calvin found the angrier he was, the better, swiftly amassing 10,000 followers.

'Twitter is best used as a stream-of-consciousness rant,' he said. 'I was in a really angry mood for a couple of days, and I doubled my followers.'

Speaking of his 10,000 followers, he said, 'It's an average figure. Mike Skinner from The Streets has more than me.'

Closer interaction with the public prompted some to question whether it was an invitation to stalkers, but in the beginning Calvin wasn't worried about any unwelcome attention.

'When I do get spotted, it's usually because I'm 6 ft 5¾ in., so the reaction I get is: "Look at that tall bastard!" I'm not destined for celebrity.'

He might have spoken too soon, for not long after he was attracting attention on the street.

'I get recognised more now,' he said. 'I got spotted waiting for a train at King's Cross yesterday. It's always a surprise being spotted in London because there are many more interesting people to spot. When I'm back in Dumfries it's different, as there's no one else famous from Dumfries.'

And he might have been modifying his opinion about stalkers when a man launched a verbal assault on him on the video-sharing site YouTube, ranting about the video for 'I'm Not Alone'.

'You are wearing honeycombs for sunglasses,' the man said. 'Are you trying to attract bees? Are they trying to sting you to blindness? If you're alone you belong in an insane asylum.'

Calvin posted the message on his own website, adding: 'This scared the wits out of me.'

When the single was released in April, Lady Gaga was sitting top of the charts, but Calvin wasn't feeling that optimistic. For a start, he wasn't happy about the new location of his studio, in a tiny room in Willesden, North London.

'It's awful,' he said. 'I moved my studio here and it's a disaster, to be honest with you. I'm in a f*cking broom cupboard, I feel like Andy f*cking Crane. It's this room they rent out on a long-term basis and I'm the unlucky tenant. I can leave if I give two weeks' notice, which is great, and I think I might do that sooner rather than later.'

First he had to hone his live sound, and finish his second album.

'I'm working on making the live show sound good, which is a lot of work. And at the same time I'm trying to finish my album. And people keep asking me for backing tracks. I really want to give them things, but I'm not getting enough sleep,' he said.

His own predictions for how well the single would do were modest, to say the least.

'Number thirteen,' he said when asked to say how high he thought it would chart. 'And I'll be gutted. I keep thinking one minute that it'll do well, then another time I think it'll bomb.'

He was worried that he hadn't done that much promotion for it. His label seemed unsure of a strategy for this and subsequent singles.

'Nobody really knows what to do,' he revealed. 'I've got three singles coming up before the album so we're sort of making this campaign up as we go along. They're saying we won't go for it on this one, or on the next one, but for the third one they'll really go for it. But what if there is no third one? This is the problem I'm facing at the moment but it's all good fun.'

Even before 'I'm Not Alone' hit the shops he was starting to trail the follow-up, even though it was not expected to be released until August, promising a change in musical style again.

But when his latest single eventually was available to buy he took to the Internet again and this time it was he who was ranting – at the price some outlets were selling it at, and in particular Tesco's price of 57p.

'That track took me two years!' he wrote. '57p! Two years! 57p! No wonder music's on its arse.'

That feeling must have been short-lived, though, as, discounted or not, sales rocketed. It shot to number one in its first week, deposing Lady Gaga's 'Poker Face', which had spent three weeks in the top spot. Calvin was in his studio when he heard the news and celebrated by eating a ham sandwich!

'I had a ham sandwich on my lap, so it seemed a good time to eat it,' he said, although on Twitter he offered an alternative method of celebration.

'Ran out of clean pants, so I'm going commando,' he tweeted. 'No better way to celebrate a number one.'

Once he had found clean underwear, he raved about how much it meant to secure a number one in his own right.

'It mattered more having a number one without Dizzee. It's better people know and like me than think I'm an idiot,' he said.

What made it even more satisfying was that it proved there was a market out there for real dance music.

'There's not many people under thirty making dance music any more so I'm ready to take over,' he said.

Calvin seemed to have convinced himself that he was only cool by association and was stunned that he had reached number one on his own.

'It's bizarre that it could be two number ones in a row, especially as I did this track on my own,' he said. 'I'm more one for piggy-backing another artist's popularity.'

He was joining rarified company, the likes of Lulu, the Bay City Rollers, Midge Ure, Simple Minds and Wet Wet Wet, as Scots artists who had hit number one.

'Respect to all of them – Andy Stewart, too. I'm very proud,' he said when he realised the exclusive club he had just joined. Once he'd had a chance to reflect, however, he realised it was a dream he always thought he had a chance of achieving.

'In all honesty I didn't think that being number one was something completely unattainable,' he said, before adding that he had worked extremely hard to get to this point – harder than he ever had.

'I've never worked so hard in my life,' he said. 'If I was to add up everything I'd done until that point – school, the fish factory, Safeway, M&S – then it doesn't compare.'

He revealed there had been an unexpected pressure to coming up with new music – particularly after his first album had not been universally well received.

'There were some one-star reviews; in the worst of them I only got half a star,' he said. 'I'm not making excuses, but that album was made at home on a crappy little Amiga for my own entertainment.'

Even in his home town the reaction had been mixed.

'Nobody in the town knew who I was. For eight years I hardly ever went out. The old boys at M&S were made up for me but my peers, guys my age, weren't loving the music,' he admitted. 'It wasn't getting any admiration at all. Maybe there was some jealousy, and I can understand that. If I was in a little local indie band pouring my heart into songs in the traditional manner but not getting anywhere, I'd be raging the first time I heard a big arse singing, "I get all the girls, I get all the girls".'

He added: 'The thing about that first album is that I was making music to please myself and I didn't think anybody else would hear the songs, but then I got signed and they came out. Now I know other people are going to hear them, I'm going to try my hardest to make it good. This time it's the idea that I like it, that you like it, that everybody likes it. I don't want to make anyone angry. I got the impression that people were actually angry about my first album.'

He went on: 'In these two years everything has been taken to the next level. There's more fun – maybe too much, and now I don't drink at all – but there's also more pressure and more paranoia.'

He paid tribute to Sean and Mark, his two old pals, who, amid the madness of the previous two years, had kept his feet on the ground.

'I've been to some beautiful places and met some outrageous divas,' he said. 'And the best thing is I've done everything in the company of two Dumfries boys in the band, Sean McCole and Mark Irving, who always make sure I get home safely.'

Calvin also revealed that the release of 'I'm Not Alone' had been the third stage of a three-step plan to delay the release of his second album.

'The first tactic of delaying the album was pretending that I lost it at Heathrow,' he said. 'That one worked pretty well. The second was the Dizzee Rascal tune, which reminded people that I existed. And the third tactic is now to put a single out and hope that it does so well that people forget I haven't made a second album.'

At the Capital FM Summertime Ball Calvin was up to mischief again, taking his ongoing spat with the *NME* to a new level. Even after the job application stunt the mag had not let up in its criticism of him, prompting some retaliation from the Scot on his website and Twitter. Ahead of the Capital FM event he printed up a bunch of T-shirts saying, 'Conor McNicholas: Editor of the NME' and planned to take them around the festivals, asking celebrities to pose in them.

'I started at the Capital FM Summertime Ball and got Lionel Richie,' he said, 'although Lionel thought I was Conor McNicholas.'

Unfortunately Calvin's plan was scuppered when McNicholas left *NME* for another mag, but Calvin was able to laugh it off.

At the same summer ball he bumped into Katy Perry, who re-iterated her desire to work with him. They pencilled in some time to meet up later in the year and it really looked like their collaboration would come off.

One person he might not be working with, though, was his fellow Scots DJ and producer Mylo. The pair kept running into each other at festivals and events and were on the same bill at the dance spectacular Creamfields in Cheshire in August. But while Calvin was generous in his praise, speaking publicly about his confidence that Mylo's new album would be 'brilliant', that spirit wasn't exactly shared by his would-be rival for the title of the nation's top dance act.

Mylo said: 'I'm not really sure about Calvin going trance but I'm thinking about sticking around at Creamfields when Calvin plays the day after me so I can check him out.'

It's doubtful Calvin cared. His career seemed to be on a different trajectory to Mylo's at the time and he was aiming his sights higher when it came to his wish list of people he'd like to work with. He was so busy he turned down requests from Tom Jones and Lulu, but there was one man he would never say no to.

'Most of the people I want to work with are unobtainable, like Michael Jackson,' Calvin said. 'With him, I'd get in a bunch of old soul musicians like Roy Ayers and Herbie Hancock and get him to make an album like *Off the Wall* again. I would feel happy that I'd taken him back to the good old days.'

In the summer of 2009, Jackson was busy planning his comeback gigs – a series of forty sell-out concerts planned for the O2 in London. The prospect then of hooking up the King of Pop with the golden boy of dance would have been a mouth-watering one – and Calvin had a novel idea of how to make it happen.

'When Jacko comes to the UK I want to grab him, take him to a cupboard in my house and write a massive dance track with him.'

Somewhat prophetically, however, he said, 'But you know that would never happen. Instead, there'd be tracks by Akon and will.i.am. It's all about selling records and not taking risks in the US.'

If that didn't come off, he was desperate for the chance to be his support act.

'I'm absolutely up for doing it,' he said, excited at the chance of seeing up close one of his all-time heroes. 'I'm the ideal opener for Michael Jackson.

'I would prime the fans, getting them excited and covered in sweat – then it would go off when he came on.

'I really can't think of anyone better to warm up for Michael Jackson in the world than myself.'

His dream of working with the best in the business was a noble one. Sadly it would not come to fruition – but not for the reasons Calvin predicted.

15

The King Is Dead, Long Live the King

FOR Calvin, 25 June 2009 should have been a day of celebration. He had just put the finishing touches to his album and had a packed summer schedule of festivals ahead. But when he returned to his flat in London he sat stunned, unable to take his eyes from twenty-four-hour news channels and the Internet.

It was the day a part of pop music died.

Michael Jackson had been found dead in his Los Angeles villa, the victim of acute propofol and benzodiazepine intoxication. When the news filtered through at 9.20 p.m. British time Calvin, along with the rest of the world, could scarcely believe it. It was a moment he will always remember.

'It was the day I finished my album and I came back from the studio on a high,' he said. 'When I found out, it was an ultimate downer and I was absolutely devastated.'

Like many fans, Calvin thought back to the Jackson records he grew up on, from the early days of the Jackson 5 through *Off the Wall* and *Thriller* to *Bad* and *Dangerous*.

'He was an influence and I was absolutely – I don't think I know anyone in music who wasn't – influenced by him. He's one of those people that a number of generations have grown up with.'

News of Jackson's death sparked an Internet meltdown. Over 3,500 separate news sources were covering the story and the sheer number of people desperate for more information caused servers to crash, affected the BBC website and forced Twitter to shut down temporarily.

Interest in the singer's back catalogue was unprecedented, with iTunes reporting rising sales of all his albums. In a day the top seven places in the album charts were all by Jackson, while twenty-three of his most loved songs entered the top 100 UK singles chart.

It seemed as though everyone turned to the web to devour news, download songs, watch videos on YouTube or take to social media to post their own reflections and memories of the pop superstar.

Hundreds of celebrities broadcast their feelings of shock and sadness, mostly on Twitter. Actress Demi Moore wrote how 'greatly saddened' she was, while Katy Perry spoke for many when she posted simply: 'Oh my God.'

Calvin was no exception. Clearly irked by some of the less kind comments online he wrote: 'Prince and Michael where I come from was our Elvis and Beatles . . . show sum Respect!!!!'

In the days that followed, as the world mourned along with the singer's family and experts lined up to apportion blame, it transpired that Jackson's former representatives were sounding out current artists to ask if they wanted to add a fresh spin to his classic tracks. It probably wasn't surprising that the UK's premier producer got a call.

But he revealed: 'I got asked to do it just a week after Michael's death – I found it quite offensive. I said, "No way." It really should be left alone because you're not going to improve it, are you?'

He later elaborated: 'I'm not going to be remixing any of his tracks. His old record label asked for a remix of Jackson 5 tunes but it's just such a cash-in and I'll never do anything like that. I'm the last person who should do a tribute. Get some proper pop stars to do it, like Justin Timberlake. Why would I do a tribute? It would be rubbish.'

Calvin might have finished his album – which now had a title, *Ready for the Weekend* – but it had been a bumpy process before it was suitable for release. He had been unhappy at the way his tunes had been mastered.

'There was no groove or vibe,' he said.

He called up the engineer and told him: 'It was kinda like I was stood in a star shape with my hair blowing back and making a face like Cherie Blair – "Oh, make it stop!"'

'I just kept rambling until he saw what I was trying to say. Which was "punchier drums", essentially.'

Clearly a perfectionist, Calvin might have obsessed about his music but he wasn't too precious not to admit they were still just pop songs.

'There are a lot of mindless moments in my tunes,' he said. 'In fact, 80 per cent is mindless – I like fantastic big riffs. But I figured that given I've already been put in this pop bracket, I should not make serious dance music but make party music instead.'

And although he wanted to put out good pop songs he knew that the cost might be his credibility.

'As soon as I put out my first single, that disappeared,' he said. 'I don't make that sort of music. I'm not one of those people trend-setters like. I'm not really sure how it works for me. I just like making tunes. I'd sooner make a tune you can hum along to, and have people say I'm a dickhead.'

It was precisely that attitude that led to him providing a song for a new European ad campaign for Coca-Cola. An agency asked him to come up with a tune for a song called 'Yeah Yeah Yeah La La La'. He gave it some thought and decided that as Prince or George Clinton's Parliament could have come up with a track of the same name, so could he. The track was indeed very Prince-esque and accompanied an advert where Critter-style creatures grooved to Calvin's beat.

Coca-Cola liked it so much they made it the basis for a £50 million campaign.

'I was well surprised when I saw that [figure],' Calvin said. 'I was right on the phone to my manager, wondering where it was all going! Nah, it was good, it was a nice opportunity to get a song played all round different countries. The first album was a disaster in most countries other than the UK. It was kinda the label's fault – I know it's easy to blame them – but it took quite a long time to come out.'

Jack White, of White Stripes fame, had recently been criticised for getting into bed with Coke, but Calvin was quite relaxed about the prospect of any flak.

'Jack White has a much higher profile and, again, he's already got that credibility. He's a purist. That's why it didn't fit with his character. Me, no one really cares. I can do that and if I get any shit, I wonder who it'd be from? I don't have die-hard fans at all. It's 2009, it's pop music. If I release a shit record – or one that just doesn't do very well – people move on to the next thing.'

Calvin, it seemed, had no pretentions to be a star – and spending time with Dizzee promoting 'Dance Wiv Me' convinced him of that.

'I'm not trying to be a celebrity, Justin Timberlake-kinda guy,' he said. 'I mean, Dizzee's on all the time. Me sitting next to him would amplify my uncomfortableness even more. That was when I really decided there's no way I can do this for much longer. That's when I thought I'm just gonna be a producer.'

That claim sounded fanciful, given he was about to release another album, but even before the new one was out he doubted whether he might do another.

'This is probably the last one,' he said. 'I don't see what else I can do.

'For me to sing all the songs, it seems like that's done now. This'll be news to the record label, but I think this is a line for me.'

There was a school of thought that he might move off in the direction of French DJ-producer David Guetta, who had masterminded a huge hit with Kelly Rowland and was about to score another with the Black Eyed Peas, but he said, 'If I'm ever gonna make a proper leap into David Guetta territory, I'm gonna have to do something – whether it's taking loads of drugs or drinking again. And if I have to, I will,' he said, before adding, 'That's a joke.'

Whether he had the motivation to keep producing albums would come down to whether they went to number one or not. The first test would come with the release of the title track as his new single in August, after it had been trailed over the summer festivals.

The new track featured Calvin singing the verses, but he had hired the powerful voice of Mary Pearce to tackle the soaring chorus. A queen of studio backing vocals, Mary had been a mainstay of the London music scene, recording with Lionel Richie, Chaka Khan and Grace Jones.

Calvin claimed it sounded 'different to anything else I've ever done' and in some ways he was right. The track was a fusion of the style reminiscent of 'Acceptable in the 80s' and the new direction in which he was heading. On first listen the chorus seemed at odds with the verses, but as with all Calvin tracks after several plays it burrowed into the listener's consciousness.

'It's not a club tune, but more of a full-on pop record – the only one I've done on this album,' he said. 'It's a bit scary to be releasing it because there is a lot of singing involved. But I don't sing the hook, which is great. I really like it, it's my favourite thing that I've done.'

With Mary's big hook about getting ready for the weekend, it was in the running to be the anthem of the summer.

'Everyone puts on shoes during the course of a night out,' he said. 'I'm uniting all shoe-wearers. That's what I'm doing there. It's the happiest, most joyful song I've done so far. It's got a diva on it, and I've always wanted to do a song with a diva. It's the ultimate dance music cliché, but done in a slightly different way.'

Semi-joking, he explained why he hadn't gone for an established name: 'She's not famous. I wanted someone I could bung £250 to and never hear from again. Royalties are few and far between these days – I just got my iTunes statement through and to be honest with you it doesn't even cover a packet of Fruit Pastilles. I'm on my arse.'

Being more serious, he added: 'She's got this great big voice and it's like a nod to an old dance classic. I love underground dance music but I also have an extreme love of commercial dance music. But only the good stuff.'

It looked like he was making good on his promise to make big 'stadium dance' tunes.

'What I'm into at the moment,' he said, 'is the idea of playing football stadiums with massive riffs, big hands-in-the-air rave anthems. The whole "minimal" thing has passed, for me.'

Where better to test these tracks out than at the big outdoor festivals? But Calvin's summer of appearances got off to a dodgy start when he ate a suspect egg sandwich and came down with food poisoning ahead of his iTunes appearance in July. But he recovered to showcase his new material and switched from performer to fan when another eighties icon, Madonna, invited him to watch her at the O2. The pop queen had paid him a mighty compliment by sampling some of 'I'm Not Alone' for her live show and invited him along by way of a thank you.

Then it was off to Ibiza to shoot the video for 'Holiday', the song he wrote with Dizzee Rascal and one for which the rapper had high hopes.

'I am looking for another number-one hit with my new single "Holiday",' Dizzee said, adding of Calvin's production, 'I like the music he makes. I like his beats. I sit pretty well on them. We work well together, but we have never sat in a studio with each other. We just do things over the Internet. We've never got together once and it was the same with this song "Holiday". He sent me mixed-down versions and asked me what I thought of them.'

A plush villa in the sun-kissed hills above Ibiza Town was the location for the video shoot, as Calvin tried to fit in beside a sharp-suited Dizzee, a host of scantily clad extras in shimmering bikinis and high heels, and the drum'n'bass star Goldie strutting around topless. Calvin lurked around while staged revelry kicked off all about him, and it's tempting to imagine him feeling self-consciously Scottish, standing there, pale, in jeans, T-shirt and trainers amid a sea of bronzed bodies.

To emphasise the point, Calvin said: 'I'm not good at dancing; I'm not good at looking like I'm having fun. I never will be, I don't think. Unless I go to a life coach.

'I'm somehow gonna be incorporated into one of the shots. And it keeps changing cos the light keeps changing. That's what they're telling me anyway. I think perhaps they just don't want me in it.'

The mood of the video was a sort of modern-day 'Club Tropicana' and as Calvin looked around him, he said, 'It's an experience.'

As the day wore on and the takes multiplied, he started to feel excluded. For a start they told him he wasn't allowed to wear his trademark fly-eye glasses.

'I am upset,' he said, after they told him they would 'detract from the look of the video'. They then demanded that he dance in front of the camera.

But Calvin wasn't having any of it.

'I'm not a dancer. So if it's a choice between being in it and dancing, and not being in it and not dancing, then I'll pick not being in it,' he said.

In the end, after travelling out there, he didn't make the final cut, but he didn't seem too bothered in the end.

'I couldn't be arsed, to be honest. It's not my video,' he said, adding that originally the song was intended for another act. 'I wrote it for The Saturdays. But they didn't like it. Or their A&R guy didn't like it. But Dizzee liked it. It happens.'

Calvin's willingness to reveal the behind-the-scenes showbiz shenanigans that go on before a song hits the charts was winning him some new admirers.

As well as 'Holiday', he had been polishing off the final mix of 'Off and On', the track originally intended for Róisín Murphy, which had ended up with Sophie Elllis-Bextor. Now, with the benefit of hindsight, not to mention new technology and better skills, he agreed with Róisín's original assessment.

'Róisín was right,' he said. 'The original version was shite.'

Craig McLean, of the *Independent on Sunday*, who joined Calvin for the shoot, described him as 'the dancefloor Andy Murray, hilariously dour and scathing about the dog-and-pony show ridiculousness of pop promotion'.

He took delight that even though Calvin had been particularly annoyed by a stunt an interviewer for ITV Online pulled (she repeatedly asked him to open a jam jar that was glued shut) he hadn't played along and instead announced: 'This is the worst feature I've ever seen. In fact, this is the worst day of my life.' Then, not to be outdone, he launched his own Jam TV show on his website, where he filmed celebrities holding a jar of jam. The odd craze caught on before Lady Gaga refused because she thought it was 'some weird porn thing'.

'In pop terms, Calvin Harris is a breath of fresh air,' McLean said. 'In a world built on spin, smoke, mirrors and Botox, he calls a spade a rusty spade.'

Calvin might have wasted an afternoon in the hills hanging around on someone else's video, but that night he was on more familiar ground, playing a gig at the Ibiza Rocks hotel in San Antonio, the island's party capital.

With the new album completed, he would be showcasing several tunes from it for the first time.

Such was the demand to see him that the hotel organisers said it caused 'the biggest roadblock since [US President Barack] Obama's inauguration'.

They raved that each 'anthem started a new party' and any doubts he might have had about whether his new material would cut it with fans were instantly dispelled.

Afterwards, in a demonstration of his versatility, he was heading to the Eden club to appear as a DJ at the 'Reclaim the Dancefloor' event.

It seemed that something happened to Calvin's tolerance levels around the time when a new album came out. Ahead of the release, he was picking fights all over the place on Twitter.

Several things had annoyed him.

First, he was irked by an early slot on the bill at T in the Park.

'I've had two number-one singles but played an earlier stage time than I did two years ago,' he said. 'I'm not sure what happened.'

'Welcome to the afternoon matinee,' he yelled when he took to the stage before launching into 'Acceptable in the 80s'.

Afterwards he added: 'I was on just after Björn Again and had to do a *TV-AM* Mr Motivator kind of show to get people moving.'

Next he launched into a rant against Sony Records and the British Phonographic Industry, as he believed they had removed the video for 'Ready for the Weekend' from the Internet.

Shot in London's Southbank, the video was another with an eighties feel and showed Calvin playing it straight before a number of glamour girls, including model Lauren Pope, took over for the chorus. YouTube removed the original mix due to a 'copyright claim'.

But Calvin fumed on Twitter: 'It's my song, you bastards.'

'It's the fucking BPI [British Phonographic Industry]. The BPI, what have you ever done for anybody you useless shower.'

He even threatened a bizarre revenge on the BPI's offices in London if they removed any more of his videos, particularly the Jam TV clips.

'I'm going to drive my car into the big window in the BPI's offices on my way to the studio this morning,' he went on. 'I'm going to hire a 4x4 for the day so I make more of an impact, and hopefully reach the online monkeys at the back of the office.'

When eventually he calmed down, he apologised: 'I got a bit caught up in the heat of the moment. Sorry to employees of the BPI but please put my video back on the Internet.'

The songs were returned to the website, and Calvin said: 'The fact I did that rant against the BPI three days after the video had been down and that the video went back up tells more about them than it does me.'

He also had a go at the Performing Rights Society (PRS), who collect money for artists based on public performances.

He said: 'The PRS took the British pop videos off YouTube. That's another body that claim they work for the artist.

'The PRS collect money for radio plays and they have only in recent years started collecting money from Radio 1 on a daily basis.

'You didn't get a true reflection of what songs are being played on the radio because they just sampled the station's plays. That meant bigger artists get money they haven't earned. The system is wrong even if it is better than it was before.

'These things get me annoyed but nobody wants to talk about it for fear of being seen in a bad light.'

Calvin did record another promo video for the single, this time using a home-made 'Humanthesiser' – sixteen bikini-clad models decorated with a new electricity-conducting body ink developed by students at the Royal College of Art in London.

'Ready for the Weekend' entered the charts at number three – the highest new entry that week – but was held off the top spot by the Black Eyed Peas' monster hit 'I Gotta Feeling', which remarkably had jumped back to number one after being deposed for a solitary week by Tinchy Stryder, featuring Amelle, with 'Never Leave You', which dropped to number two.

The following week Calvin's album of the same name hit the shops, in a change to the strategy put forward at the start of the year regarding single releases before the long player.

Calvin was right to be excited about his new material. It marked an astonishing leap forward. Nearly every song had single potential and within each track was a mini symphony with light and shade but always a killer hook.

Opening track 'The Rain' set the tone with a groovy seventies soul funk riff, big horns and upbeat lyric that celebrated life's good times. 'Stars Come Out' and 'You Used to Hold Me' were the type of thumping pop tunes lesser artists would dream of for lead singles.

Like 'I'm Not Alone', 'Blue' started like an indie track, reminiscent of an Oasis B-side (i.e. better than many of their album tracks), before giving way to a Daft Punk-esque lament in which Calvin pined for a lost love. Could that have been a message for anyone in particular? If so, then who was 'Worst Day' – a blunt appraisal of a doomed relationship – aimed at?

From the moment the chiming piano chords heralded the arrival of 'Flashback' it had future single written all over it. Designed to get hands in the air in every club, this classy melody reunited Calvin with his good friend Ayah Marar, whose playful vocal was the perfect fit for the bouncy beats.

'Relax' blended Spanish-sounding acoustic guitars with a distorted synth sound to excellent effect. With lines about girls waiting and things being there for the taking, one wondered if Calvin was sending a message to himself to sit back and enjoy his life more. Accurately describing it as a 'sunsetty thing', Calvin said he 'always envisaged it for the last track'.

The soulful instrumental 'Burns Night' acted as an ideal tempo-shifter, while after the known highs of 'Dance Wiv Me' and 'Yeah Yeah Yeah La La La', the Air-influenced '5iliconeator' sounded like the comedown after a heady night, before 'Greatest Fear' signalled one last manic hurrah, the sort of anthem for an after-hours den which only the hardiest souls frequent.

In short, it was a triumph.

For anyone looking for a simple rerun of *I Created Disco*, expectations would have been confounded.

'That's definitely the idea,' he said. 'I wanted to make something I would be proud of: "This is as good as I can do." So I don't just have that one album to my name that I'm not particularly pleased with.

'The last one was done before I was signed, so I cut corners and didn't work as hard as I should have done. I'm pleased that I managed to record it in the circumstances in which I did it, but if I were to rerecord it, it would sound pretty different now.'

Calvin described the album as 'classic dance music in a modern environment', and he explained, 'The thing I like about dance music is you can borrow from all different genres of music, all different instruments, and turn it into a dance track. In the first place, dance music seemed so varied to me, as opposed to being limited by a band with guitars, like you get with indie and whatever. I'm trying to make dance tunes that don't seem like they are dance tunes but hopefully work. I'm trying to make something that someone either hasn't heard for ages, or has never heard before. Hopefully the latter.'

The cover featured the now ubiquitous fly-eye shades, but this time on the face of an attractive woman.

'I decided to put a pretty girl on the front instead of me, thinking that if I was going to be looking at an album cover for the next year or so, it would be better if people were looking at a more attractive face than myself,' he reasoned.

As Calvin waited to see how the public would take to his second collection, the reviews were once again mixed.

The *Sunday Telegraph* called it 'one mighty slab of floorfilling summer fun', while the *Metro* said he was exploring 'new realms of synth-pop splendour'. Even Calvin's nemesis, the *NME*, awarded the album seven out of ten.

However, in some quarters the fact that he was writing music that people wanted to hear seemed to irk some journalists. The reviews seemed to be as much about the sections of society to which Calvin's music would appeal as the actual tunes.

The *London Lite* free sheet said the album was 'as commercial as zipping up your Umbro shell suit, hopping in the Fiat and nipping by McDonald's before catching *Transformers 2* at Vue multiplex'.

But Alexis Petridis, in giving the album just two stars in *The Guardian*, witheringly said the album's roots were not in seventies soul or disco but in 'handbag house', which was 'British and tinny, as evidenced by the way it made stars of the most improbable people'.

Similarly condescending reviews in *The Independent* and *The Times* also awarded only two stars.

The less-than-favourable responses prompted an astonishing outburst from Calvin. He was so furious he posted fourteen tweets on his Twitter page.

'This industry is full of rich people's kids, everywhere f*cking rich people's kids rich people kids,' he ranted. 'Rich people's kids getting good reviews because mummy f*cked the journo in the 80s. F*ck you rich people you'll not break me I don't give a f*ck. I have nothing to lose you're only rich people.

'Rich people mean f*ck all to me seriously. I'm making music for real people, real people dance – rich people stand at the back.

'F*ck the rich people's kids with their jobs as runners on TV shows or their club nights. F*ck you you've done nothing absolutely f*ck all.

'Imagine you just spent two years of your life making a record. On your own. Every single day, long hours, working to get it sounding right. Imagine the buzz of making something that you love, and after two years you finally have something you can't wait for other people to hear. Then imagine that CD landing on the desk of snide rich person's kid or pathetic London scene-FACE.

'Then them skipping through the tracks in their lunch break, and saying: "Well it's Calvin Harris isn't it? Two stars, he's a dickhead.

'I'm telling you now that it doesn't feel good.

'But, how is it that I've been playing these songs to 20,000 people at festivals this summer, and it's gone off every single time.

'Because of the f*cking rich people's kids there are people who will like the album who won't get the album because they saw a sh*t review.

'And I can't ignore it, sorry, but it does affect me and it is hurtful and I know that it's exactly what I wanted it to be, and I'm proud of it.'

Later, once he had calmed down, he added, rather amusingly, 'Anyway, morning.'

While the focus of his ire might have been blurred, he had a point. There did seem to be a snobbish tone to the reviews.

Many artists probably wish they had the courage to rail against their detractors, but while it was refreshing to see a pop star care so passionately about how they were received, he admitted his media skills needed some finessing.

'I've never been offered media training,' he said. 'It's difficult because I'm solely responsible for my musical output. I am going to have opinions and occasionally speak out and get angry about things. That is because I am passionate.'

He should have had more confidence that the lovers of his music would need more to put them off than a sneering review.

The album entered the charts at number one – vindication that the only people who matter are the record-buying public.

Calvin celebrated with his now customary ham sandwich. 'The music company sent me champagne,' he said, 'but I don't drink so I gave it all away to friends and neighbours.'

There was no danger of him resting on his laurels, even at number one. He was busy in the studio, recording once more with Kylie, along with Jake Shears of the Scissor Sisters. And even though it looked like his reign would only last one week, as the Arctic Monkeys took over, Calvin said, 'Getting to number one in the album charts is the best thing I have achieved in my whole life.'

He added: 'It was one week that I never thought I could achieve five years ago.'

But he would be back at the summit in the singles chart, as 'Holiday' topped the hit parade. Dizzee, however, was another who had missed the memo about Calvin being teetotal. The Scot said: 'I saw Dizzee on Monday and he brought me two massive bottles of champagne to celebrate being number one, even though I don't drink.'

With no obvious vices, it was all money in the bank for Calvin, but he gave an insight into his philosophy regarding finances.

'I'm terrible at spending money,' he said. 'Obviously this is not going to last for ever, so I need to save some of my money. I treated myself three years ago when I bought myself a car. But since then

I've been a bit tight and don't really want to buy anything frivolous.'

Ready for the Weekend's success was notable for another reason. For the first time since June an act other than Michael Jackson had claimed the top spot.

It signalled a changing of the guard in more ways than one.

'I never thought I'd ever knock Michael Jackson off the top of the charts,' Calvin said. 'He's spent a lot of time at number one, but he is Michael Jackson. He's the King of Pop.

'It's a good thing, but I do love Michael Jackson. I'm a massive fan. I don't know anyone who makes music who isn't. I love *Off the Wall* – when he was still disco. But he's not around to appreciate his number one. I am.'

The king was dead. Were we witnessing the rise of a new king of pop – or simply a young pretender?

16

Pineapple Chumps

AS protests go, it wasn't exactly up there with the Boston Tea Party, 'tank man' in Tiananmen Square or Jarvis Cocker's side stage mockery of Michael Jackson, but if demonstrations are measured by the coverage they generate then it certainly was effective.

At the very least the stunt Calvin Harris pulled on live TV was as ridiculous as the pop act he was protesting against.

The X Factor: a modern-day *Opportunity Knocks*. Nothing more than a singing contest but, thanks to strong ratings, the near-mythical status afforded to Simon Cowell by the mainstream media and its dominance over the charts, it has been elevated to the level of cultural phenomenon.

However its tipping point, arguably, came on Saturday, 14 November 2009, when an Irish duo took to the stage to perform a cover of Vanilla Ice's version of David Bowie and Queen's 'Under Pressure'. As the twins John and Edward Grimes – collectively Jedward – with their permanently-in-a-state-of-shock hairdos pranced around amid a general mayhem of backing dancers and props, the presence of an additional interloper at first went unnoticed. Then viewers became aware that a rather tall man had rushed onto the stage, bending over and patting his bum while holding a pineapple over his head. The intruder hugged one of the twins before jogging offstage, where unseen by viewers he was met by unhappy security staff and kicked out of the ITV studio.

Only later did it emerge that Calvin Harris was behind the stage invasion, as he confirmed on Twitter: 'Was just thrown out of *X Factor* for jumping onstage with a pineapple on my head during

Jedward. At the end of the day I had a pineapple on my head. Sorry if I caused anyone embarrassment. PS. I love Jedward.'

If only that had been the end of it. Alas no. Louis Walsh, the boys' mentor, branded Calvin an 'idiot' and praised the boys for ignoring the antics.

It was all Simon Cowell's fault, really. He had allowed the panto-mime that was Jedward to continue a week earlier, when he had ducked the chance to vote them off by letting the decision to send them home go to a public vote. The public, in their mischief, had preferred the novelty act to poor Lucie Jones, who had made the mistake of thinking she had entered a singing competition. That decision had led to a public outcry, with Sting speaking for many when he said that the reality TV show had 'put music back decades' and was little more than 'televised karaoke'. Cowell had responded saying: 'I think this show and other shows have given people like Leona Lewis, Alexandra, JLS, Susan Boyle a shot.'

Calvin's punishment for generating even more coverage for the series than the producers could have hoped for was a ban for life from the *X Factor* studios. One wonders who is regretting that more now.

It transpired he had been a guest on *Xtra Factor*, the spin-off show. An *X Factor* spokesman said that he had been at the studio all day, and added rather ridiculously that 'it is not acceptable to run on to the stage holding a pineapple on his head'.

Indeed not, but *X Factor* couldn't say they hadn't been warned. Earlier that day Calvin had posted a photograph of a pineapple, bearing the legend 'important?'

X Factor host Dermot O'Leary called Calvin 'a pineapple with a pillock attached to its bottom' and whinged: 'What on earth was Calvin Harris playing at? I was always under the assumption that he was quite cool, but invading the stage in the middle of John and Edward's performance is hardly in the same league as Jarvis Cocker, is it?'

Amid the furore, Calvin tried to explain his actions in more depth. 'I was just inspired to make a mockery of the show,' he said. 'Because it is a music competition, it is a joke and I think it should be treated as such, so when people were saying, "John and Edward, maybe they deserve to stay in this week," I was like, "Are you watching what I'm watching?"

'It's terrible, it's terrible. For the greater good of the nation I wanted to go out there and make an idiot of myself and sort of just bring the whole show into another kind of area in which it's treated as kind of a joke.'

He said: 'As entertainment goes it's pretty much down there with the worst. So compared to everybody else, it's funny, but I've noticed as the week goes on it's kind of knowingly funny, whereas first it was kind of "John and Edward, ah, they're rubbish, they should get out of there" and they were doing these terrible performances and it was hilarious.

'And then the producers cottoned on to this, as occasionally they do, and kind of make scenarios which they thought it would be funnier to put them in, and it wasn't, which was a shame.'

And the relevance of the pineapple?

'I was alluding to the fact that their hair looks like pineapples. I thought it was obvious, but nobody else seemed to get it, and just thought I was dancing with a pineapple on my head for the fun of it,' he said. 'I was gutted. I haven't watched the show since the night of the pineapple.'

Despite his criticism of them, Calvin revealed he wanted Jedward to win the series.

'I'd love them to win because where can they go from there?' he said. 'Not them, where can *X Factor* go from there? It's not a music competition.'

He also blamed Cowell for encouraging generic pop music.

'If you look at the chart, it's like a frightening stranglehold that Simon Cowell has got over the entire music chart,' he said.

Public opinion appeared to be divided between those who felt he was an attention-seeking twit and those who thought he had made a stand for real music.

Stuart Maconie, the radio DJ and music writer, fell down on the side of the twins, branding Calvin a 'disco nitwit' and sarcastically mocking his protest, saying it was 'right up there with those Buddhist monks who set fire to themselves in Tibet or that suffragette who threw herself under the King's horse'. He made the valid point that if Calvin had intended to make a mockery of the show, then 'why was he in the audience', waiting to go on a show 'designed for those not talented enough for *X Factor*'.

But he found supporters in the shape of another radio DJ, Robin Galloway, who questioned: if Calvin's attempt had been 'to make a mockery of the show, haven't Jedward already done that?!'

ITV bosses announced that in the wake of Calvin's stunt security would be stepped up the following week, which prompted comic Frankie Boyle to quip: 'It's been pointed out that it could easily have been someone with a knife. A huge missed opportunity there, Calvin.'

Jedward, to their credit, thought the whole thing was brilliant.

Edward said: 'I didn't see him when he first came on and he usually looks different because he wears sunglasses, but it was cool. I thought afterwards, "Oh my God, he came all the way to the show and brought a pineapple with him."'

John added: 'It was weird. I thought Calvin was a dancer at first. Then I thought, "Oh, it's him." I'd like to tell Calvin, thanks for coming on with the pineapple. I hope he didn't get in too much trouble.'

The twins did have an opportunity to exact some revenge when they were added to the bill alongside Calvin at T4's Stars of 2009 event at Earls Court in London. However, their plans to storm his set were rumbled. It's a good job they were, as Calvin was excitable enough – he trashed his dressing-room after a barney with his drummer, Ben Calvert. Calvin tweeted: 'I drank too much Red Bull.'

The irony was he had given up booze because he felt he kept getting into trouble when drinking. Yet he'd caused his biggest con-troversy while sober.

'I gave up drinking because bad things happened,' he said. 'Things that you just think: "I really shouldn't have done that." There have been lots of gigs when I've looked back and gone: "Oh, it was on television, a lot of people saw that, and I was totally inebriated."'

If only he could have blamed the booze on his next outburst.

The only slight tarnish on his year was the disappointing per-formance of 'Flashback', the third single (or fourth, if you include

'Dance Wiv Me') from the album. Although it had charted – at eighteen – before the *X Factor* incident, it did seem Calvin was the only party out of that episode not to benefit commercially.

A number of things may have contributed to its relatively poor chart performance. As he'd seen with his debut, demand for the singles dropped once the album was out, plus 'Flashback' didn't have quite the mass appeal of his previous offerings. The video was a slick affair, filmed in Ibiza with Calvin playing the part of a playboy trying to piece together the events of a wild night of too much excess. It was the first promo to show him on the decks, confirmation that he was seen as much as a DJ now as a live performer.

However, although the single was promoted on the Disney Channel, he suffered a blow when *GMTV* told him it was 'too dancey' for ITV1's morning show. Calvin took to Twitter with his usual restraint.

'F*CK *GMTV*! *GMTV* won't let me on their exceptionally dull programme to do "Flashback" because i'm "too dancey"! IT'D WAKE YOUR VIEWERS UP. F*CK *GMTV*!' he ranted.

Later he posted: 'A lot of people saying "Why would you want to go on GMTV?" – PROMOTION – People need to know you have a record out. Anyway f*ck em, they can give all these *X Factor* people EVEN MORE TV time, why not, you boring non-risk-taking beige death hole DEATH DEATH.'

Then, with a threat reminiscent of the one he issued to the BPI, he added: 'Look out @GMTV i'm breaking in tomorrow – i'll be the guy wearing the FLASHBACK T-shirt, setting fire to BEN SHEPHERD'S [*sic*] TIE AND HAIR.'

All that aside, he was at least able to reflect on a positive twelve months, saying: 'I've had the best year of my life not drinking, it's been great.'

After an eventful month Calvin managed to keep his head down. Plans to head out to the States to work with Katy Perry, which had been slated for December, seemed to be on hold.

Katy insisted she still wanted to work with Calvin but was worried his recent success might make him unattainable. 'We talk about doing something but he is turning into a big, fat star so I may not be able to schedule it,' she said. 'I used to think I could get him but now I just don't know. He might be just too big for me.'

Calvin was in the UK for the year's end, spreading himself thinly at New Year, playing DJ sets at both Edinburgh's Hogmanay celebrations, this time on December 30, and London's O2 at the Ministry of Sound's New Year's Eve Party. Pete Irvine, creative director of the Edinburgh festival, was delighted to secure Calvin for the HMV Picture House gigs. 'He is arguably Scotland's happening artist of this year,' he said.

That was certainly true. Yet, as Calvin knew, you were only as good as your last hit record. He had several strings to his bow now – songwriter, producer, remixer, singer, collaborator, DJ.

He was working so hard it felt something had to give. He couldn't keep all the plates spinning, could he?

17

Calvin Declines

IT would be hard to imagine Calvin Harris with a day job – clocking into an office, in a crumpled M&S suit, and driving around the country in a company car.

But when he landed a new role as an A&R man for Sony's Deconstruction record label – scouring the country for new talent – such visions sprang to mind.

Thankfully, he was quick to dispel any notion that he had turned into a music industry suit.

'Thankfully, I don't have an office,' he said. 'I've been to three weddings and wore the same suit each time. Plus there's no company car, you know what state the record industry is in – Simon Cowell has one and that's where it ends. I'm happy on my bike.'

Calvin was ideally suited to scope out new talent, given his constant gigging and DJ'ing and indefatigable work ethic. And he was looking forward to helping restore a former player in the dance scene.

'Deconstruction brought out a lot of seminal dance music back in the nineties and even had Kylie Minogue for a short amount of time,' he explained. 'Now they've restarted it within Sony so they wanted someone who was actively gigging week in and week out.'

It was Calvin's own A&R man and now Sony executive Mike Pickering who appointed him. 'Calvin mentioned he wanted to do some A&R so we offered him a job,' Mike said. 'Calvin is perfect for the role. Not only is he a top DJ, travelling all around the world with access to a lot of new acts, but he is extremely hard working.

Having been his A&R man for four or five years, I know I can trust him to do the job properly.'

Calvin had already made his first acquisition – and there must have been something in the name that attracted him.

'We just signed a guy called Burns who's been creating noise on the underground,' Calvin said. 'I like the behind-the-scenes work, I was very involved with the songs I did with Dizzee Rascal.'

Calvin might have taken on yet another role, but he wasn't about to quit any of his other vocations just yet.

Reminding fans that he was first and foremost a performer – for the time being, anyway – he released the final single from *Ready for the Weekend*. Although not the most immediate choice for a single, 'You Used to Hold Me' was nevertheless catchy with a chorus and hook made for clubs and fist-in-the-air punching. The accompanying video once again showed Calvin at the decks (when he wasn't staring at women dancing in the glare of headlamps, through the window of a monster truck). The song's release led to online speculation about the lyrics and whether Calvin was singing a 'you used to hold me beep beep beep' refrain or 'you used to hold meat', or was it even 'you used to hold me beer beer beer'.

The song performed disappointingly, only reaching twenty-seven, and Calvin pondered whether he should stop singing on his tracks for a while.

'Every time I'm writing a song, I say, "Maybe it's time to get somebody else in to sing,"' he said. 'Then I always come back to the same conclusion, which is it's going to be easier to do it myself because only I know what I want and how I want it delivered.'

Regarding his live performance, he seemed content with his band line-up, after early teething problems with the rhythm section.

'When I first got my new drummer two years ago, we just sat in front of the drum kit, going through every song and me just telling him what to play. He loved it. And once he gets the main basic, he can put in little flourishes. My old drummer used to do them all the time. It used to do my head in,' he said.

'He used to try everything as a breakbeat and it would absolutely drive me mental. I would think, "This is house music, this isn't the funky drummer. You're doing the sixteenth notes on the second

snare, you need to stop that." He never did. So I got a new one . . .
He gets it. He's amazing.'

Calvin might have sounded like a control freak, but after invest-
ing so much in his own style of doing things he had to micro-
manage.

'It's my thing,' he said. 'It's not anybody else's thing. It's basic
autopilot for them . . . No, I'm only joking.'

With his promotional work for the album done, no one would
have blamed him for taking a break, but the word did not seem to
be in Calvin's vocabulary.

After a hectic start to 2010 that had seen him travel to Australia
and New Zealand to perform at Big Day Out, a festival spread over
several major cities in the two countries, he had crammed in his
own dates out there.

He also wrote and produced a track, 'Time Machine', for
Example's top-ten album *Won't Go Quietly*.

He had been nominated for his second Brit Award but lost out in
the Best Male category to Dizzee Rascal, ironically, given the boost
he'd given his grime star mate.

If there had been a category for the hardest-working man in
music, he would have been a contender.

Amid a period of near constant performing or producing, he
bizarrely had to take to the Internet to quash rumours of his demise
– 'A lot of people are asking if I am dead. I am currently not dead.'
Then during a tour in the States he thought he was having a heart
attack after taking two energy tablets in a bid to keep going. Calvin,
who was in Miami for the Winter Music Conference, revealed on
Twitter he had tried the pills he had picked up in Canada as an
alternative to drinking Red Bull.

'I got these pills but they had three times the amount of taurine in
them as Red Bull,' he said. 'I thought, "Is this dangerous?" But I
boshed two anyway. I was in Miami, after all. However, I started
rocking back and forth in a semi-foetal position whilst I was checking my emails. I thought, "Is this a good sign?"'

Moments later he tweeted: 'I think I'm having a little bit of a
heart attack. Don't take Canadian energy pills, people – stick to
Red Bull.'

Calvin recovered in time to head to dinner with Kelis, during which they discussed a future collaboration together.

Back in the UK he went into the studio with former *X Factor* contestants JLS.

'JLS knew I liked them and they ended up coming to me – they didn't have any great hopes that I'd come up with anything good. But I was very, very set on what I wanted to do with them – which was the antithesis of most music that's coming out at the moment, that synthetic-sounding stuff with Auto-Tune. I wanted to make a modern Quincy Jones-style production like Michael Jackson's stuff from the seventies, so I had a couple of tracks like that. I knew it would work, as they've got soul voices and so why shouldn't they make a soulful dance record? It's now done and it'll be on their new album, which is good news.'

More good news came when it emerged a tune Calvin had produced for Kylie's new album, 'Too Much', a joint effort written by the diminutive pop singer, Calvin and Jake Shears, featured on *Aphrodite*, which debuted at number one, making her the first solo artist to score a chart-topping album in four different decades.

Offering more insight into how he works with other artists, Calvin said: 'I never do a song and get told what to do. If they want me, they're going to want the music I make. You can't force someone to record vocals over instrumentals – you can give them tracks and they'll pick their favourite.'

Calvin continued to work on new music but he seemed happy to work with other artists because his label didn't care if he did another album – as his didn't sell enough.

'To be honest, no one is bothered if I do another album or not – and that was the situation before the last album,' he said candidly. 'It's quite nice as the motivation is coming from me, as no one is telling me to hurry up.

'I don't sell enough copies to make the label s*** themselves if I don't release another album. Everything is ongoing, there's never an official start or end to anything, I just carry on.

'It's not hard and it's more enjoyable. Nowadays, for someone like me, the old model of doing an album then touring it and then going back in to do another album doesn't really apply. Now you do everything all at once, they all feed off each other.'

Apart from whether there was pressure from the label or not, Calvin wasn't thinking about his own follow-up just yet.

'It will be a while before I sit down and think, "Let's write the record,"' he said. 'It was the same the last time. There just came a time when I realised I had five or six tracks ready, so I might as well get it finished.

'It will probably only happen when I have a deadline from the record label. Until that point, I am quite content to mess about with ideas and end up with loads of half-finished tracks. It's only once someone tells me I have to have it completed and handed in by a certain point that I really get going. I'm a machine then – I'll be working constantly, flat out. But for now, it's nice to just mess about with whatever takes my fancy.'

Even though he was concentrating more on being a DJ with every tour, creatively he continued to be motivated.

'I might be DJ'ing and that will inspire me to make a tune,' he said. 'It's a more involved process rather than having a block of time to just tour or be in the studio – you'd get bored with that anyway.

'I know a lot of people in dance music work like that, as it's more instant and current than other forms of music – 99 per cent of the DJs I know have a set-up that they tour with.'

Calvin was unique in that he could switch effortlessly between live shows and DJ sets, which he admitted appealed to him because they were less hassle to organise.

'It's a lot easier in so many ways,' he said. 'There's no band, no rehearsals, no hassles – you just head off with your tunes and do your own thing. It makes life very, very easy and lets me keep busy without any real pressure.'

The flexibility both disciplines afforded him meant he could always be working.

'I just like to be busy all the time. If I'm not touring, I want to be off playing DJ dates wherever I can,' he said. 'Then during the week, between gigs, I'll be in the studio. I'm not necessarily work-ing on anything in particular, but I'm always messing about with something or other.

'I have lots of little ideas and thoughts all the time, ideas for tracks or things I'd like to try.'

However, while much of his recent focus had been on perfecting his set behind the decks, he was continually perfecting the live band experience. And he promised fans something new.

'It will be a completely different show, a completely different experience for me and the crowd,' he said ahead of dates in the UK, Ireland and Europe in the summer. 'You have to remember dance music comes from clubs; it's made for clubs. So inside a big, hot, sweaty tent is where it should be seen and heard at festivals.'

It was with this new philosophy that he approached the summer festivals. At T in the Park – at which Calvin was pretty much a regular now – he chose not to repeat his daytime appearance of 2009 and asked instead if the organisers could put him inside one of the huge tents. He got his wish, headlining in the King Tut's Wah Wah tent.

'I love playing in tents, that's my thing, because of the atmosphere and the lights,' he explained. 'We had the option of going on the main stage like we did last year but, for someone like me, in the middle of the day on the main stage the atmosphere isn't really right.

'So we said to them we'd absolutely love to play it this year but stick us in a tent. Let's have a sweaty rave – and that's exactly what's going to happen. What I do now is darker than before, so it's nice to have all the boxes ticked. Everybody can see the lights; it affects our mood onstage, so I dare say it affects the crowd's mood, even if they don't know it.'

He relished the idea of headlining on home soil.

'There's a tiny bit more pressure, as you're expected to be a tiny bit better than everyone else,' he said. 'That's what I expected from people who were headlining stages I was on – and they quite frequently were better. But now the focus is on me, and I'm very confident that we're going to smash it. I'm really, really looking forward to it.'

Smash it he did. Taking to the stage in a Scotland football shirt, he showed fans what a dynamic live performer he had become, blending a club and band performance like no one else.

Opening aptly with 'The Rain', given the weather that routinely plagues this particular festival, he had the crowd jumping as one. Even a technical hitch couldn't prevent a rousing finale with 'I'm Not Alone'.

Seeing the audience's ecstatic reaction must have been a relief, as just a week earlier at the Mallorca Rocks event he had doubts about his music, in the face of an impressive performance from London rapper Tinie Tempah, of whom great things were expected following his number one smash 'Pass Out'.

'At Mallorca Rocks, Tinie Tempah was on before me. He marries different styles – something fresh that's gonna go off,' Calvin said. 'I'm more traditional house. I did have a frightening moment where I thought I was horribly out of touch.'

His fears were misplaced. Calvin was very much in demand. From T in the Park he headed straight to the south of France for a lucrative DJ gig at the trendy microbrewery Brasserie de Monaco – an altogether different experience from T in the Park.

'Luxurious gigs are always really nice to play; you get a fantastic clientele,' he said. 'But the only problem is people don't really dance, they chill out at their tables and get their bottle service. It's definitely an eye-opener but not something you'd want to do all the time.'

Calvin was back on more familiar territory with Camp Bestival in Dorset, the little brother of the larger Bestival event on the Isle of Wight, but he was driven loo-py by high jinks from old-timers Madness. Calvin had apparently been less than friendly towards one of the ska revivalist's kids. And when the child's dad spotted Calvin climbing into a portable toilet he saw an opportunity for some revenge.

One witness said Calvin was in the toilet when one of the guys bolted it shut and a roadie started rattling it.

'Calvin was screaming,' the witness said. 'It was hilarious. He had to boot the door open.'

After being rescued by security, Calvin initially failed to see the funny side and, although he put the antics down to festival nonsense, he was seen stomping off in the direction of his dressing-room.

165

Madness frontman Suggs explained what happened: 'I got the f*cking blame for that. I wasn't there but our saxophone player Lee was and a couple of the others. He [Calvin] had not wanted to sign an autograph – he had the hump about something. So they may or may not have locked him in a toilet and then rocked it about a good bit. I can't say it didn't make me laugh – but I had nothing to do with it.'

Calvin hadn't enjoyed the best weekend, to be fair, and was already short on humour after an apparent date mix-up meant his slot was moved from the Saturday to the Sunday.

He summed up his feelings on Twitter that day: 'I'm in a place full of intolerable idiots. Can anyone guess where I am?'

The previous day he had posted: 'Camp Bestival tomorrow . . . was billed today but the promoters messed up . . . !'

Calvin took to Twitter a month later, when he was equally miffed because he had just listened to US singer Chris Brown's new single 'Yeah 3x' and couldn't believe what he was hearing. It borrowed heavily the synth chords from Calvin's 'I'm Not Alone'.

Calvin didn't have to spell it out when he told his followers: 'Choked on my cornflakes when I heard new Chris Brown single this morning. Do you know what I mean?'

His fans certainly did, with many expressing dismay at the obvious similarities, but Brown's champions responded, accusing Calvin of being a 'nobody' who wasn't on the US star's level.

Calvin found himself drawn into a spat and although he deleted one of his more incendiary responses – and ruled out taking legal action – he still wasn't going to take the musical plagiarism lying down.

'Because Chris Brown is an international celebrity doesn't make it OK to rip off a guy from the UK who not many people have heard of,' he said. 'I don't care that you call me a "nobody". Stealing is still stealing. It doesn't matter who you are. Of course, I'm not going to take it to court. What good would that do? I'm happy for people to make their own mind up about it. How are you going to call me irrelevant when his brand new song sounds just like my two-year-old song?'

As the row continued Calvin was accused of publicity-seeking, while some mindless 'fans' even threatened him for daring to question Brown and his producers.

'Those saying I'm doing this for publicity, that's laughable,' Calvin responded. 'I don't want or need it. This is my Twitter. I'll talk about whatever is going on in my life. That's what it's for. Believe it or not, I'm not trying to be known by you. This is way more entertaining than doing it behind closed doors.'

He also denied he was being unprofessional by speaking out.

'Unprofessional? I'm not a professional. I make music because I love making music,' he said. 'I'm not trying to present myself in any way or hide my opinions about things in order to gain fans.'

As the heat of the exchanges escalated and the tone deteriorated, he said, 'Can all these Chris Brown fans stop it now please? You are all unbelievably offensive and ignorant beyond belief. Literally getting threatened by fourteen-year-old girls right now. Racist, xenophobic and misguided. I'm sure Chris is proud of you all.'

Calvin's run of misfortune continued when it emerged that the song he had recorded with JLS hadn't made it on to their album. It sounded like a remarkable error of judgement on the boyband's behalf, given the enthusiasm Calvin had for the track.

'We made a song that sounds like '70s Michael Jackson – didn't make the album,' he said when he heard the news. 'Maybe I'll leak it on YouTube.'

Working with other people always carried an element of risk but, despite the surprise exclusion from the JLS album, Calvin was determined to carry on collaborating.

As 2010 neared its closure he thought hard about his own future direction. He had made a success of his own music, had become a successful singer in his own right – a suggestion he might have scoffed at when he was starting out. He had developed into an impressive frontman, someone who looked at ease whether it was in the intimate surroundings of a small club, a large arena or the main stage of a festival. Fans had lapped up his recent live shows, but as his reputation grew as a DJ and the list of people wanting to work with him lengthened he saw only one path ahead.

In November 2010, he made an announcement. He would not sing on any of his future tracks. He would continue to make music but only with guest vocalists. His live band he was also dismantling. From now on, his only live performances would be as a DJ.

In terms of cultural impact it might not have been up there with the Beatles' decision to quit touring in 1966, but just as that move freed up the Fab Four to take their creative development to a new level, so too would Calvin's.

'I've stopped the live shows,' he said. 'I'm going to focus more on production and DJ'ing and zero per cent of my time will go on singing. I'll do tracks with people who can sing well – proper artists, proper performers. I can focus on what I'm much better at, which is making music. I'm just not cut out for that role.

'I kind of fell into it a few years ago,' he went on. 'The live show had to happen, I had to be the frontman because I was doing the vocals on the songs. It went all right. I spent a few years trying to get it really properly good, but it dawned on me it wasn't going to get much better. I've taken the singing thing as far as I can.'

He also decided to put into practice something he had toyed with for over a year – focusing on singles rather than an album.

'The priority is making good songs and getting them out there, not making anybody wait, especially me,' he explained. 'The next thing will have a featured vocalist and it's dead exciting because these are proper artists. I get to make music and let other people do all the singing. It's a new lease of life for the sort of music I make.'

Announcing plans for a new release, he said: 'The next single will be coming up in about a month.'

Despite the announcement of new material, Calvin's decision to step back from the limelight sparked rumours he was retiring – a strange assumption given at the time he was working on a host of new tracks and was polishing a new DJ set to showcase on dates in Australia, where he would be supporting pop superstar Rihanna.

'People keep messaging me saying I'm retiring. Where the f*ck did you get that from? I love music. It's ridiculous.'

'Plus,' he joked, 'have you seen me recently? I look fantastic. Prime of my life.'

Who could argue? Here was a man who had scored a number one single and a number one album. He had the success and the money was starting to roll in. He was at ease with himself enough to make a bold pronouncement on his future career. All he was missing was the girl . . .

18

Luck in a Hopeless Place

WHEN Calvin said he wanted to get involved with other artists, this might not have been what he had in mind – but it was probably a good sight more enjoyable than many of his other collaborations.

It was late at night in Melbourne, Australia, and Calvin had just completed a storming warm-up set for pop superstar Rihanna after she'd personally asked him to be her tour DJ. After whipping the crowd up nicely, he was sitting in the second row in time for the star attraction to appear. Though still buzzing from his set, he seemed to have eyes only for the pop diva sat right beside him – the alluring Kesha.

Calvin and Kesha – or Ke$ha, as she styled herself then – set tongues wagging with their antics that night. *The Sun* reported that the American singer must have been nursing a stiff neck after pulling a bloke nearly a foot taller than her.

It was said they seemed enamoured with each other, so much so that halfway through Rihanna's set they sneaked off to be alone.

A source was quoted as saying: 'They were all over each other and didn't care who was watching. Ke$ha is a bit of an animal, but Calvin reckons he can handle her.'

Another source told an Australian newspaper: 'They were getting right into it, they were practically fornicating.'

Calvin and Kesha had known each other for years: she had supported him on tour once and they had met up regularly when in the same city. Conveniently, she had been in Australia at the same time and made a bit of an effort to hook up with Calvin. She had played her own gig after an earlier Rihanna concert but had flown to Melbourne just to meet up with Calvin, it was said, although she was due to perform at the same Future Music Festival as he was.

When it was rumoured Calvin's relationship with Kylie was more than just a working one, he had been quick off the mark with his denials. Although he had since said that in hindsight he should have kept quiet to keep the intrigue going, he was usually fast to let fans know what was fact and fiction. This time, however, both he and Kesha remained tight-lipped.

She looked harassed at Sydney airport and almost fell down an escalator as a minder shepherded her out of the way of journalists and their probing questions.

If there was any truth to the rumours, it was easy to see what might have attracted Calvin. Although she was effectively born into the music business through singer-songwriter mum Pebe, Kesha, like Calvin, had fought hard for her break and had made it thanks to a lot of hard work, perseverance, brass neck and a slice of luck. Raw demos had got to the right people, but even when her break came as an uncredited guest vocalist on Flo Rida's 'Right Round', a reworking of Dead or Alive's hit 'You Spin Me Round (Like a Record)', she turned down the chance to appear in the video, preferring to make it on her own merits. That she duly did, achieving hits on both sides of the Atlantic with 'Tik Tok' and 'We R Who We R'. Her album titles *Animal* and *Cannibal* reflected her feisty personality and Calvin was considered a brave man for taking Kesha on. She also had something of a reputation after apparently urinating in a sink at the 2009 Q Awards because she couldn't face queuing. By her own admission she also once beat up a bloke with sausages because her friend happened to like him.

'People think I'm out of control but I know what I'm doing. I haven't done anything that bad,' she said.

The pair gave hacks no further cause to gossip but the rumours continued to dog each of them for several months. A year later Calvin was still being asked about her but when pressed to say if he had ever dated Kesha, he replied somewhat cagily: 'Dated? I don't know. I've met her a few times. She's a nice girl.'

Kesha was a friend of Katy Perry, and Calvin put the disappointment of not being able to work with her properly behind him to join the 'I Kissed a Girl' singer as support for her UK California Dreams tour, which included five dates around Scotland. But something went seriously wrong.

Calvin claimed Katy's team had made last-minute plans that were impossible for him to work with. When he announced his decision to pull out of the dates, it led to a remarkable war of words between the pair over Twitter.

Katy sparked the spat by announcing: 'CalvinHarris will NOT be joining in on the fun and has CANCELLED last minute.'

Calvin responded: 'Sorry to all who wanted to see me with Katy – her team suddenly moved the goalposts, and I was to appear onstage with no production. It would have looked s***, sounded s*** – trust me you would have been more disappointed SEEING the show than u are with me cancelling.'

But Katy, in what appeared to be a dig at what had caused their previous plans to go awry, replied: 'Funny the goalpost seems to be perfectly fine for New Young Pony Club, Yelle, Robyn, Marina & The Diamonds to name a few. It's fine, I'm used to you cancelling on me, it's become ur staple!'

Calvin played peacemaker, apologising to Katy and her fans. He tweeted: 'Her show is awesome, you'll all have an amazing time without me (especially w/o me DJ'ing on a cardboard box in front of a pink curtain).'

He added: 'I am really sorry @katyperry I'm just upset because I really wanted to play but ur team made it impossible.'

As now seemed to be the norm on Twitter when anyone offered a position contrary to that of a much-loved star, his actions prompted a disproportionate response from Katy's fans.

'WTF are Katy Perry fans telling me to KILL MYSELF on Twitter for?' he asked online. 'Seriously. I'm a producer making music. Leave me alone please thanks x.'

He later tweeted his regret that the whole ugly exchange had been played out in public. 'I was trying 2 handle it pro behind the scenes but i wont let myself get ripped like that,' he said.

The furore eventually died down and Calvin was pleased to report no lasting harm had been done. 'Let's just say it's all fine,' he said. 'I'd love to work with her.'

Calvin did have better news to report, however. He had landed the first of his guest singers for a new single called 'Bounce'. It was to be Kelis, who he had first hit it off with back in 2007. Yet even though they had bonded over a fruit bowl, he hadn't been confident that she'd agree to sing one of his songs. A meeting in 2010, however, had clinched the deal.

'When I wrote "Bounce", I really wanted a female voice,' said Calvin. 'I thought about getting Kelis but then thought, "Nah, she'll never do it." But after a few phone calls I was amazed that she said yes.'

Kelis lent a soulful subtlety to Calvin's appropriately bouncy hook, which was so catchy clubbers all over the world were destined to sing it.

'Bounce' would be the first single to be recorded at Calvin's Fly Eye Studio in London, which he had moved and set up near Highbury. His previous studios had all been at home, so he welcomed the feeling of going to a different location to work.

'I used to have my studio in the bedroom but I spent most of the day sitting at my computer in my pyjamas,' he said. 'I wanted to get back to some normality where I could put on clothes, go to the studio and inhabit the real world rather than lounging around in my underpants. So with this new album, I can 100 per cent guarantee there won't be any tracks by me wearing just my underpants.'

To create the authentic retro sound for his new material he had been buying vintage synthesisers on eBay, including an early seventies Dave Smith Prophet '08, which gave him the computer-game sound effect he wanted for 'Bounce'. It took him a while to get the precise sound he was after, however.

'I was getting addicted. I bought about four [of the synths] in a row,' he said. 'Most of them go unused. But they look good in my studio.'

The B-side to 'Bounce' was a harder dance track called 'Awooga', heralding a deliberate shift in style.

'I was on tour in Australia and made an obnoxious club track, "Awooga", almost to get rid of people who liked my old music. It was so different, a hard club track, and I wanted to do it,' he said.

'I wanted to DJ and play it, and I wanted to forget about everything from my past. Even though it did well for me in clubs and I enjoyed it, I did not want to do it any more. I wanted to draw a line under it.'

Calvin also wanted 'Bounce' to mark a new way of releasing his music.

'There will be a lot of new music from me this year,' he promised. 'The album will come a little later but I'm going to be releasing a lot of singles over the summer. There will be a lot of different music, some tracks designed strictly for the clubs and "Awooga" [is] one of them.'

He flew to Las Vegas to film the video, shooting some footage in the Nevada desert before heading for the swankier surroundings of club Surrender at the swish Encore Beach resort, with its 45,000-square-foot outdoor oasis, three-tiered pools and two levels of VIP cabanas, bungalows, beds and couches.

'I am a lucky boy,' Calvin said.

Directed by Vincent Haycock, the promo only featured cameos from Kelis and Calvin, the latter in now customary DJ mode. Instead, the model A. J. English starred as a dysfunctional lout who rows with his lover, causes mayhem around Vegas and eventually finds solace back in her arms, thanks to Calvin's unifying beats.

'It was great fun shooting the video in Vegas,' he said. 'It really is a stunning location for a video. Kelis looks amazing, I look OK. It's a good one.'

'Bounce' was released on 10 June 2010. It debuted in the UK singles chart at number two and, although the next midweek sales had it at number one, it failed to dislodge Example's 'Changed the Way You Kiss Me'.

Yet Calvin was philosophical about its performance, even though it failed to emulate the success he'd had with 'I'm Not Alone', or even his singles with Dizzee Rascal, because of the respect he had for his chart rival.

'I'm a big fan of his and worked on his first album,' Calvin said. 'I think he's due a couple of weeks at number one.'

Calvin said he was happy with a top-ten placing 'because it's a new phase of the way I release records'.

He added: 'I'm not a frontman any more and it almost feels like I'm starting again.'

The song also reached number four on the US dance chart, confirming what Calvin believed – that his particular brand of music was catching on in the States.

'European dance music is taking over the world,' he said. 'America loves it more than we do. At the moment there are more resident European DJs in Las Vegas than there are in Ibiza, that's how popular dance music is.'

For Calvin, it was a fertile market and he was travelling there twice a month for gigs, appearances and meetings.

'It's not work for me,' he insisted. 'I mean, it's not like gutting a fish.'

Calvin was just enjoying this new way of working, sharing ideas, trading favours.

'I'm swapping remixes with people,' he explained. 'I've just done one for Nero. I'd love to do one with producer Nile Rodgers [the genius behind disco legends Chic].'

And he added: 'The DJ life is a lot more fun – basically I'm playing amazing parties for a living. Before, I was on the promotional circuit, on TV shows, looking awkward. Now I only do the things I enjoy.

'The live singing is over forever. Maybe I looked like I was enjoying it, but a few glasses of Jack Daniel's and shots and you can have a good time doing anything.'

He loved the fast way he could work now. 'It's a privilege,' he said. 'If I make a club track, I can have it out for download next week. I'm loving life right now.'

And the success of 'Bounce' convinced him collaborations were the way forward. 'It's important I make an album of variety,' he said. 'All of the songs have to sound different for me otherwise I may as well go and make JLS songs.'

The mention of the reality show runners-up was interesting because after his song for them did not make their album they became embroiled in another 'did-they-didn't-they' claim regarding stealing Calvin's ideas.

The boyband's 'Eyes Wide Shut' sounded suspiciously like his 'I'm Not Alone', lifting the same telltale chords as the Chris Brown track. However, by the time this latest case came to light, Calvin was in a more forgiving mood, especially as he had since been credited for the Brown song.

'It would be more gutting if the original song hadn't done well but it was number one for a couple of weeks. I can't really complain and I don't,' Calvin said. 'All I've done is commented on it and said it sounds like things I've done, but that's OK. To Chris Brown's credit he's the only one that's recognised that and is giving me a bit of a writing credit and publishing. It's not about the money, it's about where it came from.'

Calvin absolved both Brown and JLS of blame.

'I think he [Brown] was mortified, because he didn't make the track, it was the producer,' Calvin said. 'Same with JLS. It wasn't their fault and had nothing to do with them.'

Calvin's satisfaction with the way the new chapter of his career was going might have contributed to his attitude.

All of the big festivals were happy to have him back as a DJ. At T in the Park he once again headlined inside the King Tut's tent, but this time on his own. And as he prepared for that new experience he revealed it was being stuck on the Main Stage at Balado two years previously that had convinced him he had to change tack.

'I realised as I was playing at T a couple of years ago that this was as far as I could take it with me singing and with a band. I'd probably always be playing that kind of slot in the afternoon on the main stage. But it just doesn't work with my kind of music. I only want to play late at night. Dance music needs to be dark and have lights. It's the atmosphere as much as the music,' he said. 'And it's another way of avoiding afternoon slots.'

He didn't envisage feeling an urge to suddenly be centre stage again.

'I'm not going to grab the mic and burst into song,' he said. 'That's it for me. I just DJ the song. Even the songs I'm singing on, like "I'm Not Alone", will just be played, not performed. I'm not going to jump up on the decks and do a Tom Jones moment.'

He further explained his reasoning.

'I don't think I'm good enough as a singer to justify the amount of time I spent on it. Mainly it's not worth it for anyone – me, the band or the people coming to see it. That's time that could be spent on making new tracks.

'Sometimes I make a track and want to sing on it like before, so I do. If it sounds good, then that's great. My next single, "Feels So Close", is actually me singing but most of the other tracks on the new album will be other singers.

'Now that the band has gone I'm reinvigorated, making tracks again and doing the things I enjoy.'

In addition, he was now a star attraction at the big superclubs in Ibiza.

'Ibiza is always so much fun,' said Calvin, who was lined up for a date with Pete Tong at Pacha before a mini residency of ten dates for Cream at Amnesia. The response he was getting from fans meant he had no regrets about the direction change.

'I stopped the performances with the band as I wanted to focus on building an amazing DJ show,' he said. 'My music has changed. The show with the band wasn't relevant any more. So I've changed it up and there will be a big production DJ tour sometime in the future.'

Calvin was working non-stop and in one weekend played four gigs across North America and the Caribbean in just over twenty-four hours. His whirlwind tour began on a Friday night at Cave in Santo Domingo in the Dominican Republic. He was then flown to a festival in Baltimore, and just a few hours later he was heading to the Bell Centre in Montreal, before finally ending up at the Encore hotel in Vegas.

'I have just learned to fall asleep and grab some kip when I can,' he said, grateful that at least he had a private jet in which to travel. 'I can just fall asleep at the drop of a hat now. I'm pretty sure I could fall asleep standing up if I had to.'

The fruits of his labour were evident elsewhere, too. 'Off & On', the song originally offered to Róisín Murphy, was finally released by Sophie Ellis-Bextor; however, although she promoted it in the UK for her album *Make a Scene*, it was not released as a single. And the UK deluxe edition of Mary J Blige's album *My Life II . . . The Journey Continues (Act 1)*, released in November 2011, contained 'One Life', a track co-written by Calvin.

For now, his only problem was finding the right singers for his own songs. His method remained the same. He laid down the track with his own vocal and then decided who the best fit would be.

Although he had said he would never sing again, he was happy with the way his voice sounded on one track – 'Feels So Close' – so much so, in fact, that he felt confident enough to make it a single.

However, although Kelis had agreed to work with him, he struggled to find anyone else.

He offered one track 'We Found Love' to former *X Factor* winner Leona Lewis, but although she recorded it she didn't fancy it as a single. Former Pussycat Doll Nicole Scherzinger also had an option on it but passed, and Calvin's search continued.

Even his old mate Dizzee Rascal seemed to be blanking him.

'I would work with Dizzee in a heartbeat,' he said. 'I loved making those tracks with him. But as for more songs, I don't know what he's doing at the moment and whether he's making another album. He's lost my phone number or he's trying to cut me off. I thought we had a good track record – two songs and two number ones.'

He would not be deterred, however, and another boost came when Calvin was confirmed as the support once again for Rihanna for her massive fifty-six-date UK and European tour, due to start in September, which included ten dates at London's O2 Arena. He was delighted she had asked him to join once more.

'Great fun,' he said, recalling their Australian dates together. 'Her fans go absolutely crazy and she's a very down-to-earth girl, so the whole thing felt easy and I felt very welcome on the tour.'

Given Rihanna was so keen to have him around it seemed fair to assume that she might want to collaborate on a track one day. However, Calvin thought she was too big for him.

'Rihanna is great, funny and cool. It would be phenomenal to work with her but I don't think I'm at the stage I can really approach someone like that,' he said. 'I think I need to earn my stripes as a producer.'

His role model was David Guetta, but he still felt he had some way to go before he could be quoted in the same breath.

'I'm not in the same league as David Guetta,' he said. 'He has the proper hits and goes to number one in like twenty-seven countries. I need to work at it.'

To become the hottest DJ and producer in the world, he needed a massive hit. But without a singer his songs would remain code on his computer.

Calvin started to feel desperate.

'It was like nobody's wanting to do anything with me,' he said much later. 'Who's going to do the next one?'

Then, out of the blue – from the person he least expected – came the request that would change his life.

19

Field of Dreams

A BARLEY field in Bangor, Northern Ireland, hardly seems the ideal place from which to launch a bid for world domination. Yet it was there that a buzz began about a song and an artist that would propel Calvin Harris to a level of fame, power and influence he could never have imagined.

Calvin could have been forgiven for thinking he was there simply to film a video for a new single. However, a seemingly innocuous confrontation that day sparked a morality debate around the world that at one stage threatened to escalate into an international incident; the video shot that day would be poured over, resulting in accusations of glamorising drug abuse and domestic violence.

Welcome to the world of Rihanna.

For her, it was just another day. But those around her – Calvin included – must have looked on in bemusement.

In all, Calvin's involvement with her tour was proving to be the gift that kept on giving. Not only was he opening for one of the stellar acts in the business but also during the Loud tour she began work on her follow-up album and was interested in Calvin's fresh sounds.

However, during the tour Rihanna had tried to get closer to Calvin, but he had shied away from her friendly gestures. In explanation, he revealed, 'I'm not very close to Rihanna at all, but that's my fault because I'm really awkward around her. She's tried and said, "Yeah, come on and hang out in my dressing-room." She's great, she's friendly, she's nice – but I can't. I'm from Dumfries, man. I'm like, arrghh! I mean, what do I say to Rihanna? I don't know. I'm a bit weird sometimes. I'm not fully integrated into the social thing. I haven't got the chat.'

Socially he might not have had much to offer, but musically he just might. Calvin had been planning 'We Found Love' to follow 'Feel So Close', but without a female voice it was looking like it was going to be another with him singing. So much for his dream of collaborations. When Rihanna showed an interest in hearing it, however, all that changed.

The trouble was, apart from Leona Lewis's version, the only copy he had was with him 'singing falsetto like a girl'. He asked Ayah Marar to record a version.

'She did me a favour because I'm not going to play a song to Rihanna with me singing like a girl on it,' said Calvin. 'It's embarrassing enough as it is, so I got [Ayah] to do it because she sounded much better.'

As soon as Rihanna heard it 'she was obsessed with it'. Ordinarily when singers like a song they go into the studio to record their own version, but in the world of Rihanna there is no ordinary.

'The Rihanna one was fully written and all guide-vocalled and all done, and she heard it and she wanted it for her record,' Calvin said. 'And that was it. She said, "I'm just going to copy what was done." She has a team because she's Rihanna. She has a team of people that records her vocals so she sounds the same on every record.'

Calvin was with Rihanna when it was time for her to go into the studio, but his time there was short-lived.

'We were together but she doesn't let anyone into the studio when she's recording vocals, apart from the engineer,' Calvin said. 'So I was in there and I was like, "All right there, how's it goin'?", and then it was a case of "See you later!" But then, like, three or four hours later I come back and it's all done and it sounds absolutely amazing.'

Rihanna lent a magisterial quality to the melancholic yet hopeful lyrics, which Calvin admitted didn't have roots in anything particular.

Rihanna sings about finding love in a hopeless place, but Calvin said that could be anywhere – even a now defunct nightclub in his home town.

'It could have been Jumpin Jaks in Dumfries,' he said, 'although that has sadly closed down. The thing is, I don't know exactly what I was thinking about. I was just playing the song and doing non-sense singing to see if the syllables fitted the song. It was like that. I was singing nonsense and that's how the lyrics happened.'

He couldn't have been happier with the end product.

'It was great,' he said. 'I did nothing to that vocal.'

For Calvin it was an ideal situation because it meant he could focus solely on getting the music just right.

'As soon as I knew she wanted to sing it, I knew it would be incredible,' he said. 'When it was all done, I knew there was no way it could be a better record.'

Although he had been pleased with Leona's recording, it wasn't on a par with Rihanna's. 'They're very different,' he said, because Leona 'sings it dead softly, you know, how Leona sings . . . It's more like an X Factor ballad.'

It was very much a Rihanna single – but she paid him the biggest compliment by offering to include Calvin's name with a 'featuring' credit.

'She didn't have to put "featuring me" on it, though,' he said. 'She's got other records people have written and produced without them being mentioned. I guess it was a mark of respect, putting my name on it. I'm eternally grateful to her.'

It meant a change of plan to Calvin's release schedule but one with which he was delighted.

He said: 'It was going to be on my album and my third single. I had "Bounce" and "Feel So Close", then this big gap.'

'We Found Love' was slated for release in September 2011, a month after 'Feel So Close', which had matched the success of 'Bounce' by reaching number two.

Calvin and Rihanna announced plans for the single on Twitter. He retweeted her comment that she was listening to the finished version, adding: 'Sometimes it feels like we find love in the most hopeless place.'

Her fans immediately jumped on the news and Calvin got his first taste of what it was like to work with a megastar.

'It was crazy,' he said. 'Fans tweeting me, saying, "The song better not be rubbish." There was a mild threatening nature to it but it's all part of the fun.'

His next taste of the craziness came in that windswept barley field – and it was a very British style of controversy that ensued.

After an American-themed video for 'Feel So Close', the decision to film the promo for 'We Found Love' in a farmer's field signified a major change in style for Rihanna, but it was a necessity, given her touring schedule, which had taken her to Northern Ireland for three sold-out shows at the Odyssey Arena in Belfast. Behind the camera was American Melina Matsoukas, a veteran who had directed promos for Beyoncé and Lady Gaga, and had been responsible for the video for Rihanna's 'S&M', which was deemed too explicit for some daytime viewing. The concept involved Rihanna and model Dudley O'Shaughnessy starring as volatile lovers whose toxic relationship fluctuated from wild highs to devastating lows.

Councillor Alan Graham granted the crew permission to use some of his sixty acres of land at North Down for filming, as the director staged a mini-rave with Calvin on the decks. However, it became clear Mr Graham hadn't appreciated what he was letting himself in for and he was fetching his tractor when he noticed Rihanna remove what was already a skimpy red bikini during the shoot. The straight-talking Free Presbyterian promptly went over, told her to put some clothes on and find God.

'I had never heard of Rihanna until someone called me, requesting the use of my land,' he explained. 'I knew on Monday who she was. Someone explained she was as big as it gets as far as pop stars were concerned. I am a bit illiterate about those issues. I realised things had got to a stage which was not acceptable to me. Things became inappropriate and I asked the film crew to stop.

'If someone wants to borrow my field and things become inappropriate, then I say, "Enough is enough. You are not entitled to do that."'

Rihanna, to her credit, apparently took the admonishment well.

'He was great,' she said.

'She understood where I was coming from,' Mr Graham said. 'We shook hands and parted company on good terms.'

That should have been the end of the story. However, as news broke of the confrontation, the story took on a life of its own. News outlets in the UK and Ireland picked up on the incident and it spread to Europe and Australia before jumping across the Atlantic to Canada and the States.

Some people criticised Mr Graham for embarrassing Northern Ireland with a supposedly out-of-date moral code, while others leapt to his defence.

'Some people are saying I stopped the filming because she was wearing a bikini but that's a downright lie,' Mr Graham said, as the story became more twisted with every new telling. 'I understand she's a star and that's the way stars dress. They filmed for an hour and a half in the afternoon but later on, in another field, which was not facing the road, they drove a big American car into the middle of the crop of barley. That's fine, I'll not argue about that, it'll not break the bank.

'They said it was a closed set and it was at that stage that things got, in my mind, inappropriate. She took her top off and I find that inappropriate from a Christian point of view. I had let them film for an hour and a half but I felt that was going beyond the bounds of decency and asked them to stop, so they did.'

He added: 'Rihanna does not need to take her clothes off. It was fortuitous for me that I saw what was happening because I would have come in for a lot of criticism if I'd allowed that to happen. I wish no ill-will against Rihanna and her friends. Perhaps they could acquaint themselves with a greater God.'

As social media sites lit up with the controversy, the incident was debated by politicians, who were worried about the diplomatic implications and raised fears that potential US investors might have been put off after it was suggested Rihanna had been targeted because she had been wearing 'red, white and blue'. They had to be reassured that the colour of her garments had nothing to do with it.

Rihanna took it all in her stride and her stay in the country will not be forgotten in a hurry. Even though one night she kept fans waiting for over an hour, her followers were not put off, and she was mobbed by 1,000 on another outing.

And she was delighted with the finished video, which played like a mini movie, complete with a moody voiceover at the beginning that many thought was Rihanna but was in fact performed by model Agyness Deyn.

'This is probably one of the deepest videos I've ever done,' Rihanna said. 'It's all about love and love being like a drug. The good feeling of it and the dangers of it.'

However, after such controversy before a frame had even been shown, the condemnation was predictable, with religious groups slamming it for glamorising sex under the influence of drugs. French TV banned it from being shown before 10 p.m.

Critically the song received mixed reviews, with many feeling Rihanna played second fiddle to Calvin's production, which seemed strange since it was his touch that lifted it from disposable pop to a thumping dance anthem. *Rolling Stone* magazine called it 'the worst single of Rihanna's career', but in the US – which is where Calvin must have been praying it made an impact – that was a minority opinion. *Billboard* magazine spoke for many when it praised the 'gorgeous hook in a hopeless place', adding that with the song 'Calvin Harris becomes a household name'.

When it came to the video, the critics were convinced the promo was in some way homage to Rihanna's volatile relationship with Chris Brown.

O'Shaughnessy was considered a dead ringer for Brown, while the voiceover was said to be relevant to Rihanna's own troubled history.

In *Spin* magazine, William Goodman wrote:

> The evidence is stacking up.
>   Exhibit A: The clip stars a dead ringer for Brown, complete with dyed hair and bulging biceps. The actor, a British model/boxer named Dudley O'Shaughnessy, plays RiRi's booze-swilling, drug-addled love interest.
>   Exhibit B: The video opens with a Rihanna voice-over that warns, 'You almost feel ashamed that someone could

185

be that important. No one will ever understand how much it hurts . . . you almost wish that you could have all that bad stuff back, so that you have the good.'

Exhibit C: In one scene, during a heated argument between the couple in a muscle car, the Brown look-alike gives the Barbadian beauty a slap on the face. Convinced yet?

Whether art was indeed imitating life remained to be seen. There was at least one thing the world agreed on: it deserved to be a monster hit.

In the UK it shot straight to number one, selling 87,000 in just four days, where it stayed for three weeks. Although it slipped to number three, its sales made it the biggest-selling 'three' since 2003. Two weeks later it was back in the top spot and remained there for another three weeks. It would go on to sell more than a million in the UK alone.

It topped the charts in twenty-four other countries and went top ten in twenty-nine more.

In the US it started breaking records almost from the moment it was released. In its second week it rose to number nine, meaning Rihanna now held the record for a solo artist having scored twenty top-ten singles in the shortest time, beating Madonna's previous best.

After six weeks it hit the top spot, making it Rihanna's eleventh number one, tying her with Whitney Houston in fifth place for the highest number of singles to make it there. Rihanna also tied with Whitney as the third-most successful female artist, after Mariah Carey and Madonna.

The ten non-consecutive weeks it spent at number one made it the single to have spent the longest time topping the charts, surpassing her previous best with 'Umbrella'; the song went to become the twenty-fourth-biggest hit of all time, selling over 10.5 million copies.

Rihanna debuted it live during the tour and then insisted Calvin play it at the end of his DJ set while warming up for her during her ten-night residency at the O2 – another record-breaking feat, as the most shows at the venue by a female act.

'I don't normally end gigs with my own track,' Calvin said, 'but Rihanna asked me to play the single for everyone. It's all down to the fans that they've made it number one.'

Rihanna might have been smashing records but for Calvin it had a knock-on effect in the US – helping 'Feel So Close' reach number twelve. Calvin was also joining an exclusive club – as one of only eight Scots artists to have topped the US charts, and the first since Rod Stewart back in 1994.

When he realised he was part of a select group that included Simple Minds, the Eurythmics, Sheena Easton, the Average White Band, the Bay City Rollers and Lulu, he tweeted: 'Is that right?! Calvin Harris became the 1st Scotsman since Rod Stewart to have a US number 1.'

Calvin was to discover the success of the single opened doors to another exclusive club – the A-list.

Suddenly he was the hottest talent in town and the man everyone wanted to work with. After months of struggling to find vocalists for his tracks he was fighting them off. His album began to take shape.

'When I started asking for guest vocalists, I was so lucky to get Kelis to do the first one,' he said. 'I was so happy to get that. And then from then on it was like, nobody's wanting to do anything with me. Who's going to do the next one?

'So for Rihanna to come in and just take that song, it's the best thing that could have happened because after that and because it was a big success, a big hit, everyone was up for it,' he explained. 'Everyone! There was nobody I asked that wasn't up for it. Yeah, I was surprised. Even Dizzee Rascal was up for it!'

Now it was the turn of others to bemoan the one that got away.

Leona Lewis broke her silence about having first crack at 'We Found Love'.

'I worked with Calvin and we recorded "We Found Love". But he went touring with Rihanna and she ended up releasing it,' she said. 'I didn't commit to it because I wanted "Trouble" to be my first single, so I think that was another reason they went with Rihanna. It was the same version and production but mine's better. I still have the recording but I'd never leak it. That's so unprofessional.'

She tried to remain philosophical and knew enough about the business to realise such things happen, while at the same time appreciating that it was unlikely her version would have been anything like as successful as Rihanna's.

'There are so many songs I've recorded, only to hear other people singing them. It happens all the time,' she said. 'It was a bit annoying to see how big a hit it was around the world, but if I'd released it maybe it wouldn't have done as well.'

Nicole Scherzinger also later explained her reasons for passing up what must have sounded like a sure-fire hit.

'I passed on "We Found Love",' she said. 'I've got the demo of that song and I was busy at the time. They had sent me a few dance tracks and I wasn't able to get to them. And I was like, "Oh there's so much dance and I want to take a break from it." That was my fault. I slept on it.'

Calvin then exacted some revenge on the record companies who had turned him down. Tweeting that he had found some old rejection letters he named and shamed the guilty parties.

One of them, Defected boss Simon Dunmore, replied: 'Outed as the guy that passed on 1 of dance music's biggest acts ever! OUCH :-).'

It was a remarkable transformation in Calvin Harris's fortunes.

In January 2012, he celebrated in style as 3,000 clubbers threw him a surprise party in Las Vegas.

Then later that month figures posted for his company, CH Music Ltd, showed he had earned £2 million since hitting the big time back in 2007 – and those did not include royalties from 'We Found Love'. Not bad for someone who had returned home penniless after his first crack at the business in London.

Calvin was officially the most successful songwriter in the UK – but a little vignette from his tour revealed he wasn't about to turn into the prima donna just yet. A Liverpool venue revealed Calvin to be one of the least ostentatious of the performers they'd hosted.

'We've had some demands in our time, but Calvin's was definitely the most boring,' a source said. 'All he wanted was an iron, a can of polish, some newspapers, a bag of crisps and for classical music to be played into his dressing-room.'

He was riding the crest of an incredible wave. With newfound focus on establishing himself properly in America, it was reported he bought a house in California, a fairly large (yet modest by celebrity standards) four-bedroom home in the Hollywood Hills, but he wasn't getting carried away. The lad from Dumfries inside him would make sure of that.

As he looked out on that audience at the Coachella festival in California in April 2012 and saw Rihanna belting out his hit, as Katy Perry crowd-surfed and before him stood a sea of camera phones, he marvelled at how far he'd come.

'It changed absolutely everything,' he said of 'We Found Love'. 'For example, in America my tune "Feel So Close" came out about three months before. But when "We Found Love" came out, the radio started playing "Feel So Close" like it was the single after. Then that did really well, it charted well and sold a lot of copies. Then radio stations wanted to play me like I was the new act. That changed a lot of things, as they wouldn't play me before.

'Career-wise it was the best thing that could ever have happened.'

Calvin was on the road to superstardom. The question was . . . how far could he go?

20

The New Rock Star

THE man with the Midas touch – or a cynical button-pusher whose identikit beats were ruining the charts?

The only thing sure to follow success is the backlash . . . and for Calvin it came amid a period of sustained glory. Back in 2009 he had questioned Simon Cowell's dominance of the charts. Yet barely three years on Calvin was beginning a residency of the hit parade unparalleled in recent times.

He followed the success of 'We Found Love' with 'Let's Go', a thumping anthem of optimism, featuring American soul and R'n'B vocalist and writer Ne-Yo. It shot to number two in the UK charts in April 2012 and rose to seventeen in the US, where Ne-Yo is far better known.

The track gained traction as the soundtrack for a star-studded Pepsi Max advert featuring some of the world's best footballers: Lionel Messi, Didier Drogba, Sergio Agüero, Jack Wilshere, Frank Lampard and Fernando Torres. The setting was a massive outdoor beach party, with Calvin on a huge raised set of decks.

'In the ad I'm DJ'ing on a massive platform,' Calvin said. 'I spy the footballers so I press a button and footballs fly out and so they start crowd-surfing and also doing tricks at the same time.'

That month also saw the release of the Scissor Sisters' 'Only the Horses', a track born out of the collaborations between Calvin and Jake Shears for the Kylie album sessions. It got to twelve but that might have said more about the fading appeal of the band rather than anything else.

Calvin was reunited with Rihanna in May for the fifth single from her *Talk That Talk* album, 'Where Have You Been'. It gave her yet another top-ten hit, peaking at number six, while in the States it went one higher to number five.

Then a month later Calvin's touch took Cheryl Cole back to the top spot with 'Call My Name', which featured Ayah on backing vocals and became the fastest-selling single of the year, while in July his remix of Florence and the Machine's 'Spectrum (Say My Name)' took a song that only made 104 on its own merits to number one – the band's first chart-topper. Calvin's punchy treatment, which complimented perfectly Florence Welch's soaring vocals, sold over 64,800 copies in a week. It was no surprise when the BBC picked it up to use for its Olympics coverage.

In addition, 'Off the Record', a Tinchy Stryder track that listed 'featuring' credits to Calvin and the fellow Scots DJ he discovered, Burns, had reached number twenty-four when it was released back in November.

And Calvin was set for more success as 'We'll Be Coming Back', a tune featuring Example, the act that shared his musical progression most closely, was due to be released at the end of July, in the middle of a festival season that would see the Dumfries man cement his place as Britain's top DJ.

Ask any of the artists who benefitted from Calvin's touch and they extol the virtues of his contribution.

'Calvin is the man. I must admit I do love him,' gushed Cheryl, for instance, who was so thrilled at getting to number one she sent Calvin a message of congratulations. 'As soon as I heard the intro to the Calvin track I knew I had to have it. I love the energy of it and it's the perfect introduction to summer.'

Cheryl was not in the least surprised at Calvin's success, as her mentor, manager and producer, the Black Eyed Peas star will.i.am, had predicted it.

'He said to me three years ago the next pop stars would be DJs. Enter David Guetta, Calvin Harris,' she said.

Jake Shears joined in the praise: 'We had made "Only the Horses" and the song was asking for his sheen in a big way. He came in and put his magic high gloss on it.'

And Tinchy Stryder, Calvin's rival at the top of the charts before they joined forces, said: 'I've always liked his producing style and even in my sets my DJ puts his tracks on. We've always had a lot of banter together. My album kept him off the top and his singles have kept me off the top in the past.'

However, some rock acts denounced the rise of DJs and super-producers, saying they had no place at rock festivals.

Speaking after David Guetta and Calvin's appearances at T in the Park, Tom Clarke, frontman with The Enemy, ranted: 'There was a lot of whisky involved, but I was watching BBC's coverage and they cut from Noel Gallagher's set to David Guetta. If you go to any club in Glasgow or Edinburgh on a Friday or Saturday night, you can see some **** standing there, pressing play and some lights going off. It's not what I want to see at a music festival, I want to see rock 'n' roll. I want to see guys like Noel tearing it up.

'That's proper music, not "let me turn this up, oh hang on, let me turn it down now". David Guetta is an expert with a CD player. He should go get a job in Dixons.'

Turning his attention to Calvin, he said somewhat mockingly, 'I have to say, the lights for Calvin Harris were amazing. I was sitting in the bar calling our management, saying we need lasers, too, now in future.'

His opinion might have had something to do with playing second fiddle to Calvin's headline set in the King Tut's tent, but a few television viewers were also unhappy that the BBC's coverage focused on the DJs rather than traditional rock acts.

'I thought the BBC was all about "Keeping Music Live",' one said. 'We had David Guetta and Calvin Harris bouncing up and down onstage, waving a microphone and shouting, "T in the Park, show us your hands" now and again. What next? Will the 2013 event advertise artists such as Jimi Hendrix, Nirvana, Michael Jackson and Led Zep, with their records played by Dale Winton, after he has done the top 20 show from 1967? The coverage on BBC Three made the event look totally boring, which I'm sure it wasn't.'

A DJ set probably won't translate well to television, but judging by the response of the crowd inside the tent they didn't seem to mind it was pre-recorded music they were listening to.

Guetta must have been thrilled by his response because Calvin reported how the French DJ considered Balado the best venue in the world, while at the Wireless festival in Hyde Park the same month such were the numbers trying to squeeze into the tent to see Harris that double those inside had to make do dancing outside, watching him on a screen.

Calvin, incidentally, was sporting a new blond, trimmed haircut at T in the Park after coming 'to terms with myself' and deciding to ditch the hair dye for the first time since launching his pop career.

'I just don't have time for that sh*t any more in my life. And as I approach 30, I don't think it's a good thing for a man to be doing,' he said about his hair. 'It's just part of growing up, coming to terms with myself as a human being and not doing that s*** any more. Also part of it was I was this frontman of this f*cking band and all that s***. I figured I had to look similar to what I looked like before. Then when I just did the production and was not in the videos that much, I just thought I can look however I want. I prefer my more natural look. If anyone doesn't, they'd be preferring something that isn't actually real – so it's like you're preferring an imaginary idea of someone who doesn't exist. It's insane. You either like it or you don't like it.'

He shrugged off the criticism surrounding DJs, insisting that he was still a music maker, first and foremost.

'DJ'ing is DJ'ing and making music is completely different,' he said. 'I think if you go to a club there's going to be a DJ there, so maybe you're going to go to that club to see that DJ who makes your favourite music. Personally I'm not expecting the DJ to perform that music, with all manner of things. It's a club. You play tunes like any other DJ would. I don't see the problem with it. There's a lot of acts that are over-developing it to such an extent that you can't dance to it. Just play tracks. You're a DJ, it's fine.

'I used to perform with a band, putting all sorts of work into a live show and I can tell you that the reaction was worse than it is when I am DJ'ing because in a club you want to hear a produced piece of music. You want to hear the bass, you want to hear the music as good as it can sound. I think it's not a problem.'

Those comments were given to Radio 1's *Newsbeat* programme, but shortly afterwards Calvin seemed to take issue with the remarks as they were broadcast. There didn't seem to be anything controversial about his comments – he just sounded as though he was quite rightly justifying his position in the face of criticism, but he tweeted: 'Looking into taking action for that libellous broadcast. Fact is BBC *Newsbeat* pre-recorded my answers to a different set of questions. The guy wasn't even wearing a mic.'

In separate comments, Calvin talked about the music direction he had taken – and admitted that when he first struck out from his band he felt a bit of a charlatan.

'The first bit of outside production I did that was successful was for Dizzee Rascal – that was a revelation. To have money coming in and not do any promo, it felt like cheating,' he said. 'But I'm fighting for it now, I'm doing shows and giving myself deadlines – no one is giving them to me, as I'm kind of my own boss from what I used to be.'

And he had no regrets about the direction he'd taken.

'It's only been eighteen months since I released "Awooga", the first song doing what I do now. It feels like a lot longer; the guy onstage trying to sing feels like a completely different person. I'm well happy to have left it behind,' he said.

'As soon as I stopped singing, a whole world opened up to me. I could work with all sorts of great singers and still make great music. I'm aware the line is there for other people about things they do or what is cool but six years into this, I couldn't care what anyone thinks of any record I'll ever release,' he added. 'I honesty couldn't care less. My first album got slated, then my second album I was really proud of and it got slated again. Obviously I can't win. When I produce something I love, and it took me ages, people pan it.

'Then I do something that I did in my sleep, like some pop song that I put hardly any effort into, and it's the same thing.

'I'm the only guy who gets to say if what I make is good or not. So from now on, I'll do what I want and nothing else.'

Calvin found an unexpected champion in a broadsheet newspaper, where his music had largely been derided.

David Renshaw in *The Guardian* wrote that the artist who Simon Cowell had once dismissed as a joke was the one with the X-factor.

> Critics and bores may deride him as the one-beat-fits-all
> producer who's ruined the Top 40, complaining he's
> turned pop music into identikit mush and generally
> spoiled things for everyone, but the Scottish hit-maker is
> much smarter than he's ever given credit for. If DJs are,
> once again, the new rock stars, then at least Calvin Harris
> is ours. The haters claim his music is brainless, but they're
> wrong – he just makes it look easy.

There had been some drawbacks to the rise in demand for his services. For one, he had been so busy producing hits for other artists that he was behind schedule on his own album.

'It's been a pretty busy year – touring, producing for other people, remixing – so I've not been able to spend as much time in the studio as I'd have liked,' he said.

When he had carved out time for recording, his goal was to keep his sound fresh. 'The main thing I've tried to do with this album is not cover the same old ground,' he said. 'It's still sounding quite epic, but that whole "I'm Not Alone" thing has been done to death. I want to do something different, to challenge myself and feel in danger of messing up.

'Sometimes you need to do that to get the best out of yourself.'

In addition to the time constraints, Calvin wasn't always getting it his own way.

'We'll Be Coming Back', his tune with Example, was his fourth consecutive number-two hit, on this occasion being held off the top spot by Wiley's 'Heatwave'.

He was also forced to cut short two shows in Las Vegas after clubbers turned against him. First he was heckled during a gig at Tryst nightclub and later he revealed that he was 'kicked off the decks' for 'not playing Carly Rae Jepsen + hip hop'.

He added: 'No offence to Tryst, great club + staff but i don't know why i was invited there . . .! The people hated me.'

Then, in front of 90,000 fans at the Electric Daisy Carnival – one of the world's largest electronic music festivals – he had to stop an outdoor set because high winds made the Las Vegas Motor Speedway venue unsafe.

In addition, and rather amusingly, he told how new US Open tennis champion Andy Murray blanked him when the two Scottish trailblazers bumped into each other at New York's JFK airport. After Murray's historic victory over Novak Djokovic in the final, Calvin had tweeted his joy about the 'absolute Scottish hero' and 'legend' and mustn't have believed his luck when he saw him at the airport.

'I managed to thank Andy Murray because I was in New York during the tennis,' Calvin said. 'I didn't go but I was flying back on the same day as him. I saw him in the airport, walking to the boarding gate, so I just tapped him on the shoulder and said congratulations and he looked a bit confused and then walked off.'

These were hardly setbacks, of course, in what was a definite upward trajectory. The controversy surrounding the video for 'We Found Love' was all forgotten when it picked up 'Video of the Year' at the MTV video music awards in Los Angeles. It was a big night for Calvin. He performed a DJ set and won 'Best EDM Video' for 'Feel So Close'.

There had been some raised eyebrows when Rihanna neglected to thank Calvin in her acceptance speech for winning her award, but he insisted there were no hard feelings.

'It was her song and it was her video,' he said diplomatically. 'If it had been a Grammy or something, I would have preferred a nod. It was funny because I was right in her eye line the whole time. I was up in the booth, she was making her speech, there's no way she couldn't see me. I'm right there staring at her, waiting in anticipation for her to say my name – and then she just walked off. But I'm fine with it,' he insisted.

It didn't matter because soon after he had plenty to smile about. After a run that must have made Calvin think he could only get to number one with other people as the lead credit, he broke it with 'Sweet Nothing', his second chart success with Florence Welch. Calvin revealed Florence's presence was a return favour for his remix of 'Spectrum', but it was especially satisfying because he had been chasing her for years.

'I met Florence for the first time [at the] end of 2007,' he said, 'and the first time I ever saw her in my life, it was like [a] weird corporate [party] and I walked into the green room and she was definitely drunk, getting a piggy back off someone in her band, like with a bottle of champagne, screaming. And I thought, "I like this girl." And in the years [since] she just actually grew up. I wasn't expecting that. I thought she was a cool kid, one of those people who come and go and then she just smashed it. Now Florence is Florence. She's cool as f*ck as well.'

Once he'd identified her as someone with whom to work, however, he had to pursue her to make it happen, particularly when Florence's stardom rocketed after her band's 2009 baroque pop debut *Lungs* shot to number one.

'It's more satisfying when you're pursuing something. It's like chasing a girl or something. It's way more satisfying if you put in a year's worth of effort chasing and then you get the result, you get the vocal,' he told MTV *News*. 'So the Florence track was number one. She was most chased of the whole album.'

In the end Florence was happy to honour an agreement that had been in place since before the remix.

'I wanted a remix, he wanted a vocal. We just traded,' she said.

Calvin confirmed: 'The "Sweet Nothing" tune with Florence was a swap. It was, "I'll do the remix, you do a vocal." It was always going to happen. It was just a case of "I hope this is good" because you never quite know.'

Like Rihanna, Florence dispelled any fears with a powerful vocal performance. Calvin was impressed.

'I would happily work with nobody but Florence,' he said. 'She's incredible. The fact that I got to do the remix was pleasure enough. Her voice is unreal. She'd sound good on anything.'

Florence supported the track further by agreeing to appear in the video. It was another shot by Calvin's go-to guy, Vincent Haycock. His concept was to have Florence star as a club singer in a destructive relationship.

'All my videos are done by the same guy called Vince. He's in LA. He's kind of like a movie director. He has a dark side and every single treatment we get for a video for him is always extreme and then we have to kind of tone it down slightly for TV and stuff, but that was one where I just said, "If she's happy doing that, then I'm happy doing that." I'm surprised we even got her in the video. I'm surprised I even got her on the track.'

Calvin played a cameo role as a sympathetic listener, but at one stage it looks like he might get beaten up.

'I think I got about ten seconds of screen time,' he said. 'I don't like to get any more than ten. I don't want to get beat up, not on camera.'

The song gave Calvin his first credited number one since 'I'm Not Alone' and was notable because it came just a week before his new album was released. Astonishingly, Calvin had sold fifteen million singles from tracks issued from the collection and as such *18 Months* felt like a mini greatest hits. Of the tracks that hadn't already been released, nearly all had single potential.

'It's funny with this because it took so long for me to finish the album because it was never going to be an album, it was just going to be singles,' Calvin explained. 'But the sound kind of developed throughout and the ideas. From, say, "Bounce" with Kelis to "Sweet Nothing" with Florence . . . "Bounce" was kind of like a developed idea whereas "Sweet Nothing" is just a song. It changed in that respect, but it's funny to look at the track listing and track back to see all that's happened in a relatively short amount of time, like, how many singles. It's good.'

In a fascinating and wide-ranging interview with Jian Ghomeshi for *Q*, on Canada's CBC Radio One, Calvin deconstructed his song-writing process.

'For the sort of music that I produce you need three or four distinctive musical elements,' he said, 'whether it be sounds or riffs. You have a really basic arrangement, a very simple vocal, very simple where it drops in and drops out, it's almost like a formula where you replace the lyrics, the music and keep the drums the same.'

He had decided to make every track 128 bpm (beats per minute), a tempo slightly faster than the 120 bpm of Chicago house music.

'You start with a bass drum going at 128 bpm and try and think of something from there,' he said. 'Imagine trying to make fifteen different tracks all at the same speed. It's difficult, so you've got to try and think of different ways of presenting dance music and keep it interesting.'

He explained the reasoning behind the concept of 128 bpm songs: 'I was just going to do singles at first. When I stopped singing, I decided to stop doing albums basically. I thought, I'm just going to do singles. They're all going to be pop songs and dance songs and they're all going to be 128, but they're all going to sound different. That was the concept.'

Calvin said he was proud of his new album, which he felt broke new ground.

'I can listen to most things on that album and think, well, nobody did that before, even if only me and a handful of other people realise it, at least I know that I had that idea first. "Feels So Close" – nobody did anything like that before because it's an emotional – it's kind of like almost "emo" [emotional hardcore rock music] – vocal. I can't remember the last time guitars were in dance music like that and also it's just that it's all real instruments. Nothing's fake there. It's real music and it's real melody and actual emotion. A lot of dance music now, it's about being in the club and popping bottles over this cheap sounding synth, which people can make so easily and get somebody else to mix, and I'm not really about that.'

The album had given Calvin a chance to work with other DJs he admired, many of whom had approached him.

'The ones that do come directly to me tend to be from other DJs, which I love. On the album, I work with Nicky Romero, who's done a lot of work with David Guetta as well, and also Dillon Francis. So that's an example of two that wanted to work with me and I wanted to work with them,' he said.

'There's a new one with Tinie Tempah, a new one with Ellie Goulding. There's a lot of different stuff – it's half compilation of what I've done in the last eighteen months and half new stuff,' he added.

Tempah appeared on 'Drinking from the Bottle', while Goulding sang on 'I Need Your Love', plus he was reunited once more with

Ayah Marar on 'Thinking About You'. In addition, Calvin was especially pleased to have Dizzee Rascal on there, with 'Here 2 China'.

He revealed how he finally persuaded him to do it.

'We played a festival in Belgium, I was at the airport and saw him. So I said, "I've got this track, I think you'd sound really good on it, but it's not for you, it's for me." I thought he'd say no, as that's what he's like sometimes, but he was well up for it – he heard and did it,' he said.

'It's a highlight for me on the album,' he said of the Dizzee track. 'I'm glad he did it. He's owed me a vocal since "Dance Wiv Me", so that's four years ago. So I'm happy that he came up with the goods. It's amazing, he smashes it.'

The one that got away, however, was revealed to be Emile Sandé, the Scottish singer who, after an early career spent penning songs for other people, branched out on her own in 2011 and then rocketed to a different plateau after performing at both the opening and closing ceremonies of the Olympics – a feat that pushed her just out of Calvin's reach.

'I really, really wanted Emile Sandé on it,' he said. 'I was chasing her for the best part of a year. We met up. I went to one of her shows in LA and I met her and her manager and they're up for it. It's just things went insane for her. She's really, really massive now. I think she's still up for it – I hope she is because I think it would work really well.'

Calvin explained the thinking behind the album's title.

'The reason it is called *18 Months* is because it is eighteen months since I decided to stop singing and just make songs with other people. It's way more fun,' he said. 'But then "Feel So Close" was the exception because I couldn't think of anyone that would do better than that. By this stage, rather than get shy about being a bad singer I can look at it objectively and if it sounds good I use.'

Using the release of the album to give an insight into the way he worked, Calvin allowed cameras inside his recording studio for an episode of Channel 4's *360 Sessions*. It offered a remarkable window into his world.

Inside his studio it was refreshing to see so many musical instruments, from a guitar and bass to percussion, keyboards and a drum kit. He revealed the studio in Holloway, not far from Arsenal's Emirates Stadium, was an Internet-free zone to allow him to work without distractions like Twitter or phone calls.

'In here I do the things that I can't do anywhere else. The keyboards that are in here I can't take anywhere else with me, the guitar, the bass, the fact is that it sounds amazing in here so I start off in here and end in here. I'll mix in here because the sound is very true, rather than sitting with a pair of headphones on, blasting it out of your laptop speakers.

'The only advantage of being in here is there's nothing going on. It's completely silent all around. If you turn your phone off, you can just disappear and not have anything happen. No one will come in, no one will knock on the door – it's just like nothingness. You're just left to get on with it. I don't have Internet here. I can't Twitter and procrastinate; not do anything. This is the room to do music and that's it.'

He also showed off a new isomorphic keyboard.

'This is the new type of keyboard. You can play chords on it but it teaches you the relationship of the notes between other chords so you can come up with different chord sequences based on weirdness, so not actual music!' he said.

Once he's captured the sounds he wants, he can then take his music with him on his laptop. Calvin explained that he used any opportunity to keep working – on a plane, in the hours before he's due behind the decks for a DJ appearance. 'At the moment it's pretty much music, 24/7,' he said.

While it's tempting, he said, to lounge by the pool with a cocktail, he said it was important to be disciplined. 'During the day and in airports and stuff, you need to try and get into work mode because it's so easy to just go on a big long holiday,' he said.

By this stage in his career Calvin was travelling mostly by private jet, affording him more comfortable surroundings in which to operate, but despite the trappings of fame he had not lost the same work ethic of his youth. He held a constant fear that his plan of focusing on singles could 'backfire', but he hoped that while he continued to get the support of radio stations and as long as the tracks were good, 'hopefully that's all that really matters'.

One of the things Calvin was most relieved about when he recorded the album was knowing that he wouldn't have to perform the songs live again.

'I don't feel like I want to do the arenas and all that,' he said. 'I don't want to be like the Swedish House Mafia. I don't want to be playing these big shows and putting myself up there.

'I like playing in clubs. If I play again in Europe, it'll be Warehouse Project in Manchester or The Arches in Glasgow – but I don't want to try and go for f*cking stadiums.'

However, although he planned many more DJ nights, one thing he was worried about was looking after his posture.

'I take advice from Tiësto,' he said. 'He's been talking to me about his back. He did his back in and he's been warning me, if you're a tall guy and you DJ you really need to watch that. He's a mine of information for the taller DJ. You could get a stool out. But a good tip is on my rider – I ask for a very tall desk so I don't have to bend down. There was one gig somewhere in Japan where the desk the mixer and CD changer were on was three feet off the ground. I was squatting and bending over just to get to the mixer – it wasn't the best workout and I'm not taking any more chances.'

Given Calvin devoted so much of his time to music, there didn't seem to be any left for hobbies, but he was proud to announce that since he'd taken up drinking again he'd developed a taste for malt whiskies.

'I'm on the whisky wagon and it's a fantastic wagon to be on. I do enjoy a whisky for its health benefits,' he said. 'I like single malt. I'm growing to be a connoisseur. I'm working on it very hard. Ever since I've started drinking single malt, I've discovered a lot of people in the music industry are also into it, so we've traded suggestions for things to try. It's a great thing to be into. It's like a hobby, and as I didn't have any hobbies, it feels like selecting whisky is a good one to have. And I'm not talking about Jack Daniel's, I'm taking about the proper Scottish stuff.'

Calvin also opened up on life in Hollywood but admitted he was having trouble adapting to some of the cuisine.

'The food is fantastic over here,' he said. 'You can eat healthily; there's a lot more healthy options than at home, that's a fact. But when I do get back, I'm still obsessed with Marks & Spencer's stuff. There are some strange differences over here. Milk is the main one. Milk is terrible. I don't know why, it's just different. And the Rice Krispies are all flat. They are Kellogg's but flat and that's not right.'

As an alternative he'd become a dab hand at making omelettes.

'I do love an omelette at the moment,' he said. 'I've got so good at making them I was scaring myself. I had to start making scrambled eggs. I thought my calling was to be a chef. I do an egg-white omelette with smoked salmon and spinach. You've got a lot of protein, fibre from the spinach, your omega-3 from the salmon.'

Given his odd working hours, it was the perfect meal.

'You're laughing and it'll last you until 4 p.m. if you make a big one,' he said.

With the album ready for release, there came the inevitable reviews and Calvin did well to pay them little attention. The consensus seemed to be that while the stand-out tracks were 'We Found Love', 'Sweet Nothing' and 'Bounce', the other collaborations lacked star quality.

Calvin stated that he wasn't bothered by negative write-ups because 'there's all these other real people that like the music and go to the shows and enjoy themselves', he said. 'We all know that reviewers are all failed musicians, and all have huge chips on their shoulders about various things – mostly dance music because they see dance music as being a bunch of people that got lucky, whereas they grafted in their terrible band for fifteen years and didn't get signed because they were awful but they were lugging the drum kit around to small shows so they feel they actually earned the right to release records and call themselves musicians. And they were still terrible, no matter how much carrying of equipment [they did]. You know. You're still bad. I've carried a lot of things in my life. I used to stack shelves for a living,' he said.

Before the year was out Calvin had a chance to rekindle his successful partnership with Rihanna, but this time her demands ahead of recording for her next album, *Unapologetic*, were too much – even for a master tunesmith like him.

'Rihanna has been recording her next album,' he explained. 'I saw her and she said, "You have to do something for my album, you have to, we need you," and I thought, "Right, I need to do this," so you go into the studio and you go, "OK, I need to sit here, I've got two days to make probably one of the best records I've ever made in my life. Let's see how that works out."'

But he added: 'Obviously I didn't do anything, so I'm not on the record. I did a decent tune, you know, but, nah, you can't work under that kind of pressure. I can't anyway. I can't go into a studio and say, "Right, go write a hit."'

The unworkable deadline passed and an opportunity was lost.

However, just three weeks into 2013 he was celebrating again. The release of 'Drinking from the Bottle', featuring Tinie Tempah, reached number five, making Calvin the first British artist to have seven top-ten singles from one album. The track, an unsubtle, tub-thumping chant, said to be inspired by American film producer Mad Skillz Tommy Schillz, who was a regular fixture at clubs, drinking a variety of hard alcohols straight out of the bottle, peaked at number five and was accompanied by an equally raucous video in which Calvin and Tinie hung out with the devil.

He topped two other charts – as the UK's most successful song-writer for the second year in a row and the top songwriter for 2012 in the US, according to *Billboard* magazine. In addition, the posting of his latest accounts showed his personal fortune had risen to £6 million. It was hardly unexpected, given the year he had enjoyed. That fortune was about to swell massively, however, as he landed a twenty-month residency as the DJ for a soon-to-be-opened super-club in Las Vegas.

Calvin agreed to play forty-six dates at the new Hakkasan club – a five-storey, 75,000-square-foot venue at the MGM Grand hotel. He also signed up for a further twenty-two dates at the MGM Grand's 'day club', Wet Republic.

'When they told me they were going to build this massive club, it was just too good to be true,' Calvin said. 'Being an established brand, you know it's going to be quality. The good thing is there's more than one room. Often at clubs in Vegas, you kind of have a choice of one DJ and if they're not good, people leave the club and go hear someone else.

'At this club, you can listen to dance music and if you've had enough of that, you can go listen to hip hop.'

He was set to earn another whopping pay cheque after agreeing to perform at the wedding of socialite Tamara Ecclestone.

Calvin was to be paid £320,000 at the summer nuptials, which were taking place at the exclusive Hotel Du Cap and on a private superyacht on the French Riviera. Jennifer Lopez and Lionel Richie were also expected to appear.

If he was looking for a 'plus one' to take to the wedding, the tabloids were speculating who might be top of his list. Said to have caught his eye was the Russian Victoria's Secret model Anne Vyalitsyna, who he apparently met at a *Sports Illustrated* party in New York.

His socialising with the elite continued when he met up with Andy Murray in Miami while there for a massive EDM festival – and this time the tennis ace knew exactly who he was. Murray was playing at the Miami Open and, after meeting Calvin, announced online: 'Met Calvin Harris after the match in Miami, really good guy, likes his tennis as well.'

Andy had made history by becoming the first British male since 1936 to win a Grand Slam tournament – and little did he know that he was in the company of another history man.

'I Need Your Love', Calvin's track with Ellie Goulding, released in April 2013, had jumped to seven in the charts, meaning he had eclipsed Michael Jackson and entered the record books as the first musician to score eight top ten hits from the same album.

Calvin's reaction was a simple one: 'Eight Top 10s from my album *18 Months* now! So happy!!!'

In the video to accompany his latest hit, Calvin and Ellie played lovers. In real life, however, he was getting close to a certain woman. A Russian model she was not. It was Rita Ora, a fiercely determined singer with big ambitions.

Had Calvin bitten off more than he could chew?

21

Rita All About It

IT wasn't exactly what you would call love at first sight.

Calvin's first public acknowledgement of Rita Ora was to accuse her of being economical with the truth.

He felt the need to step in after the chart-topping singer claimed she'd had first dibs on 'Call My Name' but had rejected the song before it had ended up with Cheryl Cole.

Rita, who'd hit the top spot with her first two singles, said, 'I heard "Call My Name" quite a while ago because I was offered it. I turned it down. I do like the song but I didn't want to sing it cos it's not really me. I don't want to go down the dance route that a lot of other pop stars are doing. I prefer to have my own sound and do my own thing.'

That prompted an angry rebuke from Calvin, who announced on Twitter: 'For the record, Call my name was never given to Rita Ora to sing . . . she made that up, don't know why.'

Rita appeared to backpedal, insinuating her words had been twisted, when she responded: 'So for the record, don't believe media when they twist sh*t.'

Calvin urged her to 'calm down', adding, 'I was setting the record straight as you didn't at the time. It was a disrespectful comment to make, that's all.'

And she backtracked completely when she offered to explain all privately, saying, 'I hate beef and fighting. So I love u all @calvinharris call me ill explain wat actually happened they twisted it and congratulations. X'

Some clearing of the air must have happened because Rita later said, 'I love Calvin Harris, it was such a stupid misunderstanding. I feel silly for even commenting on something I wasn't clear about. The truth is I heard this song and I was like, I want this song and I didn't know Cheryl had it already. It is such a small industry, there's no point in fighting or beefing with anyone. I spoke to Calvin, cleared it up and laughed it off.'

Their heated exchange must have created frisson of sexual tension between them because fast-forward seven months and she's joining him on his private jet to Las Vegas and in the DJ booth while he performs at Hakkasan.

A day later Calvin posted a photo online of Rita boarding his jet, captioned, 'You again!'

He had his hands full, in more ways than one.

Rita might only have been on the scene for less than a year, it seemed, but already she had made quite an impact.

It was often said that Rita, whose birth name is Rita Sahatçiu, had escaped 'war-torn Kosovo' with her family, but that's not quite the case. Born in 1990 in Pristina, then in Yugoslavia, now Kosovo, she left for London with her parents before she was a year old, seven years before the war began. Rita's father, who ran a successful import/export business, and her doctor mother, the daughter of a renowned film director, were established socialites but they could see the writing on the wall.

Even then the Serbian-led government in Belgrade persecuted Kosovan Albanians, who were barred from positions of power, denied access to education and healthcare, and were intimidated on a daily basis.

The Sahatçius moved to London and started again, her mother learning English and retraining to work in the UK. When the war began back home, it sparked tension within the family, as they nervously waited for news of loved ones.

'I couldn't figure it out. All the arguments, all the tension – I knew it was coming from something,' Rita, at the time just a little girl, said. 'Like, something wasn't quite right.'

Rita was eleven when her family realised she had a talent for singing, even then possessing a voice 'like a superpower'. She won a place at the Sylvia Young Theatre School and at this time her father decided that if she was to become famous she needed an easier name. He added 'Ora' to the surname, meaning 'hour'. The name would prove ironic, given Rita is infamous for her poor time-keeping. She kept Calvin waiting four and a half hours for one of their early dates.

Rita was discovered when an A&R agent from Roc Nation caught one of her early shows and flew her to New York to meet the boss, Jay-Z. Famously he told her to be 'patient' and she waited three years before her debut album was released. It was worth the wait. Her first two singles, 'R.I.P.' and 'How We Do (Party)' shot to number one and she followed those with 'Hot Right Now', on which she featured with DJ Fresh, which also went to the top of the charts.

She appeared with Coldplay, flew to gigs by helicopter, landed a part in a *The Fast and The Furious* movie, became the face of Madonna's fashion label and attracted over three million followers on Twitter.

However, success brought interest in her private life, where there was enough to keep the showbiz columns occupied. Calvin was said to be Rita's seventh date in six months, but she enjoyed the company of women also. She was particularly close to bisexual supermodel Cara Delevingne, whom she called her 'wifey'. She dated Kim Kardashian's brother Rob, but it ended acrimoniously, and when he accused her publicly of cheating it led to the unfortunate hashtag #ritawhora on Twitter.

Calvin and Rita reportedly hit it off at the Brit Awards in February and then enjoyed a string of dates at Hollywood's Chateau Marmont hotel.

After her failed dalliances, Rita said she was desperate to find a man who could cope with a successful woman and didn't 'feel threatened' by her career. Calvin fitted the bill and after just a few weeks Rita was gushing about him.

'It's early,' she said. 'I'm not in love. But I'm definitely falling.'

Rita had an early test when Calvin had to cavort with Ellie Goulding for the video of 'I Need Your Love' but managed to keep any jealous feelings in check.

'We just laughed about it,' said Ellie, who had struck up a close bond with Calvin after they had worked together on the single.

'The whole thing was funny. We knew in that video we would just giggle and laugh the whole way through. Me and Calvin are really good friends. We make each other laugh. We text each other stupid stuff and we really get on and are similar.'

Rita wasn't the first celebrity Calvin had been linked to, but until now he had yet to fully discover the joy of being in a relationship in the public eye. Their first public appearance in the UK was a gift for showbiz hacks and gossip columnists.

Until 2013 London had only one building that worked as a euphemism for a sexual act. As Caitlin Moran mused in *The Times*:

> Yes – the Oxo Tower on the South Bank has been the sole venue to allow people to post Facebook update statuses such as: 'First date with Grace last night. I took her up the Oxo Tower.' Thank goodness, then, for London's latest landmark, which, this week, started allowing visitors to ride to the viewing platform at its apex, allowing *OK!*'s 'lifestyle editor', Natalie Posner, to be the world's first journalist to write 'On Wednesday, I was lucky enough to be taken up the Shard.'

She wasn't the only one. Rita knew that feeling too, after Calvin took her to the 69th floor of the 1,016-foot-high tower for the playback party for Daft Punk's new album, *Random Access Memories*.

The Sun joked that Calvin certainly knew how to impress a girl on a date – 'by showing her one of Europe's biggest erections'.

Calvin didn't need to scale Europe's tallest building to experience the highs. They just kept coming. And being named 'Songwriter of the Year' at the prestigious Ivor Novello Awards would take some beating.

As he collected his trophy, he quipped, 'I'll keep this speech like my lyrics – brief and repetitive. It feels like I shouldn't be here but this is easily the greatest achievement of my entire career.'

Afterwards his joy was clear to see. 'Easily, this is the best award I've ever had,' he said of his Novello. 'It's the best award a songwriter can have. It's my greatest achievement. It's the award I'm proudest of.'

After celebrating at London's trendy Nobu restaurant, Rita tweeted: 'Ivor Novello's eh? Songwriter of the year. No big deal just pretty f*cking awesome!! @calvinharris :))))'

Rita's fulsome praise of his songwriting talents made it hard to believe when Calvin revealed she didn't even like his music. As he announced dates for his biggest-ever tour, he said, 'Rita doesn't really like dance music. She doesn't really like my music – but I like hers! We're not together for musical reasons, which is great.'

Calvin's tour would take him to most of the major cities in the UK and Ireland in December, supported by fellow DJ, Tiësto, and demand was so high for his show at Glasgow's new Hydro Arena just before Christmas that all tickets were sold in just three minutes.

Rita might not have been a fan of his music, but she didn't mind accompanying him to gigs. Given his schedule, it might have been the only way she got to see him.

He played 150 shows over the year. On one crazy weekend, he clocked up an incredible 5,445 miles in his jet, with Rita by his side. From recording in his studio, he flew to Londonderry to appear at Radio 1's Big Weekend. Then it was off to Las Vegas to DJ at the MGM Grand hotel, before finally heading to LA, where he had just bought a new £4.6 million house.

Newspapers described the Hollywood home – with its infinity pool and cinema – as 'fit for a superstar DJ'. However, he wasn't happy at having photos of his new pad plastered over the web, particularly as it prompted questions from his mum about his taste in soft furnishings.

'It wasn't great having pictures of my house on the Internet,' he said, 'but they used pictures from when it was on sale so that was none of my furniture. The stuff belonged to the previous owner. My mum texted me and said, "Why did you buy that sofa? It doesn't look so good."'

After years of living frugally, Calvin was now enjoying the trappings of his success. In addition to the luxury mansion, he splashed out on a new car. It wasn't just any run-around like his first Vectra; it was a £168,000 McLaren MP4-12C supercar.

Rita's schedule seemed every bit as hectic. If she wasn't hanging out with Calvin in LA, she was partying in London with the A-list set. Although she had cooled things with 'wifey' Cara Delevingne, Rita grew close to supermodel Kate Moss. In the summer Calvin and Rita joined Kate and her husband Jamie Hince in Ibiza. They holidayed while he manned the decks.

Rita might have been becoming a darling of the tabloids, but she showed she had her business head screwed on by applying for trademark patents for her name on everything from moisturisers and nail varnish to pets' clothing and video games. Rita also covered herself in case she ever wanted to branch out into the men's market, with tie clips, briefcases and paper beer mats.

Calvin followed her lead by applying for a trademark in his name, too. It covered a host of products from video games to phone covers to recording studios. It was then reported that, in a deal similar to one signed by Jay-Z, he had agreed a seven-figure tie-in with Samsung to release a future new album on a mobile phone app. The deal meant that a certain number of copies of the album would be given away for free on the app once Samsung bought up the rights. Jay-Z, founder of the Roc Nation label through which Calvin's music was released in the US, did the same thing with his album *Magna Carta*, prompting some criticism from fans unhappy that they were forced to sign up for the app.

It was yet another indication of the portfolio of business opportunities Calvin was compiling to maximise the potential of this fertile period.

Figures released later in 2013 by *Forbes* named him as the richest DJ in the world, with a fortune estimated at £30 million.

Calvin brushed off the claims, insisting he was working too hard to count his millions. 'At the moment I barely have time to do my laundry,' he said. 'I haven't been thinking about that side of things. I know I've been doing well and I know I can buy the things I want, though I don't want a lot of expensive things. That's all I need to know for now.'

At a time when dance music, or EDM, as they liked to call it in the States, was sweeping the nation, Calvin was at the head of the vanguard. His earnings were said to be double that of other hot young talent such as *Twilight* actress Kristen Stewart, her co-star

Taylor Lautner, singers Katy Perry and Adele, and the *Hunger Games* actress Jennifer Lawrence.

'I'm sure he is working every hour that God sends,' Ricky Magowan, Scotland's biggest dance promoter, said. 'The money doesn't come without working his bollocks off. Some people can't cope with the workload that goes with keeping it all going. It is right time, right place for Calvin. It is down to him and the whole team around him.'

Magowan added: 'He is making his own music and that is where the real money is. Add to that his DJ residency in Las Vegas. Tom Jones, Frank Sinatra and Barbra Streisand are not in Las Vegas any more. It is dance music that is bringing people to Las Vegas now.'

Former editor of dance magazine *Mixmag* Dave Seaman said Calvin was at the top of the list for DJs. 'Power by association is such an important thing, especially in this day and age of celebrity culture gone mad,' he said. 'He is the go-to producer for many pop stars. Everybody wants a Calvin record because he is very good at the sound of electronic dance music, which is the sound of the zeitgeist at the moment.'

Calvin was at a loss to explain why dance music had become quite as big as it had in the States – but insisted he had been lucky.

'The rise of dance music has been astronomical in the last three years,' he said, 'and I happened to be in the right place at the right time. I made that decision completely by accident. I like to think I don't have an ego like you need to be number one – the best, the DJ of all time. I want to be the number-one songwriter-producer guy of all time.'

And he joked that the transformation in his fortunes was more likely down to two things – a healthy glow and a decent haircut.

'It's the Vegas tan that has done it,' he said. 'Growing up in Dumfries, I got no sun – I spent all my time in my room making records. When I came to America, it made me recognise the benefits of sunlight. I also got a good haircut. I used to have a terrible haircut.'

He might once have sung that he got all girls but, after building the life, he now had the lavish home, the supercar and the stunning girlfriend.

During a rare break on the beach in Barcelona, after watching his lover emerge from the waves in a white bikini, her hair slicked back – reminiscent of Bond girl Ursula Andress – he snapped the image and posted it on Twitter, saying, 'Pure Ursula vibes happening right now, by the way.'

He had the girl, he had the lifestyle – it was even said he was on the Duchess of Cambridge's playlist as she prepared to give birth – and he cemented his place in the record books yet further with the ninth top-ten single from *18 Months* with 'Thinking About You', which reached number nine.

Calvin was living the high life and it was imitated in his art, as he channelled the spirit of *The Great Gatsby* in the accompanying video. The promo showed Calvin in the lap of luxury, surrounded by adoring, scantily clad women, but it did not go down well in some quarters.

As Prime Minister David Cameron announced plans for a nation-wide Internet porn block, the focus shifted to the treatment of women in pop videos.

The growing trend for female nudity in music promos peaked with Robin Thicke's controversial 'Blurred Lines'. Here was a song with questionable lyrics, declaring 'I know you want it', and an even dodgier video, which showed a suited Thicke dancing badly with three topless models. Thicke went to number one, but Justin Timberlake and Calvin found themselves dragged into the debate with videos that, it was said, degraded women to the role of sex objects.

'It's fair to say the floodgates have opened,' said Lee Thompson, former head of music at *The Box* and an expert on pop videos.

In Calvin's behind-the-scenes programme for Channel 4, he told how his videos were put together – and often the first time he would see how the video would take shape was when his director sent him a treatment.

Vincent Haycock, the man behind many of Calvin's videos, and the one behind the camera for 'Thinking About You', denied there was a deliberate attempt to use semi-naked women to boost the commercial potential of the record.

'There might be a label out there going, "Ooh, if we do something really provocative for this young artist we might get some attention,"' he said, 'but, usually, labels will freak out about nudity, because it just won't get as much play on TV.'

Haycock insisted that the brief nudity in the video was not in his original treatment and the suggestion came from the model herself, who reasoned it would make more sense in the context of the story.

'It's just context,' he said. 'You watch Nicole Kidman get naked in *Eyes Wide Shut* and nobody goes around saying it's misogynistic, because it's Kubrick.'

Calvin made good on his promise to release songs as soon as they were ready. The first taster of his new album came in the shape of 'Under Control', featuring Swedish DJ Alesso and British synth pop duo Hurts, whose second album *Exile* had gone top ten earlier in the year.

By the time the song was released in October 2013, Calvin was under scrutiny again when 'Drinking from the Bottle' was named as one of several songs that glamourised alcohol consumption and could drive children to drink. Rita's 'How We Do' and Kesha's 'Tik Tok' were also said to be part of a culture where almost one in five songs in modern top-ten charts contained a reference to booze – twice as many as ten years ago and almost three times as many as thirty years ago.

The research by Liverpool John Moores University concluded: 'Health and other professionals should recognise increased alcohol promotion in popular music and ensure this does not reinforce the binge-drinking culture.'

While it's fair to assume that the video for 'Under Control' was conceived before any complaints were aired about previous promos, it might have done little to quell the campaigners' angst.

The video places Calvin, Alesso and Hurts' Theo Hutchcraft in an American desert town as the nation awaits news of an imminent meteor strike. As the end of the world nears, they conveniently come to the rescue of three attractive girls whose car has broken down. In a limo, all six cavort as the drink flows, with Calvin at one stage showering a girl in champagne. While the blokes remain either suited or comfortably dressed, the women are shown stripping into a change of clothing for one last rave with Calvin on the decks. When the news comes through that disaster has been avoided, it sparks a massive party.

The minor controversy surrounding his output did nothing to dampen his commercial appeal. 'Under Control' shot to number one, with sales of nearly 75,000 in its first week – Calvin's fifth chart-topper.

When the producer was asked in November 2012 about the relationship that exists between dance music and alcohol and drugs, he said, 'I think it exists. I never mention anything to do with drugs ever in any of my songs or anything. I don't do drugs. I drink, frequently to excess. I don't mention that either.

'It's just one of those things that goes with dance music. It always has done and it goes with a lot of other forms of music as well.'

Given that 'Drinking from the Bottle' was released just three months earlier, might he have been referring to his own lyrics and not those supplied by a guest contributor? Perhaps, but it could be argued that 'Merrymaking at My Place', with its references to 'stuff' being taken inside his house or smoked outside and the line 'drug-taking at my place', contradicted that statement.

It's not known how much attention Calvin paid to the criticism or observations about his songs and videos, but he appeared tetchier than usual at a gig in Miami shortly afterwards, erupting uncharacteristically at a woman who heckled him. He was playing at the city's LIV Nightclub when someone shouted that he was a 'sell-out'.

He then appeared to lose his cool, berating the clubber.

'Whose show did you come to?' he asked. 'Lift this girl up. I want to hear what she has to say.'

When the girl asked him to 'play something original', he erupted.

'That was originally written by me. That's my song. Why do you come to a f*cking Calvin Harris show where Calvin Harris is DJ'ing and don't want to hear a f*cking Calvin Harris record? You dumb f*cking bitch.'

As he started 'Feel So Close', he was heard saying, 'I'm going to play this record all night just for you. I'm going to play it again and again until you tell me to f*ck off and never come back. What's wrong with you? This girl needs to be removed from the club.'

Calvin's mood wouldn't have been improved when Rita suggested in an interview that she was single. That led to speculation
about whether pop's hottest couple were still together, but she
quashed it by then saying he was 'the sexiest guy I've ever seen'.

If Rita was sending mixed messages, this only amplified when
she was next spotted hanging out with her ex-boyfriend Dave
Gardner, a pal of David Beckham.

The debate over sexual images of women in videos refused to die
down and in November 2013 Calvin was once again listed alongside Thicke, Rihanna and Miley Cyrus for their content.

Campaign group Rewind and Reframe sought a pledge from
the music industry, including artists and music companies, to stop
making music videos that represent women as sex objects, and
wrote to David Cameron and music industry chiefs to air their con-
cerns.

Sarah Green, from one of the campaign groups, End Violence
Against Women, said, 'We would appeal to artists like Calvin Harris
to seriously think about their video's content and the kind of messages they are sending out. There are elements in the "Drinking
from the Bottle" video which are extremely dehumanising. Women
are used as props and are blatantly objectified using pornographic
film techniques.'

Singer Annie Lennox also joined the campaign, writing online, 'I
have to say that I'm disturbed and dismayed by the recent spate of
overtly sexualised performances and videos. It seems obvious that
certain record companies are peddling highly styled pornography
with musical accompaniment. As if the tidal wave of sexualised
imagery wasn't already bombarding impressionable young girls
enough, it's depressing to see how these performers are so eager to
push this new level of low.'

Calvin remained tight-lipped on the issue; it was perhaps the
perfect time to take a well-earned break from the business.

It was reported that Rita's mother had suggested the couple
plan a romantic getaway in Ireland because their schedules meant
they were seeing less and less of each other. Whether they made it
away remains to be seen, but there could be no doubt about Calvin's
commitment when he flew 15,000 miles to be with her on her 23rd

birthday. He first made a 5,000-mile jaunt from LA to attend her Studio 54-themed party at London's trendy club The Box. Early the following morning he flew 10,000 miles to Sydney to play Australia's Stereosonic festival.

Rita was working on her new album, and she must have revised her opinion of her boyfriend's music as Calvin was among several high-profile collaborators helping her. Among those quoted was pop legend Prince – one of the artists at the top of Calvin's list.

'I have met him and I have had the honour of being in the same studio as him,' Rita gushed about Prince. 'We messed around with some music and, you know, I can't believe he can play so many instruments.'

It was said Calvin had gifted Rita a song for her birthday – one that would turn out to be her future hit 'I Will Never Let You Down'.

Calvin prepared for his big UK tour but, ahead of their opening night, supporting DJ Tiësto predicted there wouldn't be too much partying going on from his Scots chum.

'I think I'm more of a party animal nowadays, as Calvin has a girlfriend,' Tiësto said. 'That has slowed him down a little bit.'

Suggesting that perhaps Calvin had liked to let his hair down previously, he added: 'He can't be with girls too much and party – so I have to party for him. I assume he's going to take it a little bit more easy on this tour, and will disappear and leave me hanging in the dressing-room by myself! It happens to everyone when you get a girlfriend.'

The tour was an unqualified success, but one incident highlighted how the digital age amplified problems that previously might have gone unnoticed. A photo of a woman with a man kissing her topless chest during Tiësto's set in Dublin went viral after it was posted on Twitter, attracting a raft of comment. Although no complaints were made to police it was feared the woman could be identified and targeted and Twitter suspended the account of the user that posted the photo.

Both DJs were powerless to prevent or even influence such incidents taking place, but Calvin was aware of his responsibilities when it came to the safety of his audience.

He revealed once in 2010 that he'd had to stop a show to ask the audience to step back to avoid people at the front being crushed and he looked to control as much as possible on his headline shows.

'You can tell really early on if something's gone wrong,' he said. 'I watched My Chemical Romance in Dublin and they had to stop the show and do this big "three steps back" thing; it was really cool because everyone did it, everyone went three steps back – so you've got to try that. I've done that before. A couple of years ago I did that and it worked.'

'It's hard to control when it's a festival,' he added, 'because so much is out of your control, but if it's your headline you should . . . you should try and control everything from ticket prices to security to everything.'

Once his UK tour was completed, he still had DJ commitments in Puerto Rico and the Dominican Republic before the year's end at Hakkasan, Las Vegas.

Rita flew out to join him and her presence sparked speculation in one newspaper that Calvin might be getting ready to pop the question.

There might well have been a rock on the horizon for the young couple. However, rather than one to wear on her finger it was more likely the large one towards which their love boat was heading . . .

22

All Ora Now

THE day lawyers call 'Divorce Day' is 2 January, because more couples file for separation then than on any other.

Calvin and Rita might not have been divorcing, but something had happened over New Year to make them join countless other couples around the world in deciding it was time to part.

Nothing official came from either star's spokespeople, but in a digital age of social media there was a modern way of telling that Rita was erasing Calvin from her life – she 'unfollowed' his Instagram account.

The tabloids agreed their workloads were to blame. Rita was heading out to Vancouver to begin filming the movie adaptation of E. L. James' best-selling erotic novel series, *Fifty Shades of Grey*.

There was further speculation that a bust-up over Hogmanay had seen Rita switch hotel rooms when they were away together.

The timing was lousy for Calvin. Regardless of the reasons behind the separation, he would be single as he prepared to celebrate his 30th birthday.

Calvin, in the only way he knew how, kept busy. As well as being the world's hardest-working DJ, he was toying with an off-shoot project – a comedy series written by *Trainspotting* author Irvine Welsh on the EDM scene, starring Will Smith and Jay-Z and with Calvin advising. It was an area Welsh knew well, and Calvin and Smith had struck up an unlikely friendship after meeting to discuss the project.

However, before the end of the month, it appeared all was not lost on the Rita front.

She again used social media to relay her thoughts, posting cryptically on Twitter that she might have been harbouring some regrets.

'Have you ever wondered which hurts the most: saying something & not wishing you had not, or saying nothing and wishing you had?' she wrote.

Then they were spotted kissing during a date in West Hollywood ahead of the Grammy Awards. Calvin was also believed to have flown to Vancouver to visit Rita on the set of her movie, where she was playing Mia, the sister of the fetishist protagonist Christian Grey.

Rita then confirmed everything was back on track by revealing details of her new single, one they had worked on together. It was to be 'I Will Never Let You Down', the song Calvin had gifted her for her birthday.

'It's one of the coolest songs I've ever heard,' said Rita, who had overcome the fears she'd had of working with the greatest hit-maker of his generation.

'You know what's funny, I never really intended on working with him, I honestly didn't,' she explained, before seeming to suggest they had come up with the idea together. 'We were sitting at home, he started humming, then I started humming, then we hummed together!' she said.

Calvin's version of events was slightly different.

'I wrote the song with her in mind. I didn't write the song for anyone else,' he told Capital FM.

And it wasn't just songs Calvin gifted. He splashed out on a Mercedes motor for her, even though she was yet to pass her test.

On 14 February she responded by posting a photo of herself online posing in her underwear with the message 'Happy Valentine's Day, baby.'

Calvin announced plans for his latest single, 'Summer', to be released in April, the first since 'Feel So Close' to feature himself on vocals – something he felt more comfortable about.

'If I have a song that I think suits my voice, I'll just do it myself,' he said, before adding: 'Most people don't even know it's me who sings.'

The accompanying video confirmed he had paid little or no attention to the disquiet the previous year about the exploitation of women.

'Summer' might have seen a change in director, with Emil Nava, the man behind videos for Ed Sheeran, Jessie J and Jennifer Lopez, but the concept was one we were used to – stunning girls with an aversion to wearing anything other than their underwear, it seemed, sitting dreamily around mansions, when they weren't racing cars in seductively unzipped jumpsuits.

Calvin made light of the thought processes behind it.

'It's just hot chicks drag racing in the desert. It's a very simple concept,' he said. 'I like my videos to be like high concept movies in the eighties when you can write the idea on the back of a matchbox. Girls, car, desert and that's it.'

For fans, the video was notable, as it showcased a new beefed-up Calvin, for whom gym sessions and his LA lifestyle were clearly paying dividends.

His transformation was such that it prompted the *Sunday Times Style* magazine to gush:

> Have you seen the DJ Calvin Harris recently? No? Well, it's actually possible you have, you just didn't recognise him. For no more is Harris a techno dweeb – a bit on the scrawny side, shaggy hair, pale but really not too interesting – now he's a rampant sex master. He's gone from an *NME* kind of guy to a *Men's Health* hunk. In other words, he's had a sexover.

Rita seemed to agree, for she too needed little encouragement to highlight Calvin's sex appeal.

'I do like it when he calls me "darlin' " in his Scottish accent. That has to be my favourite word,' she said. 'Scottish accents just do something to me. I really love them. I know all the lingo now too. I say "aye" a lot. Even my friends ask, "What are you talking about?"'

On another occasion in New York, she said of her boyfriend: 'His name is Adam. But you may know him as Calvin. Harris. He's like six-foot-sex.'

'Summer' shot straight to number one – a chart position Calvin was swiftly calling his own. It stayed there for one week but shifted over 100,000 copies. In the US its performance was even more impressive. It reached number seven in the Billboard chart but would go on to sell more than a million copies.

Calvin's single for Rita, 'I Will Never Let You Down', followed 'Summer' by two weeks. However, shortly before its release speculation about the health of their relationship mounted again after Rita ripped the shirt off actor Zac Efron's back at the MTV Movie Awards in Los Angeles. Calvin was 100 miles away at Coachella at the time. This might have been insignificant and just staged showbiz high jinx, but two things Calvin would say later about this period give the episode a different perspective.

When the time came for Rita to promote her single, she was very much on message, taking any opportunity to praise Calvin, particularly his songwriting talents.

'Adam was a massive inspiration on this record,' she said, continuing to refer to him by his real name. 'It really helps when you find someone who balances you out and really puts things into perspective. You don't want to mess it up.'

Rita said she had been working on the album for two years.

'It was pretty difficult in the beginning because I didn't know what I wanted to say, write about or feel,' she said. 'Then I met this person and he turned my whole world around. Suddenly I started to get answers and things started to run smoother.'

Referring to 'I Will Never Let You Down', she said, 'When I heard it, I really fell in love with it and it really changed me. I thought, "If it's that easy for me to fall in love with it, I need to let the world do that too."

'The song is inspired by [the time] when my life turned for the better. It's a love song basically, celebrating passion and being happy.'

She added: 'He wrote it in about an hour. And he writes as he takes a shower. What a genius.'

She explained that Calvin eventually contributed four songs to her new album, which then was slated for release in the autumn.

'There was no stress. It worked out great,' she said. 'He got something out of me that I never thought I had.'

Rita certainly sounded like someone in a loving relationship.

'I just didn't think I had it,' she said about falling in love. 'I'd never experienced it before. And I was just like in the wilderness, thinking, "Will it ever happen?"'

She talked about how much she wanted to go on holiday with him.

'We need to go away together, we haven't done that for a long time,' she said.

When asked about *Fifty Shades of Grey*, she told how Calvin, her father and her brother had all held a meeting to discuss whether it was the right project for her, given the explicit nature of the material.

She added: 'He gets me, so he brought out the very best in me like nobody else could.'

Rita recalled the animosity towards each other when they first had their Twitter spat, but when they finally met she was intrigued by him.

'I was fascinated by how his brain works, what he was going to do next, what his thoughts were,' she said.

The couple would be sharing the bill at Radio 1's Big Weekend at Glasgow Green at the end of May, but Calvin ruled out the prospect of them appearing together.

'We have our own things to do. She wouldn't like me getting in the way onstage,' he said.

Speaking ahead of the event, he gave no hint that there was anything up with their relationship, referring to Rita as 'the missus'.

'I'm lucky I can get to do music and do well and still do normal stuff unless I'm out with the missus – then I get a lot of attention,' he said.

But, in talking about how much time they managed to spend together, he didn't exactly sound like someone pining for more contact. In fact, he seemed to suggest the problem was when she was around, rather than when she wasn't.

'We see each other like four days every two weeks, so it's like an issue when she's around,' he said. 'We'd probably get sick of each other if we had a whole month [together].'

Rita also talked about the issues of a long-distance relationship.

'We're on different sides of the world all the time,' she said. 'But I've been taught that if you really want something, you make it work. So regardless of what happens, you make sure that when you are together it's incredible.'

However, she painted a picture of domesticity when they did manage to hook up. Hoping that her latest song would be her fourth number one, edging her closer to Calvin's tally, she said, 'Fingers are crossed but, you know, Calvin is great. He's a good lad. Maybe we'll start putting our tallies on the kitchen fridge and keeping score.'

Two weeks after 'Summer' hit the top spot, 'I Will Never Let You Down' matched it, continuing Calvin's remarkable run of chart toppers.

He didn't appear to be with her for her celebrations. He remained in Las Vegas, where Kesha – his ex – joined him for a game of pool.

However, that didn't mean he didn't care. He did tweet his girl-friend, saying, '@RitaOra Congratulations I told you!'

And he admitted he'd been checking the charts constantly – as he did for all his singles – to see how it was doing.

'Don't think on the week of release I'm not refreshing iTunes every five minutes,' he said. 'Even Rita's single, which I wrote and produced, I was refreshing iTunes all week.'

Mercifully, Rita said she wasn't the jealous type – but that didn't stop her being suspicious. 'I don't get jealous, I get suspicious,' she said. 'Any girl would, though. It's only because you miss that person, that's really the reason . . . I'm not a fan of long-distance relationships. If you had a choice, you want that person with you. It makes me pretty sad. But you work with what you've got.'

They were reunited for the Big Weekend, where Calvin's set rocked so loud he set off car alarms in the streets surrounding Glasgow Green.

Afterwards he said he could 'relax and watch a bit of Coldplay with the missus'.

That was the last time either of them referred to themselves as a couple. A week later, amid rumours they were no longer together, Calvin confirmed – where else but on Twitter – that after a year they were splitting up.

'To address speculation,' he wrote, 'myself and Rita ended our relationship some time ago. She is a beautiful, talented woman and I wish her all the best.'

'Some time ago' didn't suggest a week or so. Could it be that he was waiting on Rita to score her number one before announcing their break-up? It sounds cynical to suggest that they led people to believe they were still together throughout Rita's promotional schedule so she wouldn't have to deal with any awkward questions – but another thing Calvin said added weight to this theory.

Speaking on Capital FM in November, five months after the split, Calvin gave his most candid comments.

'I don't like celebrities, celebrity women. Nah,' he said. 'I haven't seen her since March. It's brilliant, it's just stress free. It's beautiful.'

His claim that they weren't together properly since March suggests they had gone their separate ways before their promotional commitments began. Or maybe it was just him.

Amid rumours that Canadian singer Justin Bieber might have somehow been involved, it was suggested that Calvin had moved her possessions out of his mansion.

Calvin didn't look like he was moping. He was spotted having dinner in Hollywood with friends, including supermodel Rosie Huntington-Whiteley, who, it was said, was after a role in one of his videos.

Rita bided her time before she commented, posting on Twitter: 'I don't usually address speculation but I've had an incredible time w Calvin & i will treasure the memories. I've moved on from this topic so i hope people will respect that and do the same. Life can only be understood backwards but it must be lived forwards.'

It didn't stop the speculation about what caused the split of one of pop's power couples. *The Sun* reported that Rita had been acting suspiciously, being vague about her whereabouts after they flew into LA for separate visits but were there at the same time.

Things came to a head when Calvin coincidentally used the same driver – and he seemed to land Rita in it.

Calvin had an unexpected opportunity to contemplate the events of the last few months when he arrived back in London and turned up at his studio to find the locks had been changed. He posted a video of his plight on Instagram, telling his 1.1 million followers: 'I haven't been in this London studio in so long they changed the f*cking locks. I'm just sitting outside on these f*cking stairs thinking about life.'

The Daily Mirror then tried to stir things up by suggesting that Calvin and Ellie Goulding's on screen romance had spilled over into real life. This was because they had been seen hanging out a lot and had left the Capital FM Summertime Ball after-party in a taxi together.

Ellie was seeing McFly and McBusted star Dougie Poynter but posted Instagram snaps of her and Calvin in the studio, with what looked like vodka and tequila bottles around them. They were working on a track for Calvin's next album.

And it was business as usual by the time Calvin rocked up at Balado for the final T in the Park to be held there. He ensured the festival bowed out in style, headlining the Main Stage for the first time – a sensational confirmation that his decision to ditch the band for his DJ set was the right one.

As if Calvin's presence wasn't celebrity enough, he had Hollywood legend and new pal Will Smith jet in to sprinkle some additional stardust on the proceedings. The pair were continuing to develop the dance music series for HBO and it was said Will wanted to see Calvin at his very best.

Smith told the stunned crowd: 'I asked Calvin Harris and I said, "Man, I've got a couple weeks off and I am looking for an experience." Ladies and gentleman, I present to you – Scotland's own Calvin Harris.'

In an amusing aside, when T in the Park organiser Geoff Ellis saw a 'W. Smith' on the guest list he assumed it was the former Rangers and Scotland manager Walter. 'It was only when I saw him arrive, I realised it was Will,' Geoff said.

Calvin was pushing ahead with plans for his next singles, with an album release scheduled for November. But one person whose plans were thrown up in the air was Rita Ora. Despite the fact she'd said her album was as good as done back in the spring, come July it was claimed it had hit problems.

Calvin had pulled the tracks he'd given her, according to *The Sun*, which quoted a source saying, 'Rita's album has hit a bit of a road block after Calvin pulled all the songs he had worked on for the project before they split. He'd made a lot of songs for her but they're now likely to go to other artists.

'Calvin wants a clean break personally and professionally. He's already given her one massive hit, so doesn't feel he owes her.'

Rita spoke publicly for the first time in August about the break-up and revealed she was still hurting.

'I'm gonna tell you the truth . . . I'm not doing too great,' she said. 'But I'm doing better than I thought. I adore him and he's an amazing human being. It was more about the situation, it was inconvenient, it was sh*t, it sucks,' she added.

If Rita was fuming at Calvin over the album tracks, she didn't say, but when she was forced to pull out of the Teen Choice Awards in Los Angeles at the eleventh hour because he had refused to grant permission, she was less guarded.

When DJ Ryan Seacrest asked why Harris had said she couldn't do it, Rita replied: 'Ask Calvin. I was supposed to perform but for anybody who doesn't understand how it works he wrote and produced the song – he's an incredible songwriter, I'm never going to disregard his talents – so he has to approve anything TV wise. He owns the rights to it and he didn't approve the Teen Choice Awards.'

Rita insisted she wasn't surprised by the decision, but then said, 'I was scheduled to perform and all my fans were texting me. We put a lot of effort and work into the show. Every time I do a show I rehearse for a month in advance. I could have got told a few weeks earlier, you know. That would have been nice. It was a last-minute change but you know it happens, we move on, we move forward.'

'Why is there this bitterness?' Seacrest asked her.

Rita replied: 'I don't know. I feel if you speak to Calvin you should ask him. I can't speak for him, but I'm not like that.'

Seacrest pressed her further, asking, 'But you were pissed?'

'Yeah,' she said, 'I'm not going to lie. I put my own money into the performance, like I always do.'

Calvin seemed to be responding to her comments when he wrote on Twitter: 'You'll only know one side of the story because I choose not to talk to the papers about every aspect of my personal life. Just know I had a damn good reason.'

When Calvin appeared on the same show two weeks later, Seacrest showed him a clip of Rita singing. Instead of the words to the chorus, she changed them to: 'I might have let you down.'

Looking visibly taken aback, Calvin said, 'Yikes. That's crazy. I think that's unnecessary. This girl – she's going to be around for a lifetime. She works insanely hard. She makes some crazy decisions but she works insanely hard.'

Refusing to be drawn on which decisions were crazy, he said, 'She is focused on her career and that is the most important thing and I respect that so much.'

'Looking in from the outside,' Seacrest said, of Rita's improvised lyric, 'you've said things that would make one look in and think she did something to hurt you.'

But Calvin refused to bite, saying: 'She's funny.'

For now that was all he would say on the matter, but one suspected there was a lot more still to come out.

23

The $100 Million Man

AFTER the Rita examination, Calvin would have been grateful for the chance to talk about anything else bar his former relationship and he was keen to share his opinion on the Scottish Independence Referendum, where the nation would have its say on whether it wanted to remain part of the United Kingdom or become a country in its own right. The debate before the vote on 14 September ignited the country, with passionate grassroots campaigning on both the 'Yes' side for independence and the 'No' camp.

Scots around the world could not help but be fascinated by what was going on back home and Calvin was no exception – although he was frustrated that he couldn't participate in the democratic process.

'It's annoying because I can't vote because I don't live in Scotland any more, so I am watching it from afar,' he said. 'I am just watching it and I'm seeing it kind of develop. Is it Scotland versus England now?'

For Calvin, the issue of national identity had personal resonance after the ribbing he used to get at school over his accent.

'When I was growing up, because I had English parents with a slight English accent, I would get lots of stick for being the English guy in Scotland,' he said. 'Maybe it was just at school. But I think there's always a vibe among a lot of people in Scotland – maybe it's just turning too much of that.'

He could see both sides of the argument – the desire of a large number of people to govern their own affairs, and the fears of others, who worried how they would fare financially in an independent Scotland.

'I see what they are saying,' he said of the 'Yes' campaigners, 'to have a country controlled by another country is kind of bizarre. They are saying we do have a lot of money, but I wonder if we do have enough money – Scotland, that is.'

As it was, a last ditch 'vow' by the three main Westminster parties, promising wavering voters that a 'No' vote would lead to unspecified new powers, was enough to persuade a slim majority in favour of remaining part of the UK.

Calvin was also grateful for the chance to talk music again and he enthused about the methodology of his next single, 'Blame'. Harris revealed young English singer John Newman, who'd won both critical acclaim and fans with his 'Love Me Again' number-one smash of 2013, had approached him via a direct message on Twitter.

'He's got an amazing voice and he's an amazing writer, which is a golden combination,' Calvin said. 'You don't really get that a lot. He approached me via Twitter DM and he said, "Hey, I've got a tune and would you like to work on it? I think it would suit your style."

'So he sent it over. It was really rough. It was him singing over and some chords and so I just took that, took his vocal and built the music around it. We went back and forth on email for a while. I finally met him. He did a show out here in LA. I went to see him. He's such a nice guy. It was a good vibe and the song came out great.'

Calvin's moody beats complimented Newman's vocals immediately and the track had hit written right through it. It went straight in at number one in the UK and reached the top spot in seven other countries. In the States it topped the dance chart and rose to number nineteen in the Hot 100.

It was Calvin's seventh number one and he had more than one reason to be happy. It afforded him the chance to get closer to stunning model Aarika Wolf, who he had met after she had made an appearance in the 'Blame' video. The pair hit it off and a picture of them kissing aboard a private jet was uploaded to Instagram.

While Calvin did not speak publicly about Aarika, he shared images of the two of them together, from the set of the 'Blame' shoot. Calvin was then photographed wrapping his arms around the twenty-one-year-old as they enjoyed some Halloween fun at the Mr. Bones Pumpkin Patch in Beverly Hills.

Calvin and Aarika – pronounced Erika – might well have had something in common. She was born and raised in Bowman, North Dakota, before she moved to Los Angeles to pursue a modelling career, and she knows something about coming from a small town. Her home town – in America's Upper Midwest – has a population of just 1,650 people.

Halloween was the cause of a double celebration. His latest album, *Motion*, which had already spawned three number-one singles, was released that day. And Calvin had assembled an even greater international guest list of talent for this one. Starring alongside him were Gwen Stefani, rapper Big Sean, R'n'B star Tinashe and girl group Haim, all from the US. Calvin confessed that working with the Haim sisters had nearly made him yearn for his days in a band again. They collaborated on 'Pray to God', which was released as a single in March 2015, and he said, 'They were fun, you share ideas. But I wouldn't want to do the tour bus thing with them.'

He added: 'I've known them for a while – we share a hairdresser because we've got very similar hair, obviously.'

Regarding the No Doubt singer Gwen Stefani, he said, 'I've never met Gwen but I was asked to work on her album and I thought, "What about mine?" She's the one artist on the whole album that I've never met.'

In terms of home-grown talent, as well as Newman, who also provided the opener 'Faith', and Hurts, there were collaborations with musical trio All About She and another with Ellie Goulding. Completing the line-up were Dutch DJs R3had, Firebeatz and Ummet Ozcan.

The result was a continuation of the polished house sound he had developed on *18 Months*. And for the first time Calvin revealed many of his songs were inspired by past loves.

'With lyrics I have a title and a concept,' he said. 'I have an idea. Partners do inspire songs. "Summer" was about someone, the Rita one, "Never Let You Down", is about someone, "Feel So Close" is about someone.'

During an interview with Ryan Seacrest, Calvin also explained from where he drew his inspiration for his infectious beats.

'The way that I was brought up was just to listen to everything – every form of music since the 1960s,' he said. 'So I get my influences from a lot of different places. Also if you know that an old record was successful . . . and the way certain sounds make you feel, like a Beach Boys record, you get certain feelings from that, you can borrow those techniques and put it in a modern environment. So you can put old sounds in new, which is why you have to listen to new pop music so you know the new techniques.'

When Seacrest put it to Calvin that it sounded like a laboratory, the hit-maker agreed. 'My dad was a biochemist, so there's something in that,' he said. 'There's the musicality and the way I just love music, but also approaching it like you're mixing different elements and trying to come up with the perfect thing.'

Calvin's run of number ones had been broken with the release of his fourth single 'Outside', with Goulding. Although Emil Nava contributed another visually stunning video to accompany the track, it failed to peak higher than number six.

And *Motion* also just fell shy of the top spot, entering the album charts at number two, being held off by Ed Sheeran's *X*. In America it gave Calvin his first top-ten album, reaching number five.

The critics were largely still unimpressed, yet although Calvin had only two years previously said he couldn't be bothered with reviews, this time one really got up his nose. In awarding *Motion* the customary two stars, Will Hodgkinson in *The Times* described Calvin as 'the world's most lavishly rewarded space bar-presser'.

Calvin took to Twitter to point out that he was the 'sole writer and producer of shitloads of hit records . . . but i understand not convenient to mention this'.

He added: 'I bit . . . I admit it . . . still beats giving them idiots interviews tho. Only downside is media people assume a lot of things . . . they wana know how I did it so badddddd . . . I just want you to know, not them.'

He went on: 'I'm proof you can do it too . . . producers writers singers you can do it . . . I'm from a small Scottish town. I did this no help. No connections in music media entertainment nothing . . . I don't have the big mouth either – I don't speak to anyone talk myself up etc lol.

'Just wrote music loved it produced it mixed it for 15 years and now I get to work with the best singers/writers in the world . . . I'm lucky.'

But Calvin had a message for aspiring musicians and DJs out there.

'If you write produce sing dj whatever and you feel isolated or like you can't get thru the door, have hope it really is possible,' he said.

The reviewers would continue to sneer, but Calvin continued to pay attention to the only critics that mattered – his paying public. And when new figures emerged at the end of 2014, naming him as the top-earning DJ on the planet for the second year in a row, it was a resounding vote of confidence in his talents.

Calvin had raked in a staggering £40 million in the previous twelve months – a rise of £12 million on the previous year, earning more than Jay-Z, the actor Leonardo DiCaprio or Brazilian super-model Gisele Bundchen. In just two years he had earned £68 million – or $100 million.

When you totted up the success he'd had, it was truly staggering – a triumph of ambition, dedication, talent and know-how.

'Summer' had sold more than one million copies in the US alone, where appropriately it had become the song of the season. Then there was the success of 'I Will Never Let You Down', plus his remix of Fatboy Slim's 'Eat, Sleep, Rave, Repeat'.

In addition to his residency at Hakkasan, there were his festival appearances and tours. As well as headlining T in the Park, he starred at Creamfields in Cheshire, the Isle of Wight festival, the Electric Daisy Carnival in Milton Keynes and Lollapalooza and Coachella in America, earning between £500,000 and £1 million an appearance. He also appeared in Prague, at SonneMondSterne in Germany, the BBC's Big Weekend in Glasgow in May, and the 2014 Malaysian Formula 1 Grand Prix. He ended 2014 with a Stereosonic festival tour in Australia.

He became the first UK solo act to notch up more than one billion plays worldwide on the Internet music streaming service Spotify. 'Summer' was his most popular track on the service, streamed more than 160 million times. If you were to add up all the minutes his music had been streamed, it was the equivalent of more than 5,000 continuous years. As Spotify gives 70 per cent of its revenues to rights holders, it is seen as the future of mass-music consumption, with falling music sales showing that an increasing number opt to stream than to own their songs. While Mark Terry, the co-president of Calvin's label Columbia Records UK, announced his congratulations for Calvin, the artist tweeted simply: 'Thank u world.'

Add to all that the commercial reach of his 4.6 million Twitter followers and 9.1 million fans on Facebook, it is easy to see why he is one of the most powerful people in pop.

There is no sign of him resting on his laurels or letting his cash sit in the bank gathering dust. It was reported that he had splashed out £15 million on five mansions in the hills overlooking Los Angeles. His plan was to knock down two of the houses in posh Benedict Canyon to build tennis and basketball courts.

And we can look forward to him starring in his first feature film – appearing as himself in the movie version of the American TV series *Entourage*. Calvin will appear alongside fiction actor Vincent Chase, played by Adrian Grenier, whose exploits in Hollywood with his gang of mates from New York are loosely based on those of Mark Wahlberg.

If there was a fear that he was doing too much, however, a timely wake-up call came in November 2014, just as he was due to make a triumphant return home to perform at the MTV European Music Awards in Glasgow. Just a day before Calvin was supposed to open the event in front of a television audience of 500 million, he dramatically pulled out, announcing on Twitter: 'No EMAs for me this weekend. Got some heart problems. Heading home to see if it can be fixed.'

As fans started to panic, he deleted the tweet, leaving everyone wondering what exactly was going on. Although he actually won the award for Best Electronic at the SSE Hydro event, MTV bosses failed to mention it to the packed audience. Thankfully Calvin was spotted safe and well in LA and he said later, 'I had an exhaustion thing. But I'm good now.'

He was fit enough to honour his commitments in Australia and landed in Perth for his festival dates accompanied by Aarika – a sign that their relationship was blossoming.

And another indication that he was in the best shape of his life came when Calvin signed another lucrative deal to become the face – and body – of Emporio Armani. It was an incredible trans-formation from the geeky-looking kid in garish hoodies we were introduced to back in 2007. The promotional photos released to mark the announcement of the modelling deal showed a toned and lean Calvin, complete with sculpted six-pack and defined pecs. Announcing the news, Calvin, who had once said he only owned one suit, revealed, 'This year was the first time I wore an Armani suit. When I was trying it on, as soon as I put it on, I felt amazing. The material was awesome and I felt really good in it.'

It didn't seem to matter who they were: everyone wanted a piece of Calvin Harris.

Yet in this world of private jets, supercars, stunning models, multimillion-pound contracts, number-one records, movie deals and media speculation, two recent stories stand out to remind us of the person behind the global brand that is Calvin Harris.

When volunteer Ross Thompson asked the DJ and several other celebs for help buying a van to collect food donations for homeless people in Northumberland, he did so more in hope than expecta-tion. Ross had only £110 towards his fundraising target of £4,000. But within minutes of Ross messaging him, Calvin topped up the total to £4,000 and then replied, tweeting simply: 'Done x.'

Ross was gobsmacked.

'I cannot describe how happy I am at the generosity that has happened here. We are now able to get a van and get the essentials to the people that need them more quickly. I am for ever in your debt,' he said.

And at Halloween in 2014, when Calvin jetted out to Puerto Rico for an exclusive party on a private island in the Caribbean Sea, for a gig that earned him a cool $1 million, who might he have been expected to invite? His model girlfriend, some celebrity mates, new potential business partners, perhaps? In fact, it was a group of his old pals from Dumfries, who he invites regularly to watch him perform in Las Vegas. Calvin might be one of the most in-demand artists in the world, but he hasn't forgotten his roots.

At Christmas he made sure he had time to return home and spend time with his parents. On Christmas Eve he was spotted in his local Tesco store, picking up some last-minute provisions.

Taylor McCormick, an auxiliary nurse, who has seen him live several times, said Calvin was happy to chat and pose for photos with well-wishers. 'He was nice,' she said. 'He asked me how I was and wished me a happy Christmas. He got bombarded after I spotted him but didn't mind. He was happy to speak to people.'

At the close of 2014 he posted a self-portrait on Instagram, smiling broadly. Happy, he most certainly was. Alongside the photo he wrote: 'That's me smiling because it's been an unbelievable year maybe the best year of my life, the success of "Summer", "IWNLYD" ["I Will Never Let You Down"], "Blame", "Outside" blows me away and the *Motion* album. I got to work with some absolute superstars and make some incredible music videos. So this is me saying thank you to anybody who bought a song, came to a show, streamed a song or even just liked a pic on Instagram. I appreciate all of you and this life so much thank you and God bless.'

Calvin Harris is at the top of his game and his dominance of the dance scene and the charts shows no sign of abating.

Tim Barr credits the DJ/producer/singer/songwriter's success to his remarkable talent, a skill for adapting to the times – and a little slice of luck.

'I think what marks Calvin out is the fact that his sound anticipated so many of the trends that have become mainstream in modern pop,' he commented. 'When he began his recording career, the EDM phenomenon wasn't even on the horizon. The music scene at that point was dominated by guitar bands – I can remember being at the filming of a music TV show around the time he released "The Girls" and he was the only act on that night to have a synth onstage (though he did have a guitar player too). At that time, the level of success he's achieved would have seemed quite incredible.

'He's been amazingly astute – and lucky in parts, I'm sure – in terms of guiding his career and aligning with musical developments at just the right time. Through timing, determination and some choice collaborations, he's ended up being exactly where most of his critics would never have imagined he'd be – whether that's drawing a record crowd for his main stage set at Coachella or premiering a new video in cinemas around the world. It's easy to underestimate just how much effort that takes.'

Stature-wise Calvin Harris – Adam Richard Wiles – might just fall a quarter of an inch short of achieving official giant status, but some people don't need a certificate to be considered a giant among their peers.

Epilogue

THE rippling muscles, the solid six-pack, the pose more reminiscent of David Beckham than a lad from Dumfries. Looking at the stunning images of Calvin lounging in his Emporio Armani underwear, it is hard to believe this is the same person who as a nervous teenager hid at the side of a stage.

As 2015 began we saw a relaxed, confident Calvin comfortable in his own skin. Success, recognition and fortune all help, of course. However, as he said in response to snide remarks on Twitter after posting the photos: 'Comments on my Twitter looking at my Armani picture like, "He's changed now he's got money, funny what money can do" . . . That wasn't f***ing money, man, that was six days a week in the f***ing gym.'

If his physique is anything like his career it has come purely through hard graft. And, like his music, the Armani images went global, sparking a sensational response worldwide. One reader even wrote to a British national newspaper thanking them for printing the images and making her day!

The photos took on a life of their own, but Calvin nearly experienced the flip side of celebrity fame when it was claimed naked images of him were being circulated online. It was unclear if such images existed or if so how they had been acquired, but in the wake of 2014's celebrity Internet storage thefts one could not be too careful. Showbiz websites wisely sought legal advice and a potentially embarrassing episode was quietly averted.

That was but a solitary cloud in an otherwise perfectly clear sky. More photos emerged of him looking happy, enjoying some rare downtime on the beach with girlfriend Aarika. He announced a new three-year deal with Hakkasan, one that would earn him £265,000 a gig at the Las Vegas nightclub, Wet Republic at MGM Grand Hotel and Casino, and Omnia Nightclub at Caesars Palace.

At the 2015 Brits in February he was up for British Single of the Year and British Video for 'Summer'. He lost out to 'Uptown Funk' by Mark Ronson featuring Bruno Mars in the single category. British Video was to be decided by a Twitter vote, the winner decided by the number of tweets bearing a hashtag for the nominees. However, although Calvin correctly predicted One Direction would triumph with their video for 'You & I' because of their sizable fan base, he didn't help his own cause by giving his Twitter followers the wrong hashtag to tweet. From as far back as 12 February 2015 he let fans know the tag, believing it was #BRITCALVINHARRIS. Only on the night of the Brits on 25 February did he realise his mistake. At 8.18 p.m., once the event was underway, he tweeted: 'For fucks sake it's #CALVINHARRISBRIT'.

Despite that mix-up, he was in jovial mood that evening – as well he might be, because if reports were to be believed, that was the night he hooked up with Taylor Swift.

The twenty-five-year-old pop superstar was one of the few artists who could dwarf even Calvin's sensational fortune. Worth an estimated £130 million, she became the youngest female ever to make it onto the prestigious Forbes World's 100 Most Powerful Women list. Effortlessly making the transition from country star to pop phenomenon, she was arguably the hottest talent on the planet when Calvin caught her eye. Taylor had famously stepped out with a few celebrities, like One Direction's Harry Styles and actors Jake Gyllenhaal and Taylor Lautner, and earned a reputation for writing about her failed flings in her songs.

However, in clean-living Calvin she had found a kindred spirit. After they hit it off at the Brits, it quickly emerged he was newly single after splitting from Aarika. As the weeks progressed, Taylor was spotted in his DJ booth, and they were snapped coyly holding hands and decked out in similar attire at Hollywood hangouts and Whole Foods stores. They took their relationship to a new level when he met her pet moggies at a house party. But the cat was well and truly out of the bag at the Billboard Music Awards in Las Vegas in May. Taylor was the star of the night, scooping eight gongs, but all eyes were on the public display of affection she reserved for her Scottish beau.

For Calvin, it seemed a match made in heaven. He had the lifestyle, the fortune, the success and now, just as he'd sung in 2007, it looked like he'd finally got the girl.

On the night he and Taylor got together, he had been asked by an interviewer to name his highlights of the previous twelve months.

'I headlined T in the Park, which was amazing,' he replied. 'I had three number one singles, which was amazing.'

It was amazing. However, one wonders whether if asked the same question now he would answer differently.

Looking to the future, and with his personal life seemingly content, it is hard to see what, professionally, there is still to achieve. A Brit Award or Grammy one day might be the icing on the cake, but one throwaway comment he gave that night at the Brits seemed to reveal what Calvin Harris holds dear – more than baubles and industry gongs.

As the interviewer remarked how 'enormously successful' and how 'very well respected' he had become, he turned and, nodding, said simply: 'I'm good with that.'